The Russian Capitalist Experiment

To Paul Lawrence and Igor Faminsky

Who helped us go behind the factory walls
as the capitalist experiment began

The Russian Capitalist Experiment

From State-Owned Organizations to Entrepreneurships

Sheila M. Puffer
Northeastern University,
Boston, Massachusetts, US

Daniel J. McCarthy
Northeastern University,
Boston, Massachusetts, US

Alexander I. Naumov
Moscow State University,
Moscow, Russia

Edward Elgar
Cheltenham, UK · Northampton, US

Published by
Edward Elgar Publishing Limited
Glensanda House
Montpellier Parade
Cheltenham
Glos GL50 1UA
UK

Edward Elgar Publishing, Inc.
136 West Street
Suite 202
Northampton
Massachusetts 01060
USA

A catalogue record for this book
is available from the British Library

Library of Congress Cataloguing in Publication Data
The Russian capitalist experiment : from state-owned organizations to entrepreneurships / Sheila M. Puffer ... [et al.]
    Includes bibliographical references and index.
        1. Industrial management—Russia (Federation)—Case studies. 2. Business enterprises—Russia (Federation)—Case studies. 3. Privatization—Russia (Federation)—Case studies. I. Puffer, Sheila M.

    HD70.R9 R862 2000
    338.947'05—dc21   99-045193

ISBN 1 85898 633 8
Printed and bound in Great Britain by Biddles Ltd, www.biddles.co.uk

Contents

About the Authors

Sheila M. Puffer is Professor of International Business and Human Resources Management at the College of Business Administration at Northeastern University in Boston. She is also a Fellow at the Davis Center for Russian Studies at Harvard University. She has been a faculty member at The State University of New York in Buffalo and the University of Ottawa, and served for six years as a personnel administrator for the Government of Canada. Dr. Puffer holds BA and MBA degrees from the University of Ottawa and a Ph.D. from the University of California, Berkeley. She also received a diploma from the Executive Management Program at the Plekhanov Institute of the National Economy in Moscow in 1980. Dr. Puffer is editor of *The Academy of Management Executive*.

Daniel J. McCarthy is Professor of Strategic Management at Northeastern University in Boston. He has served as the Philip R. McDonald Professor of Business Administration and as associate dean and director of the Graduate School. He has been an assistant controller at Tufts University, production manager at Johnson & Johnson, and president of Computer Environments Corporation. Dr. McCarthy has been a consultant to numerous organizations and is a director of Clean Harbors, Inc., Tufts Associated Health Plans, and Managed Comp, Inc. With expertise in corporate strategy and high technology management, he has taught in more than a dozen countries. He holds AB and MBA degrees from Dartmouth College and a DBA from Harvard University. He is also a Fellow at the Davis Center for Russian Studies at Harvard University,

Alexander I. Naumov is Deputy Director of the School of Business Administration at Moscow State University where he received a Ph.D. in management. Dr. Naumov was a Sloan Fellow at The Massachusetts Institute of Technology in Boston in 1975-1976, a research scholar at The State University of New York at Albany in 1977, and a United Nations staff member in New York from 1979 to 1985. He was executive secretary at the Institute for External Economic Affairs in Moscow in 1987-1988. Dr. Naumov has taught as a visiting faculty member at Northeastern University, consults for numerous Western and Russian organizations, and is the cofounder of the Russian Association of Management Development.

1. Introduction

We set out to study Russian enterprises with the objective of developing longitudinal case histories of different types of enterprises as they evolved during Russia's economic transition in the 1990s. More specifically, we wanted to learn how managerial decision making evolved over time in these enterprises. The Russian author and one of the American authors on our team began researching this topic in 1988 in an intensive field study comparing decision-making practices in four Soviet and four American manufacturing firms. The results were described in books that were published in English and Russian (Lawrence et al., 1990; Naumov, 1991). In another study, the two American authors analyzed changes in decision-making power perceived by Soviet managers in 1990 (McCarthy and Puffer, 1992). The authors also compared the decision-making authority of these former Soviet managers to American managers for the same period (Puffer and McCarthy, 1993a). An additional study presented these Soviet managers' predictions of the decision-making authority they would possess as the 1990s progressed, compared to the authority they had earlier (Puffer and McCarthy, 1993b).

In this book, we examine decisions in strategy, operations, financing, investments, marketing, R&D, and human resource management. Additionally, we analyze the key external forces influencing these decisions as changes continued in the economic, social, and legal-political environments during the transition. We began this project in 1993 by interviewing and tape-recording executives of ten Russian enterprises. To follow their development, we continued our research for six years, in most cases conducting annual interviews at company sites.

We believe that a longitudinal perspective of different types of enterprises will help business practitioners, academics, and students better understand the evolution of Russian enterprises as they operated in an environment that changed from a relatively predictable state to one far less certain. We hope that this work can be useful to academicians involved in research on Russian management, business, and the economy, and to students in international business, economics, and Russian studies. Business practitioners may use these findings as background material when making decisions involving different types of Russian enterprises. We also believe that the analysis presented in this book will be helpful in understanding economic transitions in other countries in the former communist block.

Several characteristics of this book are of note. First, it is based on primary data gathered during lengthy on-site interviews with founders and other senior executives of the enterprises. Second, we developed our own conceptualization of the period covered in our research by identifying four distinct phases of the Russian government's policies toward business and its role in the economy. Third, the longitudinal perspective is a major validating feature of the book since the information was gathered annually from 1993 through 1998, and in some cases in 1999, rather than having been collected as a retrospective account at the end of the period. Additionally, the categorization of enterprises into three types allows a comparison between new entrepreneurships, state-owned enterprises transitioning to private ownership, and hybrid firms that have characteristics of the other two types.

The information in each company's chapter is presented in chronological order, and represents the managers' descriptions and interpretations of their situations at the time of the annual interviews. These company chapters then served as the database for our summary, conclusions, interpretations, and scenarios presented in the final two chapters.

PLAN OF THE BOOK

The 1990s are widely recognized as a period of transition in Russia's economic development and have been filled with a seemingly endless stream of changes. Within the transition, however, we have identified a number of discrete stages which we call Commercialization, Privatization, Nomenklatura, and Statization. These phases of the political and economic environment are described and analyzed in Part One.

The ten enterprises are classified according to three categories. Two enterprises are still owned primarily by the State, three have hybrid ownership shared between private parties and the State and receive some State funding, and the remaining five are new entrepreneurships. The state-owned enterprises are very large, with many employees and diversified operations. Both were closely tied to the defense sector in the Soviet economy, and each is trying to adapt its products and services to commercial markets. The Central Research and Development Institute of Robotics and Technical Cybernetics in St. Petersburg is primarily a research and educational institute, while Toriy Research and Production Association is a radio electronics and scientific research and manufacturing operation headquartered in Moscow, with branches in other cities. These state-owned enterprises are discussed in Part Two.

The executives of the three hybrid companies drew heavily on their contacts and experience in large state-owned organizations to continue receiving some state funding at a time when government policy called for minimizing such subsidies. Mikromashina, with a relatively new plant in Moscow, manufactured small consumer electrical appliances for domestic consumption, and for export through its joint venture with Western partners. Tonar, an abbreviation that translates to "products for the people," is headquartered in Moscow, with operations located throughout Russia. The company continued to receive government subsidies because of its mission to develop and manage large-scale projects providing social benefits to the public. The third hybrid company, Ekip, an abbreviation meaning "ecology and progress," is another firm with a social mission to utilize technology in designing and developing ecologically friendly products. These enterprises are described in Part Three.

The five entrepreneurships include Premier Bank of Moscow, which was one of the first private banks registered to conduct commercial banking in the late 1980s. BusinessLink of St. Petersburg began as an executive search firm serving Western multinationals, but diversified into several different businesses including advertising and real estate development. Aquarius Systems Inform started out in Moscow as an assembler of personal computers, but diversified into building products and started its own bank before refocusing on the computer business. Another Moscow-based technology firm, Platinum Russia, established a branch in St. Petersburg, and extended its software offerings to include systems analysis and consulting. Vybor, which means "choice," opened its business in Moscow as an import-export company trading in consumer goods, but later focused on distribution of imported shoes. These five entrepreneurships are the subjects of Part Four.

Part Five contains two chapters. In the first, we review and summarize each company's major activities and responses to environmental opportunities and threats. We present summaries according to the three company types – state-owned, hybrid organizations, and entrepreneurships – rather than by individual companies as in earlier chapters. For these three company types, the analyses are organized by the four stages of the economic transition which we observed during the decade – Commercialization, Privatization, Nomenklatura, and Statization. This format thus provides a conceptual framework for analyzing the progress of different types of companies during Russia's capitalist decade. This approach allows a comparison among the three company types and a better understanding of how different types fared during the country's transition. In the final chapter, we look to the future and describe three plausible scenarios for Russia's political and economic environment. Based upon our analyses in the previous chapter, we consider which types of firms would be most viable under each scenario.

HOW THE RESEARCH TEAM CONDUCTED THE STUDY

Our three-person research team, composed of two business school faculty members from Northeastern University in the US and one from Moscow State University, was a binational collaboration that yielded a number of important benefits. By pooling our contacts, we were able to gain access to key individuals in diverse businesses. Additionally, the reputations of our two institutions appear to have instilled confidence and trust in those we interviewed. Among the major advantages of having a Russian team member was the assurance that information about Russian society and the business environment was accurately interpreted from a Russian perspective. Two Americans, on the other hand, could provide frameworks and raise questions important in interpreting these situations for Westerners interested in the changing Russian business environment of the 1990s.

The companies we studied were not selected with the objective of fulfilling the requirements of statistical sampling. Rather, the criteria for selection were our familiarity with these businesses, and our perception of how well they represented a number of different industries. The latter basis for selection, we believed, would allow us to make comparisons among types of companies. Based on the personal and business reputations of the executives, we believe that the individuals and their companies generally exemplify ethical and forward-thinking business practices. In short, our objective was to present examples of some of the better business practices and decision-making processes in Russian companies.

Another selection criterion was that the firms should reflect three primary ownership and funding patterns – state-owned enterprises, hybrid firms, and entrepreneurships. Our rationale was that type of ownership largely determines firms' access to funds, as well as their autonomy and flexibility in decision making. This approach also had the advantage of including companies at different stages of their life cycles, a factor which we believed would be another significant influence on managerial decisions. Half the companies selected were new entrepreneurships since, in our view, that segment was becoming the most vibrant and promising in the Russian economy. Entrepreneurships provide an opportunity for their owners and managers to exercise discretion and employ a variety of decision-making styles. In contrast, managers in the three state-owned enterprises were perceived to be more constrained by their experience and enterprise conditions, both of which were the legacy of the Soviet centralized economy. Managers in hybrid firms were likely to exhibit characteristics of both the entrepreneurs and the state-owned enterprise managers.

In conducting the research, we acted as a team with all three researchers present at most interviews, and with two interviewers in attendance otherwise. In all companies, we interviewed the founder or CEO, and in most we interviewed at least two other senior executives, and sometimes other employees as well. Interviews centered on a series of questions about the firms and the environments in which they operated. The majority of interviews were conducted in Russian, with the remainder taking place in English. On most occasions, two of the interviewers present were fluent in Russian, allowing a thorough understanding and verification of responses. We continued to use a consistent set of questions each year as a framework for the interviews.

Several measures were taken to ensure that the information was as accurate as possible. All interviews were audiotaped and some were videotaped. Many of the audiotapes were transcribed in the original Russian, translated into English, and reviewed by at least one Russian-speaking team member. All team members asked questions to clarify information or to address new circumstances that had arisen during the current year. Notes were taken by all team members and were later compared to obtain agreement about interviewee responses. This process not only validated content, but also enabled us to interpret responses within the context of circumstances during that particular year. In some meetings, research assistants who were also present added their input to interpretations of various responses. In most companies, we toured the facilities, viewing production, administrative, and marketing operations, as well as retail outlets and R&D and test facilities. The team usually had lunch at the enterprises with the CEO and other key employees. On a number of occasions, executives also invited the authors to dinner and other social functions. Over the years, the team developed a strong rapport with most interviewees, which built trust and facilitated an open atmosphere during meetings.

In the time between our series of annual interviews, the team worked in both Russia and the United States summarizing materials on each company, and tracking the evolution of circumstances within each company as well as the country. Case studies were written about two of the companies, and with the approval of the respective managers, were published in journals in the United States, Europe, and Russia (McCarthy and Puffer, 1997a; McCarthy, Puffer, and Naumov, 1997a, 1997b). The situations of other companies were periodically summarized and brought up to date. Managers were contacted as needed by the Russian team member for clarification and additional information. Our goal during these interim periods was to remain current with the companies' situations as well as the economic and political environments. By analyzing and interpreting information at recurring points over the decade, we were able to document trends as they developed.

ACKNOWLEDGMENTS

We are indebted to many people for their involvement in this project. We are especially grateful to the executives and staff members of the ten enterprises that are the focus of this book. Their willingness to cooperate with us on annual interviews allowed us to follow the longitudinal development of their companies' progress. Coming to know them as individuals as well as business professionals added a personal dimension to our work. In a number of cases we also had the opportunity to meet their families and socialize with them. For their openness and generosity we will remain always in their debt.

In addition to the executives who participated, many others were involved in our research efforts. Numerous research assistants at Northeastern University and Moscow State University performed valuable tasks to help us accomplish our work. Among them were graduate students from the two institutions including Russell Levine, Nadezhda Peeva, Christopher Landry, Thomas Levanant, Sophie Derevianko, Irina Naumova, Tatiana Kozlova, Aleksandr Makhanko, and Alexei Prigozhin. Executives from other organizations assisted us in various ways, including Gordon Lankton, Edward Rivera, Barry Potter, and Daniel Ryan of Nypro Inc. of the US, Stanislav Shekshnia of Millicom, Moscow and CIS, and Andrew Vitvitsky of the US AID in St. Petersburg.

We also appreciate the encouragement of administrators at Northeastern University and Moscow State University, as well as their financial and personal support of our work. We acknowledge Northeastern's College of Business Dean Ira Weiss and Senior Associate Dean James Molloy, former Dean David Boyd, and former Senior Associate Dean Roger Atherton. We also thank Oleg Vikhanski, Director of Moscow State's School of Business Administration, for his support throughout the project. The Davis Center for Russian Studies at Harvard University provided us with valuable background information as well as opportunities to present progress reports on this research. Financial support from the International Research and Exchanges Board in Washington, and the BURK and BFET fellowship programs at the Russian and East European Studies Department at the University of Pittsburgh is also acknowledged and appreciated.

Sheila M. Puffer	Daniel J. McCarthy	Alexander I. Naumov
Boston	Boston	Moscow

PART ONE

Political and Economic Environment

2.   Four Stages of Russia's Economic Transition of the 1990s

TRANSITION FROM A CENTRALLY-PLANNED ECONOMY

Russia's communist-controlled, centrally-planned economy had existed for nearly 70 years prior to perestroika in 1985 and the dissolution of the Soviet Union at the end of 1991. During the period of state ownership of the means of production, which lasted from 1917 to 1991, the major objective for enterprises was to fulfill plans dictated by centralized industrial ministries. Managers were rewarded for meeting production plans, and made virtually no decisions about product mix, pricing, customers, suppliers, distribution, or competition. All such decisions were made by central ministry officials, and no cash was exchanged among enterprises to pay for goods and services. Such transactions were centralized in the ministries, which were also the source of financing for capital investments, wages, social benefits, and other expenses.

Profit, in the Western sense, was not an objective. Instead, a primary driver for managers was the efficient use of resources, which was rewarded by ministries with bonuses and investment funds. Enterprises rarely knew their exact costs, and few could determine costs for individual product lines. Yet, managers were required to submit reports to ministries on financial performance measures and other aspects of their businesses. Managers were under pressure to meet rigid production plans as well as other demands associated with enterprise operations. A consequence of strict governmental demands was that managers became exceedingly skilled in finding ways to meet their imposed goals. Their practices included employing excess workers, hoarding raw materials, vertically integrating operations, and networking with other enterprise managers and government officials. Typically, they reported performance results which showed them fulfilling the plan and meeting other targets.

In contrast, managers operating in the economy as it evolved away from central planning were required to make decisions in the context of a highly volatile and ever-changing political and economic environment. This environment, however, can be viewed as having had a number of distinct phases, and the requirements placed upon managers varied during each one. Differences occurred in their decision making, but their strategic thinking remained relatively constant as they maintained a consistent view of their financing goals. Ultimately, survival was the overriding strategic objective.

This chapter describes four stages of development that we observed during our research. These periods, which can serve as background for understanding the dynamics of business in Russia during the 1990s, focus on two variables— phases of the market economy and the government's activities in regulating the economy. The four phases are not distinct time periods, and a substantial overlap occurred among the periods. At the end of 1990s for instance, all four phases existed simultaneously, but in different degrees from earlier periods. We identified them, however, as occurring in a specific sequence, with the Commercialization stage running from the late 1980s through 1992, the Privatization stage from 1993 through mid-1994, the Nomenklatura stage from mid-1994 through 1997, and the Statization stage from the beginning of 1998 through the end of the 1990s.

The relationships between government, business, and the economy shifted markedly during each of these four stages, requiring managers to act differently in response to the high degree of uncertainty as well as the changes that characterized each era. These stages are described below and form the context in which evolving managerial activities and processes took place. The material in this chapter should be useful for understanding subsequent chapters on business practices of various types of companies in Russia during the decade of the 1990s.

COMMERCIALIZATION STAGE—LATE 1980S THROUGH 1992

The Commercialization stage began when the government established policies encouraging the creation of cooperatives, small businesses, and joint ventures (Blasi et al., 1997). The objective was to help alleviate the inefficiencies of state organizations in such areas as consumer goods and services. A system of privately-owned banks was also established to support the development of a private sector. Not all cooperatives were created as private enterprises, since some were established inside state-owned organizations. In such cases, cooperatives employed workers from the enterprise, and rented resources such as space and equipment to conduct commercial activities. This period saw the first real attempt at liberalizing the economy during the Communist regime, although limited attempts had occurred under Krushchev in the 1960s and Brezhnev in the late 1970s (Owen, 1995). Gorbachev's reforms in the second half of the 1980s paved the way for a fuller transition to a market economy.

This transition was unleashed further with Yeltsin's market reforms coupled with the fall of the Soviet Union in late 1991 (McCarthy and Puffer, 1997b).

This period was fruitful for entrepreneurs and others who welcomed the freedom to start and manage their own businesses (Zhuplev et al., 1998). During this phase, managers were able to establish entrepreneurships and acquire more decision-making authority in state-owned enterprises (Vlachoutsicos and Lawrence, 1996). They were also able to establish objectives of achieving profitability and serving emerging needs of the new industrial and consumer markets. To many managers, strategic opportunities seemed unlimited.

The government hoped that commercialization would reduce the inefficiency of state organizations and central planning by developing more flexible and rapid responses to changing market needs. It was not expected to totally and immediately destroy state ownership, which in fact coexisted throughout the period with private commercial activity. To foster private enterprise, it was clear that a commercial banking system was required, and the government took several measures that led to its rapid development. In the late 1980s, the government also established legislation encouraging cooperatives and joint ventures, which represented the earliest types of private and quasi-private enterprises to emerge at the beginning of the market-oriented economy. Although some of these enterprises were private, governments at various levels, such as the Moscow city government, often participated in ownership and management. The Commercialization stage, in sum, saw the beginning of a market-oriented economy as well as private enterprises, but with the simultaneous and pervasive involvement of the government in the economy. This phase can be divided into two stages: the Gorbachev period that began in the late 1980s and which prevailed until late 1991, and the initial Yeltsin period starting in late 1991 and lasting until the beginning of the Privatization phase in early 1992.

The Gorbachev Period

Perestroika, the policy of economic restructuring, was initiated in 1985 by then-Communist Party Secretary Mikhail Gorbachev and was intensified during his term as President of the USSR from 1988 to 1991. This policy ushered in enormous changes in the economic system. The Law on Soviet State Enterprises of 1987, for instance, introduced many features of a market-oriented economy, including foreign joint-venture partners and self-financing by enterprises. Enterprise managers were also permitted to select customers and suppliers, to have greater flexibility in work force management, and to exercise far greater freedom in product and production decisions. Another pathbreaking piece of legislation was the New Enterprise Law of June 1990, which virtually dismantled the Soviet central ministries (McCarthy and Puffer, 1992; Shama and Sementsov, 1992).

The government's main goal of this period was a build-up of capital to better prepare the country for the subsequent Privatization stage. Yet, policies initiated at the time also gave rise to a class of wealthy and influential individuals, sometimes called New Russians. The term referred to people who prospered personally from the changes that occurred with the liberalization of the economy. Many of these individuals were able to divert for their own gain resources allocated by the government to state enterprises. The government directed funds to state enterprises to help create cooperatives housed within state enterprises, as well as joint ventures with foreign firms as permitted by newly passed legislation. Because directors and general directors of these state organizations simultaneously managed state enterprises and commercial enterprises within their organizations, they were able to manipulate funds to their own advantage. In this way, it was often difficult to determine who held the controlling interest within these organizations. Control was nested in a series of structures, often referred to as the Matreshka principle, since the structures resembled sets of Russian dolls having layers similar to an onion.

Some joint-venture partners of these Russian enterprises, or sub-units within enterprises, were not able to fully discern who actually owned or managed the joint venture. The Western understanding of joint ventures is that they represent a third organization created to exploit the strengths of two or more partners. In contrast, the Soviet or Russian version of a joint venture often holds that the party entitled to the greatest benefits is not the one who invested the most money or resources, but rather the one with the most personal influence. In many joint ventures, it was the directors and general directors who had the most influence, and thus they reaped the greatest benefits. Naturally, such a situation did not suit many foreign partners, and was a primary reason for the short life of thousands of joint ventures that were created during this stage.

Similar situations occurred with cooperatives and small businesses that existed within state structures. In many cases, these organizations used state resources for the private enrichment of individuals. This practice was in contrast to the more open and market-oriented operations of many small private businesses and independent cooperatives that operated primarily in the service sector. Even as perestroika was coming to an end by 1991, the republics of the USSR continued their attempts at making the difficult transition to market-oriented economies (Puffer and McCarthy, 1993b). Many processes of perestroika started primarily in production-oriented enterprises; the government subsequently began commercializing the banking system, as well as scientific institutes and educational organizations.

The Yeltsin Period

Boris Yeltsin's rise to power in mid-1991 radically changed the development of private and commercialized state organizations, and accelerated the transition to a market-oriented economy. Two major events occurred at the beginning of 1992. The first was the freeing of prices of most goods from state control. The second was the cancellation of many state orders to enterprises, coupled with the substitution of a freer, decentralized method for orders and procurement of goods and services. These decisions were in the same spirit as an earlier historic decision, the repeal of the 1986 wage reform, which, as one expert noted: "For the first time since industrialization, the setting of wage rates and norms (output quotas) is to be totally decentralized" (Filtzer, 1991). These and other related changes also precipitated rampant inflation, with prices rising sharply to near world levels, with the exception of raw materials. In 1992, for instance, prices rose by 2,400 percent, wages by 1,200 percent, and incomes by 900 percent (*Economic Newsletter*, March 1993).

President Yeltsin negotiated directly with industrial enterprise managers who were identified as holding one of the keys to economic revitalization (Englund, 1992). An unanticipated outcome was that, because of their powerful positions, some private and quasi-private organizations reaped large benefits, while others with less influence were ruined. Businesses that survived were primarily those that restructured their relationship with state organizations in anticipation of privatization, as well as those that changed to more market-driven strategies. In the process, however, many cooperatives, small businesses, and joint ventures were unable to compete, and were forced out of business. What followed was the commercialization of many state organizations, primarily through the creation of both open and closed stock companies, depending upon the conditions for share ownership. Thus, preparation for the next stage, privatization, was underway.

PRIVATIZATION STAGE—1993 THROUGH MID-1994

The economic situation remained unstable as the country entered 1993. Industrial production in January compared to January 1992 showed a decrease of 14 percent in oil and natural gas output, 12 percent in coal, and 16 percent in steel production, and predictions for the remainder of the year called for even further decreases (*Economic Newsletter*, March 1993). It was in this environment that privatization of state enterprises began.

The first phase of privatization, called voucher privatization, began in early 1993 and consisted of issuing vouchers representing ownership shares in enterprises and organizations that were formerly owned by the state (Boycko et al., 1995; McCarthy and Puffer, 1995). This stage was most associated with Anatoly Chubais who headed the State Property Commission that was responsible for the privatization process. The idea behind the commission's system of voucher privatization was that every Russian citizen was to obtain some ownership of the enterprises to be privatized. In addition, enterprises undergoing privatization were able to choose from three methods of distributing the shares of their enterprise among managers, workers, and individuals outside the enterprise.

At first, the proposals were not expected to set any limits on ownership of shares by outsiders in order to provide enterprises with some possibility of external management. Many enterprise directors, however, seemed not to want real market reforms. Their resistance often stemmed from their inexperience in managing enterprises under competitive conditions. They also had a large majority of the communist-dominated parliament, the Duma, on their side, and had created a strong lobby with the executive branch. Coupled with the relatively weak position of democratic and liberal forces in the Duma, the result was a restriction on external ownership of enterprises.

The former communists, many believed, had decided to undertake privatization for a number of reasons. First, it was an ideologically attractive move to win votes. Also, by gaining control of enterprise assets through privatization, many former communists accumulated substantial personal power. This power was more personally rewarding than the collective influence they had gained in the past through service to the state and the communist party. Finally, the weak financial controls or audit trails on enterprise income provided additional opportunities for personal gain. Rather than supporting real privatization, such opportunists as Boris Berezovsky and Vladimir Potanin wanted to accumulate ownership and power for themselves, and formed large conglomerates. In a great many cases of enterprise privatization, substantial shares of stock were thus amassed in the hands of the same top managers who headed the former state enterprises. This phenomenon was especially prevalent in production-oriented organizations that had extensive capital assets. And although ownership was redistributed into private hands, no new capital was infused into the enterprises.

By the end of privatization's first phase in mid-1994, more than 19,000 of the 29,000 designated enterprises were privatized *(Economic Newsletter*, June 1994), stock accrued to over 40 million citizens (Kranz, 1994), and more than 60 percent of the labor force was employed in the private sector (Sachs, 1995). Moreover, virtually all the smaller and medium-sized organizations that were formerly state-owned were at least partially in private hands by the end of 1993 *(The Economist*, 1994). New entrepreneurships began to flourish, and many adapted to the freer environment more quickly and successfully than did larger former state-owned organizations. By many accounts, the privatization program was considered quite successful at the time.

Thus, at first glance, it appeared that privatization was moving in a positive direction. Yet, in many privatized organizations, the state remained a partial owner, and the former senior managers continued to operate overstaffed and inefficient organizations (Standing, 1997). Some analysts reported that more than 70 percent of the shares of privatized companies ended up in the hands of enterprise workers and managers (*The Economist*, 1994). Also, the objectives of many top-level managers had little to do with generating profits for reinvestment in their enterprises. They were often more concerned with satisfying workers' demands for job security, and in accumulating enterprise shares for themselves. Many workers expected that they would start receiving dividends within a year of buying shares of their enterprises. While an attractive prospect, this positive outcome rarely materialized.

The former state enterprise directors sought to choose the form of privatization that would allow the largest portion of shares to be distributed to them and their workers. Many bought large percentages of shares very cheaply, and eventually became the primary owners of their enterprises, but then often stripped the enterprises of their assets. Many senior managers thus ended up owning shares of enterprises that were destitute and incapable of producing anything. Still, some managers were able to initiate effective market strategies and restructure and reorient the activities of their enterprises in new directions.

Private business owners initially showed a great deal of interest in the privatizing process and the newly privatized enterprises. Initially, some tried to buy shares of former state-owned enterprises engaged in activities similar to their own. For instance, a private electronics manufacturer might look for opportunities to buy a former state-owned factory, or the part of it that produced related electronics. However, the form of privatization chosen by the former state-owned enterprise directors often prevented outside firms from buying a controlling block of shares. Consequently, private business owners gradually lost interest in such pursuits, and the privatized enterprises lost opportunities to gain an infusion of new capital.

As the period progressed, many owners of the newly privatized enterprises, as well as new private businesses, rushed to buy other businesses and assets that appeared to have value. Their objective was to diversify their activities and establish themselves solidly in the Russian market. As a result, many of these businesses over-diversified and often became involved in unrelated activities. A significant number went bankrupt or experienced serious financial difficulties. Some business owners, however, were able to exit their ill-conceived expansions and concentrate on their basic activities, while others developed their basic operations even further.

Thus, although 70 percent of large former state-owned enterprises had been declared privatized by mid-1994 (*Economic Newsletter*, August 1994), many observers recognized that little had actually changed. Most privatized firms were still operating in essentially the same way that state-owned enterprises had for decades. Few changed their product offerings in response to market needs, and continued to produce for inventory to maintain employment, even though workers were often not paid on time for their labor. With sales withering, such enterprises were unable to invest in new plant and technology, and still relied upon government subsidies for continued operation. One analyst estimated that the total value of credits received by enterprises during the summer of 1994 exceeded 13 trillion rubles (Lloyd, 1994). The percentage of enterprises receiving subsidies was greatest in the defense sector in which less than half of the major organizations had been privatized.

Some analysts argued that what had occurred was not privatization, but "destatization." While a large percentage of state enterprises had supposedly been privatized, 43 percent of industrial production came from enterprises where the state was still the sole owner. An additional 40 percent came from firms where the state continued to own a significant share. Few improvements occurred, and industrial production for the first ten months of 1994 shrank by 22 percent compared to the same period in 1993 (*Economic Newsletter*, July 1994).

Overall, the results of privatization's first stage turned out to be less successful than expected. Although much ownership had been redistributed into private hands, little new capital had been infused into the enterprises. Another important requirement for progress, a change of management, also failed to occur. The same people continued to run the newly privatized enterprises, except that many of the best managers left to work in private business. Thus, managers who were in charge when their enterprises reached a state of crisis during the communist and post-communist periods remained in charge. Industrial decline continued, unemployment grew, and the public expressed increasing dissatisfaction with the privatization process.

NOMENKLATURA STAGE—MID-1994 THROUGH 1997

The Nomenklatura stage began in mid-1994 with the start of privatization's second phase, which had the objective of infusing new capital into Russian enterprises. Government officials believed that such funds would enable former state-owned enterprises to operate as private enterprises. The specific objective was to find strategic investors for the most economically important enterprises, primarily in the natural resources, metallurgy, telecommunications, high technology, and food industry sectors. In contrast to the earlier period of voucher privatization, shares at this stage were sold for money in open auctions to the highest bidder. However, many people expressed skepticism about the openness and honesty of the auction process.

As might have been expected during a period of major rapid changes, inconsistencies developed. At the federal level, a large-scale sale of state property was undertaken. Yet, the opposite occurred at the local level, which saw the Moscow city government repurchasing the automotive giants AvtoZIL and Moskvich. In another instance, the government's June 1994 decree allowing the ruble to float in the currency market was a significant step in market reform. However, because of the government's onerous taxation policies and restrictive foreign investment measures, new funds for enterprise investment under privatization's phase two did not materialize to any significant extent. Additional hindrances to capital infusion were the government's problems in freeing the ruble, and President Yeltsin's announcement in mid-1994 that the role of government institutions in regulating the market should be strengthened. These events resulted in increasing uncertainty about the government's real objectives, and gave rise to questions about whether it even had a clear policy on privatization.

Some government officials argued that the market had not yet developed to the point where it could significantly influence changes in the behavior of enterprise managers and workers, which might increase their effectiveness. Many in the government, therefore, saw it necessary to become more actively involved in regulating the economy. It appeared to many observers that the government was trying to move in two directions simultaneously—liberalizing market transactions, while also increasing government controls. One source reported the rapid increase in barter caused by the government's uncertain directions and onerous tax policies. He cited a survey of more than 200 enterprises which revealed that barter of goods, debt swaps, and other non-monetary deals accounted for 73 percent of all transactions in 1996 and 1997 (Kramer, 1998).

A further deterrent to successful privatization was that, in cases where funds were received by enterprises, they were often appropriated by the senior managers for their own gain. Most of these individuals were not only holdovers from the past, but had also accumulated large ownership positions by receiving stock from the government, and by purchasing additional shares from employees and other citizens. They were often said to be assisted in their financial dealings by government officials. Some enterprise managers were described as being internally focused, looking to the past, resistant to change, close-minded, and slow to react to new ideas (Longnecker and Popovski, 1994; Shama, 1993). It appeared that such managers were more interested in maintaining their own positions than in improving the condition of their enterprises. In contrast, the government had the stated objective of achieving positive financial results in the enterprises. Although the two groups seemed to have divergent goals, they often collaborated in self-serving activities.

Together, these members of the industrial, government, and former communist party elite were referred to as the nomenklatura (Mikheyev, 1997).

The term refers to a new elite, the leaders of large commercial organizations as well as a significant number of high-level state and local bureaucrats. These influential decision makers cooperated in the development of a new group of oligopolies built from powerful former state enterprises. These oligopolies were established in major financial and industrial groups called FIGs which, under the friendly eye of the state, were able to conduct business without real competition, and thus control prices. This situation was most egregious in five or six large conglomerates such as Menatep, which had major holdings in banks, enterprises, and natural resources. The leaders of these and similar enterprises became known as oligarchs who, with their government allies, gained substantial control over the economy. In 1993 the first FIG was registered consisting of 20 industrial enterprises and one bank. The number increased dramatically by the end of the Nomenklatura period.

The rise of powerful commercial banks was a major force that eventually contributed to restraining the development of a market economy, even though a strong banking system was deemed necessary to implement such reforms. These new banks played a key, but negative role by making loans to the government to help pay its debts and implement its policies of increased control over the economy. When the government was unable to repay its loans, these banks began obtaining controlling shares of large state enterprises as repayment. Recognizing this practice by the banks, one analyst noted:

> Of special importance was the episode of 1995 in which Yeltsin, acting through Anatoly Chubais [the privatization minister], in the loans for shares scheme, bought in a particularly blatant way the financial and political support of leading bankers and businessmen—a group soon to be known as the 'financial oligarchs'—by letting them acquire major state assets at little or no cost to themselves. (Reddaway, 1998)

Gaining control of large amounts of fixed assets, however, actually increased the need for additional capital by these banks. Lacking significant resources to finance their growing businesses, they tried to attract large quantities of foreign capital. One of the most outstanding illustrations is found in the activities of Vladimir Potanin. In mid-1997, for instance, he convinced the international financier George Soros to put up $980 million to assist him in buying 25 percent of Svyazinvest, the state-owned telecommunications company, as well as borrowing over $600 million through syndicated loans from foreign banks and Eurobonds. In addition, British Petroleum in late 1997 paid Potanin $571 million for a 10-percent stake in Sidanko, Russia's third largest oil producer (Kranz, 1999).

Some very large financial-industrial groups emerged including Onexim, Menatep, Inkombank, and Alfa. Most started as banks which grew rapidly during the stages of commercialization and voucher privatization, and remained the largest banks in Russia, at least until the country's financial crisis of August 1998. Their acquisition of major former state-owned enterprises, including many from the rich natural resources sector, made them the most powerful conglomerates in the country. Little is actually known about how they acquired their initial capital, but it is clear that they obtained funds from the state budget and that this funding financed their growth. The banks were charged with managing this money for various governmental purposes.

Transactions using money from the state budget turned out to be very profitable, especially during periods of rapid inflation. One such activity was the purchase of treasury bills from the government by the powerful banks. Called GKOs and OFZs, these treasury bills were issued by the government to finance the state budget, since tax collections proved insufficient. This practice began at a modest level in 1993 and 1994, but by 1997 these financial instruments amounted to over 14 percent of the country's GNP, and increased to 15 percent in 1998. These bills often carried annual interest rates of over 200 percent, and by the end of 1997, 35 percent of all banking assets were held in the form of GKOs, and they produced 41 percent of all bank earnings. Thus, these banks and the new private enterprises to which they made loans were closely linked to the state budget. And the government's voracious appetite for bank loans also severely limited funds for the entrepreneurial sector. In addition, many state enterprises, as well as semi-privatized firms whose controlling share packages still belonged to the government, deposited their funds in the commercial banks to earn high interest rates (*Economic Newsletter*, October 1998).

In addition to offering high rates of interest, private commercial banks were a mechanism for enterprise managers to avoid state control of their business transactions. Thus, the managers of commercial banks and their enterprise counterparts established a common bond facilitated by the use of state funds. Their manipulation of state budget funds, at a time of continuing budget deficits, significantly weakened the government's ability to develop sound financial policies that might have been used to support market reforms. The alliance also deterred the development of a market economy since a significant portion of the funds was controlled by a small number of elite banks and their favored customers. They became ever more deeply entwined with high-ranking government officials, and the situation gave rise to the term "crony capitalism."

Although many bankers, industrialists, and government officials were making huge sums from these financial transactions, little was reinvested in developing the country's economic potential. Instead, large amounts of capital were spirited out of the country to personal accounts and investments abroad. According to the World Bank's conservative estimate, $88.7 billion fled Russia from 1993 through 1996, and a later study by a team of Canadian and Russian academic economists estimated the figure to be $140 billion from 1992 to 1997 (Reddaway, 1998).

Commercial banks during these times had a powerful lobby with various levels of government, including President Yeltsin's closest advisors. Some bankers, such as Potanin and Berezovsky, became leaders of influential finance and banking groups. Simultaneously, government officials such as Vasiliev and Kokh went to work for the banking groups. By this exchange of senior executives and bureaucrats, the nomenklatura became positioned to significantly influence the economy. Members of the group managed to get the best of former state property for themselves and their organizations. One Western expert concluded:

> Yeltsin and the governments he has appointed have become so beholden to the 'oligarchs' and other established interests that they have lacked the will and the power to effectively implement any reformist policies, perfect or imperfect, that involve painful change for the establishment ... [which is seen as] pursuing their private interests with no regard for the national interest. (Reddaway, 1998)

All of these self-serving activities occurred while the government, under phase two of privatization, was ostensibly trying to attract strategic investors to privatized enterprises. These investors, it was hoped, would improve the management of privatized firms, including those in which the government still owned a significant share. Workers in these firms, however, had become disenchanted with their ownership of shares which had not produced the dividends they expected. Many sold their shares, often to managers and their allies who solidified their control over the enterprises by amassing significant blocks of stock. While they gained control of enterprise activities, no real improvements occurred. Owners simply did not know what to do nor how to do it, and if they did know, they often were unwilling to do so. A complicating factor was that they lacked managerial training, the majority having had technical education in engineering or the natural sciences. Even when investors had been backed by foreign capital, the management of privatized enterprises did not usually improve. Foreign investors often had short-term profit goals, and a desire to quickly capture market positions through strategies that did not require large investments in developing human resources. But it was precisely this type of investment that many believed was required to improve the management and operations of these large enterprises.

In contrast to the deterioration of large enterprises, which experienced a decrease of 10 million employees from 1994 to 1997, the number of employees in small businesses grew by 600,000 from 1995 to 1997. The entrepreneurial sector therefore seemed to be growing successfully, and one source predicted that "if there is any hope for growth in the economy, it will have to come from that sector" (*Economic Newsletter*, December 1998). The same source noted that the number of new businesses rose by about 20,000 from 1996 to 1997, and that Russian statistics estimated 2.7 million such businesses were operating in 1997.

Healthy development in the entrepreneurial sector, however, did not occur without difficulties, the most severe of which was the pressure to pay bribes and protection to various groups. According to a major study of over 200 entrepreneurs in 20 regions conducted in 1997 and 1998, 39 percent said they had been the victims of threats and force from time to time, while another three percent reported encountering such problems often. Seventeen percent of the respondents believed that, with respect to Russian business in general, threats and force occurred frequently, while 62 percent believed these situations occurred from time to time. Still, 58 percent reported that it was possible to conduct business without being subject to threats and force, while another 34 percent believed it was possible, but with difficulty. Finally, 56 percent reported that during the last few years there had been no change in the frequency of such problems, while another 30 percent reported a decrease (Radaev, 1998). Thus, there was some degree of optimism among entrepreneurs, even in the area they viewed as their major problem. This is not to imply that all such problems had disappeared, since another survey noted that dealing with corrupt government officials was more harmful to business than threats from the mafia (*Economic Newsletter*, July 1999). Another source noted that "any money that reaches Russia from abroad risks being siphoned off by organized crime, in cahoots with the state" (*The Economist*, 1999c, p. 19).

Although the privatization process did not improve the performance of most large enterprises, the economy was on a fairly even keel for 1997, with GDP increasing 0.4 percent and industrial output 1.9 percent. Inflation seemed to be under control, with prices rising only 11 percent during 1997 (*Economic Newsletter*, February 1999). It was apparent, however, that the economy was still very fragile. Foreign investors, as well as Russian managers and workers, needed to show patience and systematically develop their businesses using effective long-term strategies so as to become more competitive. Nonetheless, this was generally not the disposition or objective of any of these parties, nor of many government officials during the Nomenklatura period. Many managers and their government allies were more interested in solidifying their power and wealth by accumulating ownership in the assets of former state-owned enterprises. In many cases, they sold off these assets, or created their own private companies to own such assets.

Many of the most valuable former state-owned enterprises, with the cooperation of government officials, were acquired very cheaply by the conglomerates of a few powerful oligarchs who were the leaders of major FIGs. The first one was registered in 1993, and by late 1997 there were 72 FIGs consisting of 1,500 enterprises and organizations and nearly 100 financial institutions. This concentration of power, coupled with ever-changing and often contradictory government policies, eventually resulted in the deterioration of the emerging market economy, and its replacement by a much less free market. These events were occurring simultaneously with the weakening financial condition of the Russian government.

In retrospect, both phases of privatization, the latter of which included the Nomenklatura stage, were seen as failing to achieve their goals. The hoped-for infusion of new capital into enterprises, through the purchase of additional stock, did not materialize to any great extent because of continuing political, legal, and economic instability. The initially positive view of Phase One's accomplishments changed over the years as ownership of shares became consolidated into the hands of a few individuals, specifically senior enterprise executives and the leaders of a number of large conglomerates. These developments contributed to the reluctance of new investors to purchase shares in these closely-held organizations (Filatotchev, Starkey, and Wright, 1994). Instead, many large foreign companies, especially from North America and Western Europe, chose the route of direct investment in their own Russian subsidiaries, as well as selective participation in partnerships with Russian enterprises and government organizations (McCarthy and Puffer, 1997b; Puffer, McCarthy, and Zhuplev, 1998).

The transition from state ownership to privatized operations was an extraordinarily difficult process. Most privatized enterprises became engaged in struggles for survival, especially as the government, which was unable to collect taxes effectively, continuously reduced subsidies. Enterprises were expected to finance themselves through profits from their operations and by attracting new investment capital. Such developments seldom materialized. Most enterprises were grossly overstaffed with personnel who were often unable to adjust to the new conditions, and unprecedented layoffs of millions of workers occurred. Plants and equipment were often outdated, and products were unable to compete with imports. Marketing, which might have facilitated a smoother transition, was virtually non-existent in such enterprises.

The move from central planning toward a market-based economy placed an onerous burden on managers of newly privatized enterprises. They were now free to set their own production targets and determine the prices and markets for their products, and they had to develop their own sources of supply. Although they were required to be self-financing, bank loans were scarce and, if available, came with exorbitant interest rates. Inflation was a devastating reality during the early 1990s, as exemplified by 1992's rate of 2,400 percent (*Economic Newsletter*, March 1993). Restrictive and ever-changing government policies, coupled with unrealistic and unpredictable tax laws, made managing enterprises a difficult task. Freedom to manage was accompanied by severely limited resources, while a lack of market-oriented experience and training hampered managers' ability to operate under the new conditions. This situation was a traumatic change from prior times when the single objective for managers in state-owned enterprises had been to fulfill a centrally-mandated plan.

STATIZATION STAGE—1998 THROUGH THE END OF THE DECADE

The government had vacillated for years between loosening and tightening its grip on the economy. In early 1998, significantly tighter controls were imposed when President Yeltsin announced that the deteriorating economic situation made it necessary for the government to become more deeply involved in regulating the economy. GDP, in fact, had begun to decline in May of 1998, after a period of relative stability. The downward trend continued so that by the August crisis, GDP was down more than 8 percent, and industrial production by 11.5 percent, compared to a year earlier. September saw a further drop in GDP of 9.9 percent over the prior September. For 1998 as a whole, both GDP and industrial output had declined approximately 5 percent relative to 1997. Inflation had also become a major problem, with prices having risen 84 percent during the year. Another signal of impending problems was foreign capital investment which, in the first six months of 1998, was at the same level as the corresponding period for 1997. By contrast, in 1996 foreign investment had increased by 2.3 times over 1995, and further increased in 1997 by 1.8 times over 1996 (*Economic Newsletter*, January 1999).

The country's financial situation was exacerbated by the mid-February 1999 allegation that the Central Bank had channeled $50 million into an offshore account in the UK (*Economic Newsletter*, February 1999). PricewaterhouseCoopers, the international accounting firm retained by the International Monetary Fund to audit the Bank's policies and accounts, verified this violation when auditing the bank's activities with the offshore institution, Financial Management Company. The auditors also found that the Central Bank was keeping double books for transactions with this organization (*Boston Sunday Globe*, 1999). Further allegations of wrongdoing and money laundering surfaced in September 1999. American, British, and Russian investigators announced that there was "strong evidence" that 780 Russian officials used a bond-selling scheme to send billions of dollars out of the country in 1998 a few hours after the IMF deposited a $4.8 billion loan into the Central Bank. The investigators also suspected that the Russian mafia and Kremlin authorities may have siphoned as much as $15 billion out of the country through the Bank of New York and other financial institutions (Kelley and Stanglin, 1999).

Given these circumstances, the Statization stage was perhaps the logical culmination of the Privatization and Nomenklatura stages. With power being heavily concentrated in fewer and fewer interlocking hands, and the economy rapidly deteriorating, a return to a more pervasive role of government was virtually inevitable. The country's difficult situation was exacerbated by Yeltsin's ineffectiveness at governing, as well as by constant changes in government officials and their policies, growing resentment and discontent among citizens, and the increasing power of the communists in parliament.

To facilitate the government's plans to take a leading role in bolstering the economy, a policy was formulated of utilizing the oligopolies instead of developing small business. By late 1997, major enterprises, with the help of the government, had stepped up the pace of vertical and horizontal integration of industry, as well as linking bank capital with industrial capital. As in the past, government officials believed that this approach would improve the economy by increasing the strength of larger enterprises. However, the problems of managing these enterprises were again ignored. Enterprise troubles were invariably attributed to a lack of money, with managers seemingly saying: "Give us enough money and we'll fix everything." A larger role was seen for the government, such as introducing strong protectionist barriers, or possibly rebuilding the economic infrastructure of socialism. Whether consumers would accept the offerings of these monopolies was questionable, however, since many had become familiar with high-quality imported products. Consumers might, it was thought, be resistant to the inferior quality of goods produced by state-supported monopolies. What were really needed, in fact, were enterprises that could produce competitive products, but the existing managers would not or could not make this happen.

The move toward large enterprises, coupled with the close relationships between a small number of oligarchs and government officials, set the course for increasing state involvement in the economy. The financial crisis of August 1998, which saw the government default on its internal and international debts, ended any semblance of financial stability and confidence in a free-market economy. The IMF postponed a $4.3 billion payment of a $22.6 billion rescue package after the Russian government defaulted on $40 billion of its domestic debt in August, and allowed the ruble to devalue precipitously (Filipov, 1998a). Without such relief, according to the Russian finance ministry, the economy could contract by 5 to 7 percent in 1999 (Kranz, 1998b). Some Western and Russian analysts, however, believed that it was the ill-conceived policies of these Western-controlled world financial institutions that had caused the crisis in the first place, with their large infusions of cash lacking proper controls and accountability (Reddaway, 1998).

Some sources believed that Western countries and organizations should not make the same mistake again:

> This time, however, the rich countries should steel themselves and say, "Sorry, not until you put your house in order." Unless Russia gets a radically new economic regime, any further western money is likely to be squandered. (*The Economist*, 1999b, p. 17)

Another source reported Russia's debt to be $150.6 billion, of which $16 billion was obligated to be serviced in 1999. Despite such staggering liabilities, tax collections were reported to be only $1 billion in January 1999. It seemed likely that Russia would be able to pay off no more than $7 billion of its debt, putting enormous pressure on the government to successfully reschedule its obligations (*Economic Newsletter*, February 1999).

Many believed the government was largely responsible for the crisis and the events leading up to it, while many also blamed the self-serving oligarchs:

> The Russian media have branded these so-called robber barons as the main culprits in the August crisis. While there is plenty of evidence to support these allegations, it was the federal government—and not a cartel of prominent Moscow banks—that aggressively developed the domestic and international market for Russian treasury bills and other public debt instruments. (Berzonsky, 1998)

One Western source, however, laid the blame directly on the President, stating: "Today, the immense power Yeltsin enjoyed is seen as the primary reason for Russia's worst crises of recent years" [including the 1998 economic turmoil] (Filipov, 1998b).

The crisis underscored the increased power of the communists as seen in their ability to block the appointment of Viktor Chernomyrdin as prime minister. Chernomyrdin had held the position earlier and was Yeltsin's choice for the important post. This nomination and its denial by the communist-controlled Duma might have seemed a surprise to some, since Chernomyrdin's proposed approach seemed very consistent with communist goals. One Western source commented:

> Chernomyrdin's strategy is straight out of the old Soviet book. The former chairman of gas monopoly Gazprom believes that the backbone of the Russian economy is its industrial enterprises.... Chernomyrdin wants to turn these companies around by flooding them with cash.... The only way the prime minister can do that is by printing rubles. (Kranz, 1998a)

The same source offered an explanation of why the communists in the Duma, and even the noncommunist upper house of parliament, opposed him: "Chernomyrdin is expected to allow favored private banks run by his powerful business supporters to channel credits to industry. That could further strengthen the grip of powerful financial industrial groups on the economy" (Kranz, 1998a). These groups, of course, had fallen into disrepute for being among the instigators of the crisis.

The September 1998 appointment of Evgeny Primakov, a 68-year-old Soviet-era cabinet minister, confirmed in the eyes of most observers a return to increased state control and involvement in the economy. He himself announced: "State intervention in economic life is essential to establish economic order" (Thornhill, 1998). One of his first decisions was to appoint a leading communist legislator, Yury Maslyukov, as minister for the economy.

Primakov's strong support in the communist-controlled Duma came as no surprise, but his broad support in the mostly noncommunist upper house of parliament did surprise some. Among his supporters was Grigory Yavlinsky, head of the Yabloko party, who supported major market-oriented reforms such as privatization of property. The situation which brought Primakov to power might be explained in part by a poll conducted by the All-Russian Center for Public Opinion Research shortly after the August crisis: 83 percent of Russians surveyed favored a return to state control over prices, 70 percent supported the nationalization of the major companies that had been privatized since 1992, and 50 percent wanted to nationalize commercial banks (*Economic Newsletter*, October 1998).

Even his ousted predecessor, Sergei Kiriyenko, "felt that Primakov was a good compromise leader and that he had managed to obtain political stability" [however, at a price of economic inaction] (*Economic Newsletter*, December 1998). Perhaps the reasons for Primakov's broad support were best expressed by former Soviet President Mikhail Gorbachev:

> In the very beginning, the communists said the Primakov government was a bourgeois government, whereas the pro-Western people said it was a communist government that would drag us backward. These different views mean that this is exactly the government we need, because our wild extremists on the left and on the right equally dislike it. (Puffer, 1999)

Probably the reason Primakov appealed to so many in the time of crisis was his reputation for putting the country's interests first. According to one Western source: "He is a man who by temperament focuses on the national interest and can be expected to do his best to rein in, perhaps sharply, the private sector 'oligarchs'" (Reddaway, 1998). Primakov's dilemma and subsequent inconsistency in policy making, though, might well have been foreseen given his early statements. He said, for instance: "Reforms are necessary, the present situation cannot be overcome without them" (Filipov, 1998c). Yet, he also called for a strong state role in the economy, something the communists had been demanding. It was clear from his vacillations that he saw the country's major priority as being internal stability rather than meeting its financial commitments to outsiders.

However, it was the economic events triggered by the August crisis, rather than actions by the Primakov government that took their toll on the oligarchs. The three-month moratorium on the redemption of the GKO-based government debt declared by Prime Minister Kiriyenko in August "meant that the banks with such a large percentage of their assets invested in GKOs had in effect become insolvent ... and in no way could provide their depositors with their deposits [because] their money had been frozen" (*Economic Newsletter*, October 1998). This default by the government, coupled with the subsequent ruble devaluation, effectively cut off the cash flow needed by the major banks to continue doing business. The immediate result was that 18 of the country's 20 major banks failed (Matthews and Hirsh, 1998).

In describing the precipitous fall from power and influence of Onexim Bank's founder, one source noted:

> Potanin is not alone. Russia's six other banking tycoons—Russians call them "oligarchs"—have been brought to their knees by falling commodity prices, Russia's financial crisis, and their own greed and mismanagement. [Yet it is] widely believed that most have stashed millions in bank accounts outside Russia. (Kranz, 1999)

The same observer quoted the editor-in-chief of the Moscow newspaper, *Segodnya*, as saying: "The oligarchs have money enough to live…. But they have lost their influence." Still another source editorialized: "The arrest or bankruptcy of one or two of Russia's oligarchs, as the most influential tycoons are known, would go down well both with Russians and with westerners wondering whether to bail the country out again" (*The Economist*, 1999a, p. 51). This almost occurred when a warrant was issued for the arrest of Boris Berezovsky. His close association with Yeltsin's daughter not only spared him this fate, but it is reputed to have been the major reason for the later sacking of Prime Minister Primakov (Matthews and Dlugy, 1999).

Another source, in describing its ranking of the leading industrialists, also noted the fall from power of these oligarchs:

> It is the owners and directors of processing or manufacturing plants that have moved up, and the bankers that have moved down if not entirely off the list, unless they are bankers that have been blessed by the government in one way or another. (*Economic Newsletter*, November 1998)

To help ensure their survival, three of the major oligarchs, Potanin, Guzinsky, and Khodorkovsky, joined forces and merged their banks into a single holding company (Watson and Matthews, 1998). It was not clear, however, whether these events signaled the beginning of the end for the nomenklatura. Although these particular oligarchs had lost their influence at least for the time being, their return to power, or their replacement by similar opportunists, could not be ruled out.

In this volatile environment, Primakov's appointment added an element of stability, but many saw his lack of a clear economic direction as a sign that the country would not make any significant economic progress:

> Unimaginable though it seemed when he took office in the chaotic days after the ruble fell out of bed last August, political stability has broken out…. Mr. Primakov's success so far rests on avoiding controversy by doing very little. His inactivity—over collecting taxes, reforming prices, sorting out the banks, paying wages that have sometimes gone unpaid for a whole year—has been masterly. (*The Economist*, 1999a, p. 51)

The West, and particularly the IMF and the World Bank, had demanded a plan of austerity and tough measures, such as cutting federal spending, to bring the economy back from the brink. External pressures notwithstanding, Primakov's initial plans showed none of the toughness needed to improve the country's projected $5 billion deficit. It was seen by one analyst as "a vague and contradictory economic crisis plan ... that amounts to a tactical retreat from market reforms" (*Boston Sunday Globe*, 1998, p. A9).

The same source saw the plan as a "hodgepodge of concepts ... which failed to resolve the country's central dilemma: how to pursue socially popular policies such as price controls and higher wages while still meeting IMF demands for fiscal discipline and market reforms." A noted Western expert on the Russian economy summarized the situation by stating: "More than that, his [Primakov's] government consists of so many different factions that it will be impossible to take any significant action" (Goldman, 1998). The same commentator also noted: "There never was a consensus in Russia on market reforms, and there isn't one now" (Goldman quoted in Browning, 1998). Another authority commented that the country had reached a stage of "stalled transition" that could restart in a number of different directions, most negative, but some positive (Colton, 1999).

A cornerstone of the Primakov plan that worried many analysts was a restructuring of the banking sector. The banking sector would be overseen by the Central Bank and its recently appointed director, Viktor Gerashchenko. In his previous tenure in that role from 1992 to 1994, he had resorted to printing large quantities of rubles to support failing state enterprises. This in turn caused hyperinflation and wiped out the savings of millions of Russian citizens. One source noted, however, that the IMF had "criticized the [government's] plan to bail out 15 of the country's largest banks that found themselves short of cash when the ruble crashed in August" (Wheatley, 1998). The same source noted that the plan would classify banks in order to decide which ones were strongest and might be saved, but saw this as being "susceptible to the kind of favoritism that allowed Russia's poorly managed banks to grow in the first place." Another source quoted a Goldman Sachs forecast that the value of the ruble, which had been six to the dollar before the crisis, would fall from its level of 16 in late 1998 to 100 during 1999. He further stated: "It is now clear that this government will do little more than muddle through" (*Financial Times*, 1998).

Primakov's lack of a credible plan was one reason given by Yeltsin for replacing him in May 1999 with Sergei Stepashin. Some observers, however, believed that Primakov's ouster was the result of his endorsing the arrest of the oligarch Boris Berezovsky, a close friend of Yeltsin's daughter (Goldman, 1999). Berezovsky's power, in fact, seemed to remain intact as did his close ties to Yeltsin's family. His August 1999 dispute with an American company over the ownership of the highly respected and politically independent newspaper, *Kommersant*, was reported as an attempt to gain control of key media outlets prior to the fall 1999 Duma elections (Higgins, 1999).

Almost concurrent with this dispute was Yeltsin's naming of his fourth prime minister in 17 months. His August 10, 1999 appointment of the head of the Federal Security Service, Vladimir Putin, to the prime minister's post was seen by experts as purely a survival strategy on Yeltsin's part: "It's not about policy, it's not about Chechnya, it's not about reform or no reform. It's about the survival of Boris Yeltsin and his family once he steps down from power," said Ariel Cohen, a Russian analyst at Washington's Heritage Foundation (Nichols, 1999). The same source reported Clinton administration officials as saying that the change should not affect US-Russia relations. Yeltsin may, in fact, have sensed the increasing power of a new political coalition headed by Moscow Mayor Luzhkov and Former Primer Minister Primakov. Their objective was clearly to siphon support from both the Kremlin and the communists, and they seemed to be succeeding (York, 1999).

In spite of the many erratic decisions by Yeltsin, the IMF had seen it necessary to approve a $4.5 billion loan program for Russia in July 1999 to help stabilize the economy. Then-Prime Minister Stepashin, in fact, had been seen as instrumental in securing the loan during a reportedly successful visit to the United States. Stepashin was quoted as stating: "Our primary task for the long term is to develop a free and attractive investment climate" (Weymouth, 1999). In fact, although total investment in Russia plummeted after the mid-1998 financial crisis, foreign direct investment fell far less sharply. The crisis triggered a 75-percent devaluation of the ruble, which made imports far too expensive for most Russians (Weymouth, 1999).

Ironically, the devaluation spurred investment in plant and equipment on the part of Western companies, as well as many Russian firms. Russian companies were reported by a long-involved Western executive as becoming even more aggressive in their investments than foreign organizations to take advantage of what they saw as a window of opportunity (Tappan, 1998). Among the multinationals, the same observer found in an informal survey in late 1998 that 97 percent of the foreign executives he interviewed said they planned to stay in Russia despite the problems. Other sources noted that Danone of France had committed to building a $100 million plant in Moscow, Nestle of Switzerland planned a $30 to $50 million plant, while Cadbury of the UK, IKEA of Sweden, and H. J. Heinz, Procter & Gamble, and Gillette of the US were among the multinationals that planned major capital investments to ensure their market positions (*Economic Newsletter*, July 1999; Matlack, 1999).

Although serious problems persisted in the economy, such investment was only one of the relatively positive indicators in 1999. The economy, in fact, showed some signs of recovery during the first and second quarters, particularly in the area of raw materials such as oil, gas, and metals. The ruble's devaluation contributed to an increase in exports of such products.

GDP had not yet shown an increase, but the decline in industrial production which had begun to abate somewhat in late 1998 actually ended in May 1999. That measure turned remarkably positive with a year-to-year increase of six percent in May 1999 over May 1998, nine percent in June, and a reported eleven percent in July 1999. And although consumer prices continued to rise, they did so at a slower pace. The Russian stock market, while considered very risky, rebounded strongly and showed one of the steepest increases of the world's financial markets during early 1999. Germany continued to be the largest investor in Russia as well as its major trading partner, while the United States followed closely behind (*Economic Newsletter*, June, July, August, 1999).

So although the Statization period marked an increase in the government's involvement in the economy, its activity was relatively benign. The country continued to edge its way out of the mid-1998 crisis, albeit at a relatively slow rate. Still, the signs of a potential turnaround, or at least a cessation of the downward spiral, had begun to emerge by early 1999. The mid-year picture showed other positive indications for Russian businesses in some sectors. The solid basis for this relatively positive view was noted several months earlier by a British expert on key Russian industries (Hill, 1998). A parallel positive development was the increasing investment activity by Western multinationals. The US-Russia Investment Fund, sponsored by the US government, also adjusted its strategy. After temporarily halting lending and investments following the August 1998 financial crisis, it reinstated its programs by the end of 1998. The fund then assigned Russian banks to specific risk categories and attempted to work with the strongest institutions (Torch, 1999). In fact, a few positive developments had begun to emerge in the banking sector. Some medium-sized banks had invested less heavily in government-issued GKOs and remained relatively strong, and the Russian government had also begun to allow foreigners greater participation in the Russian banking market (Tappan, 1998).

It was clear during mid-1999 that the international community would continue to support Russia, but not without imposing conditions and recognizing the inherent risks. The type of developments desired is illustrated by the Gore-Stepashin Commission's publication in July 1999 of *Basic Guidelines for Codes of Business Conduct*. The US-Russia Business Development Committee and the Chamber of Commerce and Industry of the Russian Federation had cooperated to produce these guidelines for Russian business based upon widely accepted principles of good business practices. While recognized as a good beginning, it was understood by all involved that putting such guidelines into practice was what Russia needed to secure its position in the international business community (*Bisnis Bulletin*, 1999).

IMPLICATIONS FOR THE CASE STUDIES TO FOLLOW

The economic evolution that transpired in Russia during the 1990s, beginning with the Commercialization phase, seemingly offered unlimited opportunities. And the Privatization phase began with great promise, but never materialized to meet expectations. Still, many enterprises, including most of those to be described in later chapters, continued to grow and prosper. Clear strategies were developed, objectives were set, growth was achieved, and some organizations began to evolve toward broader levels of participation in decisions. Strategic thinking was in place, and decision-making processes reflected successful organizational growth and development.

The Nomenklatura phase, however, was accompanied by stagnation in economic development. Nonetheless, many organizations, like some of those we analyzed, continued to build their businesses, primarily because of strategic orientations which allowed them to both pursue their goals and remain flexible in their plans and tactics. Even in the early phases of statization, many such organizations were able to make some progress, although strategic choices became more limited.

Moreover, an additional 7,000 entrepreneurships were created during the first half of 1998 – prior to the country's financial crisis in August, which caused many smaller businesses and entrepreneurships to close their doors. And even after the crisis, there seemed "to be a significant increase in the number of people doing business." Many of these businesses, however, were "operating without officially registering, and in many instances, of course, off the books and illegally" (*Economic Newsletter*, December 1998). The primary reasons for operating in this way were to avoid drawing the attention of criminal groups and tax officials. In one study, entrepreneurs reported that corruption and taxes were their two major problems (Radaev, 1998).

Noting that the crisis did open opportunities for some, one Russian expert on the country's entrepreneurial sector stated that the crisis allowed some new entrepreneurs to start businesses in place of others who failed. However, they often operated with a more cautious approach to their businesses. They severely limited the number of relationships in which they became involved to a few close and trusted associates, and placed less emphasis on family ties in business than in the past. What had become most important to many entrepreneurs was the professional reputation of the individuals with whom they did business (Radaev, 1999). Another cautionary note was sounded at the political-economic level:

> In Russia's return to statist capitalism, the vibrant part of its economy could be damaged. Alongside cash-strapped industry has grown a dynamic private sector encompassing everything from retail stores to computer software companies, to small consumer-goods manufacturers. Now, they are caught in the financial

31

squeeze, unable to withdraw their funds from banks or to pay for imported goods. (Kranz, 1998a)

With the mid-1998 financial crisis, all the organizations we studied established survival as their primary goal, while attempting to maintain their strategic directions. In early 1999, it was still unclear whether the strengthening of the state's influence and control on the activity of large enterprises would be achieved through legislative, financial, or personnel methods, or a combination of these approaches. It was becoming clearer, in any case, that the result would be at least the partial dismantling of free-market mechanisms. Some analysts predicted that the Duma and presidential elections of 1999 and 2000 would bring even more power to the anti-market forces, particularly the nationalists and the communists who were allied with the directors of many large former state enterprises. Such events would bode very badly for organizations such as the ones we analyzed, which were attempting to develop in the fast-disappearing market economy.

Some Russians, however, still hoped for another approach. The country, they believed, could possibly implement true privatization of most resources, including land and minerals. This notion, in fact, was a cornerstone of the program put forth by presidential hopeful, Grigory Yavlinsky in late 1998: "He would institute land reform, which he argued was a prerequisite for economic reform. Land was the country's main asset, and if private it could serve as collateral for borrowers. In his view, there could not be other reforms until land itself had been privatized" (*Economic Newsletter*, January 1999). Like others, Yavlinsky called for major reforms in the banking system in order to restore confidence among investors and ordinary citizens. Additionally, he advocated reducing the power of monopolies, especially Gazprom, one of the world's richest corporations, but whose wealth was enjoyed by very few in Russia. Such actions as those proposed by Yavlinsky would undoubtedly benefit most of the organizations that we analyzed.

The probability of this market-oriented alternative, however, seemed rather illusory in 1999, given the resurgence of the large monopolistic enterprises which were moving ever closer to renationalization. To accomplish real privatization, the country would need to pass laws to separate private property from government control. The state, moreover, would have to be prohibited from participating in most activities in which it would profit, such as the development of land and mineral resources. Rather than being directly involved with business and the economy, the state would have to concern itself with the political arena, and support the development of privatized businesses and the economy. Those espousing this view argued that previous Russian governments had already failed in their attempts to build a productive economy through state ownership of land and operation of the country's natural resources and means of industrial production.

Some analysts believed that the weakening of the market economy might bring about a further fragmentation of Russia into independent regions. Some regions, as well as their financial institutions, had emerged from the 1998 crisis in stronger positions than the central government. As one analyst reported:

> Some regional banks have come through this crisis in far better shape than the high-profile competitors from Russia's capital. Because these regional banks engaged in very little speculation in GKOs or similar debt instruments, their portfolios suffered relatively minimal damage when the debt moratorium was announced in August. (Berzonsky, 1998)

The same source noted that these banks had become more creditworthy than the Russian government. Some regions by 1998 had already ceased paying taxes to the central government, such as Sverdlovsk, Khakassia and Kaliningrad, while others, like the Sakha republic and the Kemerovo region, had begun accumulating their own gold and foreign currency reserves. One Western analyst suggested that they might also begin issuing their own currency as one region had already threatened, and also noted that they would likely take other measures to make themselves independent of Moscow (Reddaway, 1998). It is unclear how such a scenario would affect businesses like those we analyzed, but it is likely that some could prosper while others would suffer.

In viewing the post-crisis events in Russia, including the appointment of Primakov as Prime Minister, the Russian business daily, *Kommersant*, declared in a headline that Russia had reached the end of an era. The newspaper also stated that Russia was no longer a strictly presidential republic, but a land where parliament would have a larger say. In fact, one post-crisis poll in the fall of 1998 indicated that two-thirds of the population wanted Yeltsin to resign (Nettleson, 1998). Whatever course Russia does take, its prominence in the global arena necessitates that the rest of the world, especially the West, support positive policies and developments whenever possible.

It is hoped that a stable environment can provide a reasonable platform for positive economic developments based upon the socio-political and economic route the country cultivates for itself. In an insightful summary of Russia's situation in 1999, a Western authority concluded:

> The question the Russians and foreign observers will be asking eighteen months hence [after the presidential elections in 2000] is whether the winner will have the desire and ability to restart systemic reforms—economic and political—or whether he will try to lead the country neither backward nor forward but laterally, onto a kind of historical spur line where it could be marooned for many years. (Colton, 1999)

Most foreign analysts, as well as many knowledgeable Russians, agree at this point that only Russia can solve its own problems. It was in this context of an ever more constrained and uncertain economic and political environment that Russian business managers, such as those we analyzed, were required to navigate their strategic directions as they approached the year 2000.

PART TWO

State-Owned Enterprises

3. Institute of Robotics and Technical Cybernetics

PRESTIGIOUS RECORD UNDER CENTRAL PLANNING

The Central Research and Development Institute of Robotics and Technical Cybernetics functioned as one of the most important R&D centers in Russia. This unique scientific and educational organization, established in 1968, reported at that time to both the Ministry of Science and the Ministry of Higher Education. The Institute was associated with the Leningrad Polytechnical Institute, the largest of its type in Russia, which in the early 1990s was renamed St. Petersburg Technical University. The Institute conducted leading-edge scientific research and development as well as production of highly sophisticated equipment for the Soviet defense industry using lasers, robotics, and other technologies. Because of the Institute's position as an affiliated organization of St. Petersburg Technical University, the director, Vitaly Lopota, also held positions in that university. As vice-rector, he was the university's second highest ranking administrator. He also held the title of professor in recognition of his stature as a scientist.

In the early 1990s, the Institute had 1,500 employees, nearly half of whom were technical and scientific specialists. An additional 2,000 to 4,000 students and faculty members from adjacent St. Petersburg Technical University worked as temporary employees at the Institute. The Institute's main complex included a very large building devoted to a number of research and development activities, as well as production facilities for creating bench models and prototypes. A major feature was a tall tower that housed an antigravitational simulator used to test equipment designed for space travel and communications. The Institute also had facilities in seven other locations, including a military testing site on Lake Ladoga 200 kilometers from St. Petersburg, a space center in Moscow, and a cosmonaut training center in Kazakstan. The Institute's activities were classified as secret until 1993.

The Institute is typical of many enterprises in Russia's defense sector whose circumstances changed abruptly from the privileged position they enjoyed before privatization. The defense sector had been the Soviet government's top priority, with the result that this enterprise had been well funded and equipped in order to provide its key customer, the government, with sophisticated products. It had also attracted and retained the best scientific talent within its technological fields. In 1990, however, the enterprise suffered a double blow—government orders declined drastically for military R&D and production, and these declines were then followed by severe reductions in financial subsidies. These two crucial events left the Institute with virtually no established market and extremely limited means to support its operations.

Research and production activities were concentrated primarily in robotic systems and manipulators, scientific and analytical devices, and information technology. In its specialized field of robotics, the Institute developed robotic systems and manipulators designed to function in extreme conditions such as high radiation fields and outer space. Other products included robotized laser equipment and analytical devices used in various sectors of the Russian economy.

In the field of analytical device engineering, the Institute created devices based on ionizing radiation, as well as other types of detectors used to perform monitoring and control tasks often dealing with ecological problems. For instance, the Institute had been heavily involved in assessing the aftermath of the Chernobyl nuclear disaster in the mid-1980s. Two hundred of its personnel were assigned to Chernobyl along with specialized equipment which was deployed in places inaccessible to humans to monitor radiation levels and establish measurement and control systems. Later, during the 1990 Persian Gulf War, the Institute's robots were used to defuse bombs and mines, and its thermal monitoring equipment was installed in reconnaissance aircraft deployed in United Nations missions over Iraq.

The Institute's extensive experience had positioned it with the technological capability to provide equipment and devices for the aerospace, medical, and petroleum industries, as well as others requiring sophisticated scientific instrumentation and equipment. Its products included monitoring and control equipment for power supply systems, radiation monitoring devices, fluid and gas flow parameter meters, wide range air pressure transducers, mobile X-ray television systems, and medical diagnostic devices. In the field of space research, the Institute had developed a simulator for Russia's cosmonaut training center, and the chief scientist and his team had developed the world's first lunar module soft landing system. Other specialized applications in computer information technology included a terrestrial computer system for radiation detection, a computer-aided control panel for industrial plants, and cartography software.

The Institute's 600 scientific and technical personnel were reputed to be among the most talented in Russia in their areas of specialization. Additionally, its relationship with St. Petersburg Technical University helped provide the Institute with a continuous flow of technical ideas and talent.

FORCED TO THE MARKET BY 1993

The Institute remained a government-owned entity after the country's privatization program and was designated as one of 42 State Scientific Centers in 1993. It was expected to function in the emerging market economy as a quasi-privatized organization, continuing to receive government subsidies, but required to provide 50 percent of its own financial needs. The Institute was forced to seek commercial business to replace the government defense orders that had previously been its sole market.

Like many scientists in North America and Western Europe, these technically sophisticated people assumed that technical virtuosity alone would produce success. But as elsewhere, the Institute's managers were to find the market a demanding master in which customers often had numerous alternatives, as well as high expectations that their particular needs would be met. Attempts in early 1993 to align the Institute with North American and other Western partners produced few tangible results. Russian customers had little need for, or were unable to afford, the Institute's highly specialized and expensive products. The lack of financial resources inhibited work on adapting products and equipment to commercial requirements. Maintaining the highly skilled employees remained a priority for Dr. Lopota, and he consistently paid employees' wages on time during a period when few state organizations did so. However, it was still difficult to keep some employees from leaving for more attractive positions in private companies.

MANAGING THE TRANSITION IN 1994

Organization, People, and Management Systems

The Institute did little to change its organizational structure during 1994, retaining the pyramidal hierarchical model so prevalent in Russian enterprises. Three deputies for technical areas reported to Dr. Lopota, along with the chief engineer who was responsible for production and equipment repair. One deputy explained, however, that his job had changed from simply managing technical projects to being responsible for marketing, and he encouraged his staff members to take on additional responsibilities as well. The director, however, noted that one of his major problems was "the psychology of people," especially getting them to think of customers' needs. Although he considered his top people to be excellent scientists who were developing well as managers, Dr. Lopota felt the need to be personally involved in many areas of the Institute, claiming that he knew "all that goes on in the organization."

He added that a financial control system was needed, but believed that he was making good progress on a local area network based management information system. This system was expected to provide information on many areas of activity such as contracts, customers, and work orders, as well as cost and revenue information. One of his personal goals was to gain financial control over the organization's activities in order to improve its management, and help ensure its survival during the transition. He described managing as being like "a Russian salad with so many things to do and needing to be an expert in many areas."

By 1994, the Institute had stemmed the loss of talented young scientists to private business that had begun in 1989 and lasted around five years. A "brain drain" to the US had also been a problem during that period. One manager noted "a good trend" in that more students were enrolled in the Technical University, and were beginning their work with the Institute. Dr. Lopota noted the importance of this event, recognizing that these young people were a source of creativity and new ideas: "Within Russia, much of an entire generation between the ages of 25 and 45 left science and education to go into business, and they were the smartest." But not all the best people were lost, since "some of them preferred to continue doing science rather than sell beer," Dr. Lopota added. Turnover of long-time employees had stopped, but of the recently hired graduates, about half had left to work in business.

In order to motivate managers and other employees, changes were made in the Institute's compensation system. For the first time, employees were rewarded with bonuses according to their work results, a system that most people saw as fair. Additionally, people were paid bonuses for their involvement in special projects, and for obtaining contracts with customers. Another positive feature for employees was the absence of layoffs since the work force remained at the same level despite reduced state funding, and temporary employees were hired from the University to staff projects. Yet salaries were low, and were frequently eroded by high inflation.

Operations and Markets

Thanks largely to state funding and some regular customer orders, production operations continued uninterrupted throughout 1993 and 1994, although at a reduced level. The same situation prevailed in research and development. The Institute had upgraded its technology by introducing a local area network and Sun Microsystems Computer Aided Design (CAD) equipment. It had also obtained e-mail capabilities using state funds. The Institute wanted to exchange scientific information with the West so as "not to reinvent the wheel." Managers were planning to set up a data bank on the premises that could be accessed via the Internet. Additionally, they had plans to establish a fiber optic cable linkage with Finland for teleconferencing at Helsinki University. The project also involved other Russian organizations including the St. Petersburg Physics Institute. Dr. Lopota mused: "There are so many things that I would like for the Institute. For instance, I dream of having a full CAD-CAM capability for the laser center."

The Institute's basic strategy was to reduce its dependence on state orders from 70 percent to 50 percent of its business. In addition to laboratory directors and virtually all employees being responsible for finding new markets, the Institute was active in exhibitions, and utilized advertising for the first time. Another dramatic change of attitude was described by one of the three deputy directors: "Before, we got state orders and funds, but really we just wanted the funds and avoided doing boring work by becoming involved in challenging and interesting work. Now, whatever brings funds is interesting, since we are trying to keep a stable work force." He described four major projects on which the Institute was working "which Dr. Lopota gave us," referring to the crucial role of the director in obtaining contracts and funding.

The deputy director noted that the Institute's radiation protection technology showed the most promise, with a large potential market in the ecological equipment segment. The target market for this technology was Russian government agencies. He added that the Institute was seeking large orders for a Russian space technology contract involving robots, and also an order for a power station. He spoke of products for many potential markets, such as X-ray technology which could be utilized in air guidance systems, robots which could work in virtually any hostile environment, and various technologies which could be utilized in security systems such as customs operations and airports. He was very proud of the Institute's technological achievements and its potential, but recognized that "it's hard to get business and markets." In late 1994, the Institute still dealt primarily with Russian customers, especially state and local governments, but also did some business with China.

Financing as the Key for the Future

The Institute's financial health depended very much upon remaining a quasi-state agency. Not only did this provide some state funding, but it also ensured a favorable tax status. Dr. Lopota explained: "This is the only way to survive now. Later, when the Institute becomes profitable, we might want to rethink our status." He had met with Western venture capitalists during 1993 and realized that they were not interested in investing in long-run potential, but were looking for a quick profit. He added that "some Western private investors have been burned, and won't come back to Russia." Exacerbating the Institute's financial problems were the difficulties in getting paid by customers, which often took two to three months. The Institute responded by holding back shipments to the government and other customers, and it was more difficult to collect from the former. Also, due to late payments, the Institute was forced to cut off services to a TV station that utilized Institute equipment, with the result that the station was not able to broadcast its programs.

To ensure the Institute's status as a state enterprise and to secure funding, promote contacts, and solicit orders, Dr. Lopota spent a great deal of time with government officials and members of the scientific community. These activities required his travelling to Moscow at least twice a month. One of his deputies stated: "The director spends a lot of time with government officials, lobbying and selling, and our orders really depend upon his negotiating skills." Dr. Lopota emphasized that financing the Institute's operations was his major problem: "We in Russia must be responsible for ourselves and not depend upon the West. So for the future, it's a question of developing products for our success."

Dr. Lopota explained that, as director of the State Scientific Center, he was often required to be in Moscow as a member of various councils working on national strategic issues in his fields:

> Most of the decision makers in the fields in which my organization operates are in Moscow, and our processes are closely tied to the activities of these decision makers. For instance, if we have a contract signed with Gazprom, I have to go to Moscow to solve problems associated with this agreement.

A 1994 Plan for Business in the New Environment

By early 1994, the Institute's difficulties led the director to develop a business plan which he presented at a conference at the Massachusetts Institute of Technology in the US. Several Russian organizations presented business plans to a group of American industry, financial, government, and academic experts attending the session, which was cosponsored by the MIT Enterprise Forum. The essence of Dr. Lopota's plan was a flow diagram showing how he would harness the Institute's resources to produce financial returns. It included ideas, people, quality, and time. A specific objective was to retain and motivate the Institute's 1,000 employees, including 600 scientific and technical professionals. The director believed that technical expertise, in addition to a low-cost labor force, were valuable assets for the Institute.

The plan anticipated, but could not count on, an annual $10 million government subsidy. Some business objectives were to integrate the Institute's medical and scientific laser technologies and products, develop strategic plans for niche markets, and seek suppliers willing to work on the basis of countertrade or barter. Other objectives were to create a technology center to focus the Institute's technical expertise on developing new commercial products. Yet another project was to establish a center to exchange information with Western scientists.

In response to the plan, most panelists viewed it as rather theoretical, excessively dependent on technology, and not oriented to customers. Dr.

Lopota was advised to focus his energies on a few applications, and target them to specific customer segments. One expert also cautioned against integrating laser and robotic technology, and suggested keeping them separate. The major recommendation was to add customer input to each element of the flow diagram in the business plan, since customers are viewed as the driving force in a market economy. A related suggestion was to find scientists interested in developing applications for their work, with one panelist noting that "most scientists prefer just to do the science." A similar view was expressed by another expert who remarked that the Institute must avoid the "disease of inventors" who fail to analyze customer needs or who become too arrogant to see the potential problems for their work in the market. Another expert noted that the weaknesses of this plan were the same as most business plans prepared by American high technology companies, and that the excessive technological orientation was not unique to any country.

Dr. Lopota was disappointed with the responses, and regretted that his business plan was seen as theoretical. He believed that it was actually quite practical, and that focusing on specific products would not be a problem. The Institute had, in fact, modified some of its laser equipment for commercial needs, but there was insufficient demand for the product in Russia. As support, he showed the panelists a drawing of a laser cutting machine tool which had been redesigned to exacting German specifications. Overall, he felt his plan was quite concrete by European standards, and included payback periods. He noted, however, that the term, business plan, might be inappropriate for his proposal, given the explicit connotations of that phrase in the United States. He emphasized the seriousness of the Institute's financial problems, which he believed could be solved only by successfully commercializing its products.

DR. LOPOTA'S VIEWS AND OBJECTIVES IN 1995

In 1995, Dr. Lopota felt that the Institute was in a stronger position to attract more funding because at that time it was of a caliber similar to the prestigious Bauman Institute in Moscow. Moreover, the Institute had become closer to the government. The work force remained at the same size, and salaries were paid on time, although inflation had continued to erode the value of the ruble. All projects that had been described in the prior year were reported as still being active. All laboratories continued to operate, and half of the Institute's profits were used to purchase new equipment.

Dr. Lopota talked at length about his personal views and the importance of science within Russia. He also voiced his opinion of scientists in general and the country's obligations to young scientists, as well as his views on the Russian work ethic. He spoke also of his own background, and considered himself a patriot dedicated to the progress of his country. As a specialist in laser technology, he had been the chief scientist of a very large, well-funded laboratory in the defense sector, where he had been able to work on cutting-edge technological projects. He described this period as "the wonder years" of his career and considered his lab the best in the world in his area of R&D. With the end of the Cold War, the lab was closed in the mid-1980s, leaving Dr. Lopota to consider new directions. He considered going into business and becoming involved in a joint venture, but in 1991, at the age of 40, was selected to head the Institute.

He was proud of his alma mater, the Polytechnical University, which had an illustrious history as Peter the Great Polytechnical Institute, and was the first in Russia to be designated as a technical university. His own Institute had been associated with the University, which he noted had played a key role in Russia's industry, technology, and R&D, but had gone bankrupt in 1990. Being director of the Institute, reporting to the rector of the University and being second in command there, did not seem the most promising prospect. He did not really want the job as director, but explained: "Patriotism made me take it. I could not let the Institute go down the drain."

Human Resources Strategy

Dr. Lopota spoke of his problems in motivating employees and attracting and developing scientists. He believed that the "psychological problems" of workers was his most serious issue after financing, more so than economic and technological problems. He believed that "people have to earn their money, but most want to sit around and wait for it to come." He tried to promote initiative by offering bonuses based on performance and by providing opportunities for employees to earn money using the Institute's specialized technological equipment. He believed that Russian employees had difficulty making decisions for themselves. In his view, this problem was attributable to child-rearing practices and the educational system, which created a dependent mentality whereby children were trained to ask for permission to do most things. By his own admission, his early attempts to motivate employees had failed, mostly because he tried to force new ideas on them. Not only did he believe that "people need a new way of thinking," which he tried to explain to others, but also that they must become convinced of their ability to be generators of new ideas.

Dr. Lopota explained that Russia's economic conditions had hurt the creativity of the scientific community, including his Institute. He identified four age groups or generations in science, which must work in concert to produce a creative environment. These groups ranged from an older cadre of experienced scientists who usually functioned as teachers or mentors in the institutes, to a less experienced but highly capable group of younger scientists who became the new generators of creative ideas. It was necessary to continue

44

attracting a cohort of young graduates to feed the creative cycle. However, many of the best older and younger scientists, as well as young technical graduates, had been enticed away by better financial opportunities in business. He noted that this drain of talent left the Institute with 90 percent of the scientists in generations two and three, and without a solid creative nucleus. The director believed these scientists needed to work with younger counterparts in order to fertilize their own ideas with an infusion of new thinking, while also developing themselves as teachers of the younger scientists.

In response to the situation, Dr. Lopota made a strategic decision to balance the generations of scientists within the Institute. He explained the importance of the Institute's linkage with the University as being a source of experienced teachers as well as young students. In his dual roles at the Institute and University, he was able to facilitate this transfer of talent as well as to work directly with the middle generation of scientists to help them become mentors and teachers.

In summing up his views of his technical employees and Russian workers in general, Dr. Lopota stated that this was a unique time for the country when managers like himself could develop a new generation. There was an opportunity to get rid of unproductive workers, and motivate people to work and live in an interesting way:

> We need to motivate and retain the best people, and be ready for the new young people aged 25 to 35, and for our obligation to provide a challenging technical environment for them. We need money from Prime Minister Chernomyrdin so as not to waste these resources. Some in the Academy of Science think that everything is fine in Russian science, but it is not.

He noted that some questioned his long-term approach in revitalizing the Institute when they felt things needed to be fixed right away. He acknowledged that both the short and long terms were important and, likening himself to a computer, remarked that he was running at 100 megabytes per second, while most others operated at a far slower pace of 100 kilobytes. He felt that only rarely did he act tough, but realized that he had to push even the best people and "gently lead this revolution."

Scientific Objectives and Strategy

Dr. Lopota had a high regard for Russian computer programmers who were typically proficient in writing concise code, since they usually worked on older computers with very limited memory capacity. His programmers had built their own versions of IBM's 486 and 586 computers, but their major problem was how to test their work given the lack of the necessary equipment. One of his programmers had left to work for Hewlett-Packard and had become a top

Unix programmer. He later returned to the Institute, a decision that Dr. Lopota regarded as a very positive sign. Programmers, in Dr. Lopota's view, were a valuable resource in Russia's scientific and business future. As an illustration of the Institute's programming capability, he noted that a 5-million-ruble order had been received from the City of St. Petersburg for a small expert system.

The Institute was linked with a number of other universities and institutes in a fiber optic network around St. Petersburg, and was the only scientific center in Russia with a direct fiber optic cable connection to the Internet. The Institute had a web server and management wanted to hook into a worldwide information system, but lacked the money for such an undertaking. The Institute was one of six centers worldwide that planned to participate in the 1996 Internet World Exposition coordinated by an American organization. The Institute's antigravitational testing tower, which was leased to a local television station for broadcasting its signal, had the capability to provide real-time information remotely, but required a fiber optic cable to do so. Again, the lack of funds prevented progress on developing this communications system.

Dr. Lopota viewed telecommunications as having the greatest potential for the Institute, and was devoting 60 to 70 percent of his time to that area. Although his specialization was laser technology, in the early 1990s he had studied telecommunications intensively at Hewlett-Packard and at Stockholm University. He felt that the Institute was "at the top of the field in communications and fiber optics." One example was the Institute's work on a telecommunications network for the energy industry in northern Russia.

To capitalize on the Institute's telecommunications capabilities, Dr. Lopota had worked for three years to try to convince government officials of the importance of information technology and telecommunications to Russia's future. He felt that most scientists were not able to negotiate effectively with government officials on such matters, and that he had to be the leader of this effort on the Institute's behalf. He advocated reallocating funds to this growth sector, away from poorly functioning, unprofitable, large enterprises that were still receiving government subsidies. Regarding the Institute's needs and objectives, he stated:

> We must in three or four years get 50 percent of our orders from outside of Russia to keep this place running, or we might have to close our doors. Fiber optics and telecommunications is our strategy today. This is our tomorrow, for both the Institute and Russia. I am always optimistic, but realistic. I don't want to brag, but I do keep trying.

A MORE FOCUSED STRATEGY IN 1996

By late 1996, Dr. Lopota's strategy had crystallized. He wanted the Institute to focus on research and development rather than production, and to invest in equipment and human capital: "Our equipment and technological output are at the highest level, and are not designed for consumers or large production quantities." His intention was to develop highly specialized technological outputs for governments and a limited number of large organizations. The Institute's work force was nearly the same size as the previous year, but 100 of the 1,000 employees were put under a government-mandated status in which they received only two-thirds of their salary. They had no real work at the Institute, and would be required to leave after a year or two. Dr. Lopota considered this measure preferable to layoffs.

Information technology had become the Institute's technological focus, and was to be the platform for its research directions. Dr. Lopota stated: "Regardless of what scientific directions we choose, information technology is the foundation of all directions." Yet, the Institute, as a state-owned organization, was also obligated to keep key specialists in other technological areas since it was the only Institute in Russia responsible for these specialties. Noting that the Institute had to find financing, Dr. Lopota added:

> It is still necessary to move the psychology of people toward earning their pay. This is new to Russia, but it is necessary to accomplish this, and it is an important part of my job.

Financing

Dr. Lopota's financial strategy was to remain 100 percent government-owned in order to retain the advantages of state financing and favorable tax status. He explained: "I don't pay taxes on land, real estate, or added costs. If I were not state-owned, I would have to earn twice as much in order for the Institute to end up with the money that we have now." State ownership brought other advantages such as easier access to military orders and to important information networks, as well as a high degree of freedom in operations. Dr. Lopota explained: "A major advantage of state ownership is that I am in charge of everything here. I don't coordinate with anybody and I don't have to communicate with the government about everything. What's important are the scientific results we produce."

The Institute required $500,000 a month to operate, and Dr. Lopota added: "If I were to receive half of that from the state budget, things would be easy for me." Usually, however, the Institute received only $100,000 to $150,000 from the government, and needed to earn the rest itself. Government funding was always uncertain, and in 1996 no funds were received from June through September. Collecting receivables from state-owned agencies also continued to be a problem, and work was stopped on some orders in August and September due to nonpayment. During such periods, the Institute had to work on lower-level technology projects to bring in income and to survive. Dr. Lopota cautioned:

This has no future, but I have to earn money doing such work. At that point, we need to come down from the heavens of high technology to the level of today's technology and make what we can get paid for. That's a waste of qualified people, but we are forced to do it. Only 10 percent of our employees were forced to stop working. It's good that the remainder have work, not from state orders, but from our other orders.

With regard to international contracts, most efforts had not yet produced results. The Institute was close to receiving an order from the Chinese government for a spacecraft soft landing system. Another source of funds came from selling technology in Germany for which there was no Russian market. The Institute earned from 100,000 to 150,000 DM annually in such joint scientific projects with German firms.

Information Technology Becomes the Major Focus

Dr. Lopota explained that many people, especially Russian companies, would like to be competitors, but lacked the Institute's technical expertise. He added that he was spending a lot of money on computer technology, especially information technology:

> We are now a highly computerized firm, and have our own production of computers and networks. I have enough modern computers, and people here are gradually learning to use them in their work. When you're involved in future-oriented high technology, these things are really needed today only by governments. It is the same in America.

Although the Institute was pursuing a relatively large number of scientific directions, Dr. Lopota described information technology as the basis for the Institute's survival: "In the next few years it will be an area of special attention for me. This is the heart around which things are formulated. I looked for something general, something essential that could be supported by many scientific directions." In essence he was describing the Institute's technological platform from which new scientific initiatives and products would emerge. These included a technology for creating a high-speed transport environment for information on a fiber optic line of communication called Asynchronous Transport Module (ATM) technology. Dr. Lopota claimed that there were no American specialists in this technology which the Institute was attempting to develop as the basic network of the University, and later for the commercial market. He added that the Institute was one of 11 locations in the world experimenting and communicating with this technology.

To keep up with technology, the Institute's scientists had many formal and informal relationships around the world, and followed closely what was going on in America. Dr. Lopota added: "There is a big computer 'mafia' in the world, in a good sense. These are intellectual people who know each other regardless of the country they live in. My specialists are actively participating in these discussions." Another area of high interest to Dr. Lopota was the development of high quality home pages for Russian companies and government agencies. These home pages, which utilized unique and highly efficient technologies developed at the Institute, offered high quality image resolution and rapid Internet access.

In the past year Institute scientists had also worked extensively on an optical fiber network linking organizations in St. Petersburg to a global network. This technology enabled them to successfully participate in the 1996 Internet World Exposition, as targeted in the previous year's plan. They had also prepared an information base which was now available on-line to organizations around the world. However, they sometimes had difficulty updating it because of the Russian government's delay in providing the information. The Institute had also developed a low-cost capability for worldwide videoconferencing with the work station they designed. These cost $3,000 to $4,000, in contrast to Sun Microsystems' work stations which reportedly cost $20,000 to $25,000. One of the first uses of their equipment was to broadcast a conference of high school students in Russia and the United States communicating with one another on the program, "A Night Without Violence."

Dr. Lopota was particularly proud of the Institute's ability to develop its own equipment such as computers and networks at very low cost. He felt their computer networks, some of which they had produced themselves, were very modern, and that they had the latest software. In the past two years, the Institute purchased $1.5 million in new equipment such as routers and special computers, and had invested in fiber optic cable installations. He added: "The state form of organization of an enterprise allows very effective use of money, and therefore we can afford to invest a lot." Although components were not sourced from Russian firms, Dr. Lopota noted: "We're working on getting Russian manufacturers to participate in our production. It is a very complex process and is taking a lot of time. Even if it doesn't happen now, it's developing a relationship between people."

The Institute also sold older equipment, with a three-year guarantee, to customers whose needs were not as technically rigorous. However, Dr. Lopota did not want to commercialize this type of business:

> I do not like to work in this market because it is uncivilized. It's wild. There is a lot of dishonesty. Also, the market requires computers of a low level, and I specialize in high technology. I don't sell separate computers, I sell networks.

The Institute produced around 150 units per month for sale. When asked whether he was preparing for the market, he responded: "Yes, but it's not visible in what you see here now. I try to invest every spare ruble in the Institute's development."

Emphasizing his objective, Dr. Lopota clarified the need to set priorities: "Last year our corridors were better lit. This year, we have an energy saving program going on. We don't have money to remodel the walls and the roof, or even to pay salaries sometimes." However, employees' salaries had been paid late only on one occasion, with a delay of only two weeks during, what he termed, the worst of times. He noted that the Institute's relationship with the University constituted "a whole complex that is a quintessential technical university, with its own production facilities that could bring ideas to a real result."

Human Resource Strategy

Dr. Lopota explained how human resources fit in his strategy:

> If I start to produce simple technology, then my specialists wouldn't grow, so I make the highest speed products since I must think about the future. Last year I talked about my plans to improve the balance of the four generations of scientists in the Institute, and the most important thing I have done is to provide a stream of students from the University. Typically, in scientific organizations, there are no students, only graduates. But here, the students work in our laboratories, even though they still have two years of university to finish. They are the future.

He was able to hold onto his more experienced technical specialists "because they don't have the opportunity to have such equipment anywhere else." He noted that many competitors, especially American firms in St. Petersburg, were trying to attract such people with "very big money," as much as $4,000 to $5,000 per month compared to $1,000 at the Institute. He added: "I really like this team, and none of them are leaving, because they understand that they are making their own future here with their own hands." As to whether older employees were able to make the transition to the newer, more demanding conditions, Dr. Lopota stated: "I give everybody a chance. If they take advantage of it and learn the new technology and new equipment, then they have the right to stay. If they can't do that, I need to give them a year or two and then they'll have to leave." He noted that it was still the psychology for many people in Russia to consider the State or the director or some other figure to be obligated to them, and that such people could not survive in the new system.

Looking to the Future

"Organizations such as mine need to be supported," Dr. Lopota asserted. He felt that Russia's future depended upon maintaining a technological capability in key areas such as information technology and telecommunications, and that the government had to support such initiatives. He disagreed with arrangements between the Ministry of Science and George Soros, the American investor-philanthropist who had directed very large sums toward projects in Russia. He felt that such projects were not benefiting Russian enterprises, and that American firms were gaining major advantages such as control over key communications crossroads. He pointed to a major fiber optic system between St. Petersburg and Moscow: "It has been a very sound policy for America, but absurd for Russia." He felt that Russian government officials involved in such agreements did not understand the implications of these pacts for the future. Rather than pursuing such avenues, and rather than investing in decaying state enterprises, he believed the government must continue to fund key Russian research organizations such as his Institute.

BETTER TIMES IN 1997 AND PRE-CRISIS 1998

Although the economic situation was never very favorable, Dr. Lopota explained that the Institute had a number of accomplishments during 1997 and 1998. He stated: "In general, times are better recently." One reason for this success was that he was an advisor to the Governor of the St. Petersburg region on science and technology policy. This role allowed him to lobby, "in the positive sense," he added, on behalf of the Institute.

He noted that the Institute had completed an automated radiation television monitoring system on the Russian-Finnish border. This system, the largest of its type in Eastern Europe, was estimated by Dr. Lopota to have a value between $500,000 and $1 million. It was a very important undertaking that led to a similar contract for another border-crossing area. As another example of the Institute's achievements, he noted that work was nearly completed on the development of an antiterrorist robot that operated X-ray and television systems. The product was developed under contract with the Russian security service, and was ready for production. The entire project was a new development derived from the Institute's basic robotic research.

While the Institute had been diligent in paying employee wages on time, customers did not always pay their bills. Dr. Lopota stated: "The government cannot pay its liabilities, and therefore I am forced to raise money from a variety of projects. I have orders from different companies, and allocate part of the profits to research projects." Subsidizing the Institute's state orders with commercial contracts, in his view, was not a contradiction. He explained that his strategy included "managing operations in such a way as not to be dependent on a single customer." The Institute's business was evenly divided among four segments. One segment was business with state-controlled enterprises, another consisted of orders from the Russian Space Agency for work related to its commercial activities, while a third segment was work conducted for other customers. The remaining 25 percent of the Institute's work was devoted to projects financed from its own funds, primarily scientific programs of basic and applied research:

> We make a certain amount of money today, and people understand very well that if a new niche appears tomorrow, we'll make even more money. Therefore, I allocate no less than 10 percent of revenues to promising new research, while many American companies allocate only three to five percent to such purposes.

Dr. Lopota was interested in developing international business, noting that seven to eight percent of the Institute's business consisted of international commercial contracts. As an example, he cited the company's contract with Daimler-Benz of Germany to develop robot-technology systems that might ultimately be used in monitoring satellites. He was currently in negotiations with companies from China, Germany, and France, as well as with an American chief engineer responsible for developing an international space station under the Alfa program.

Information technology was still a top priority of the Institute and Dr. Lopota discussed the interesting research being conducted on a new system that allowed management information technologies to be monitored on a global, regional, or local scale. The research was based on a technology called telenetics which allowed users in real time in any location on the planet to use communication channels and high-speed technologies for information processing. The result was uniting the intellectual and technical resources in real time, regardless of their locations on the earth. "Our mission is to create synergy in cyberspace," he declared. Such a capability, he believed, was needed to develop a viable international space station. In 1998, he had presented these concepts and the Institute's capabilities at an international congress devoted to the principles and philosophy of building Internet 3. He compared this event to American Vice-President Gore's appearance at a conference on launching Internet 2. When asked when his project might be initiated in earnest, Dr. Lopota responded: "It's a question of time and money, money and time. Nevertheless, certain technologies are being implemented since we try to actively participate in the servicing of Russian information channels." Dr. Lopota stated that the Institute had a professional and well-maintained information network called Rusnet that was being used by a number of Russian organizations:

> We work with companies operating in the fields of energy and television utilizing our ATM [Asynchronous Transport Module] technology and equipment. We also work with companies from Germany, Finland, and Sweden, and are ready to work with American partners such as Bay Networks with whom we have some association.

Another commercial development was the Institute's new laser purity instruments derived from one of its newly developed laser technologies. The devices were used in the gold processing and jewelry industry in Russia and the Czech Republic. The instrument was an innovation in using chemical processing to determine gold purity. Another product was a laser drill that could create any shaped hole such as triangles or rectangles. Other developments included a new radiation control system, and an Internet news company, St. Petersburg News, which provided information on Russia.

SURVIVING THE CRISIS OF AUGUST 1998

Dr. Lopota explained the impact of the country's economic crisis on the Institute as follows:

> We have had a very difficult summer. Today it is very difficult to survive and be successful. I think that my staff deserves at least 10 times better compensation for their work, but I can't afford that at the present time. If my monthly revenue was not the current $500,000, but $5 million, such compensation would be reasonable, I could employ more people, and maintain our buildings. We had begun to refurbish hallways, restrooms, and the canteen, but the crisis set us back.

Dr. Lopota felt that the country badly needed stability and leaders who would remain in office for no less than five or six years, rather than changing every year as had occurred in recent times. "I don't see anything good in that," he declared. "Of course, I would not like to see extreme changes in the staff of the Ministry of Culture or the Ministry of Science," referring to the agencies with which he worked closely. "In Russia, in the process of creating new things, we should be patient and not act to destroy what we currently have. We seem to have the mentality that we need to destroy everything old to its foundations and then start building. We should not work that way."

For the foreseeable future, Dr. Lopota's core strategy for the Institute was to remain a state-owned organization. He explained that this status allowed him to pay lower taxes, and that the Institute did not pay real estate, property, or value-added taxes. Also, if he did not have money to pay electricity or heating bills, he could delay payment because of his state-owned status and not lose these services. He stated: "I find this more profitable. I have an advantage over private companies because our product cost is lower and I can be more competitive. I would definitely like to have my own private company, but I would be deprived of many advantages."

Noting that 25 percent of his business was with state-controlled organizations, Dr. Lopota stated that in recent times these contracts were obtained only through competitive bidding. If these customers evaluated the Institute's project as being superior to others submitted, it would be awarded a contract. He added: "So I have forgotten long ago what it is like to be subsidized. Today, the principle on which money for scientific purposes is allocated is competition."

Regarding customers, Dr. Lopota explained:

> Nobody just sits and waits anymore. We all actively look for contracts. For instance, we participated in a high technology congress recently where the only exhibitors were Russian companies, but foreigners attended as well. We established contacts with customers at such exhibitions, and every half-hour had meetings with potential customers on site. We have a marketing department, but normally marketing activities are part of the responsibilities of every laboratory head, and we have become more aggressive in that direction.

Dr. Lopota summarized the Institute's competitive strategy:

> We have not changed the profile of our organization, and are implementing the same strategy as previously. We value our professionalism. We create networks, infrastructure, serve large corporate clients, and we try to work with these large corporate clients. This is all in the sphere of information technologies. We can develop even further on the basis of these technologies.

Regarding how he spent his own time, he explained that financing and human resources were priorities:

> Well, the crisis has set us back several years in terms of our financial resources. Until now, I had resources for six to eight months ahead. But now, they are even scarcer, and I have resources for a maximum of two and a half months. So, I have to work very aggressively to keep close track of all payments. I have to work many more hours pursuing contracts, and after working hours, work just as intensively with my own staff to educate them. By this I mean that, because we lack finances to motivate people, it is necessary to convince them and lead them. I work with a lot of young people in our organization, many of whom come from the Technological University. The average age of our employees is 36. I never start with giving them responsibilities. I start with providing them with interesting ideas and good equipment, and then I look at what the young people will demonstrate. I provide them with equipment in exchange for their efforts. In a sense, I could say this is the capitalist way.

Regarding the more experienced scientists and how they fared after the crisis, Dr. Lopota added: "They are forced to maintain themselves in good shape, or the young people will replace them." He emphasized that his human resource philosophy had not changed.

All of these heavy responsibilities, coupled with his frequent work as a member of the Russian Academy of Sciences, left very little personal time for Dr. Lopota to devote to his family and other pursuits:

> Yes, this is a lot of work. Every morning I come to work and have to decide what responsibilities to delegate. I have to think things through. But my major

occupational activities are in no way changed, and I still go to Moscow every two weeks. I have a very interesting life.

4. Toriy Research and Production Association

THREE DECADES AS A HIGHLY REGARDED ELECTRONICS ENTERPRISE

The Toriy Research and Production Association was created in the early 1960s to conduct basic and applied research and produce electronics-related products for military, industrial, and medical applications. Products included gyrotrons, clystrons, television sets, sterilizers, and scalpels. The general director, Dr. Igor G. Artiukh, had been employed at Toriy for his entire career, beginning in 1963, and was appointed to the top position of general director in 1986. He had an engineering degree as well as a doctor of science in economics. His first deputy, Dr. Alexander Mikhalov, the technical director and chief engineer, had worked at the enterprise since 1971. Until the early 1990s, Toriy's work was classified as secret, and the organization was closed to outsiders.

In 1993, Dr. Artiukh reported that he spent about 60 percent of his time at the enterprise and the remaining 40 percent in leadership positions of two major industrial enterprise associations. As president and co-founder of the Moscow Association of Entrepreneurs and Producers, he lobbied the government on behalf of 90 large enterprises and several thousand entrepreneurships. As vice-president of Arkady Volsky's Association of Industrialists, he and his colleagues represented 2,500 large enterprises nationally. The group also organized a league to represent the defense industry, and even supported its own political party. With regard to his managerial style, Dr. Artiukh admitted that he didn't listen enough to his staff, and that they had criticized him for this shortcoming.

Seeking Status as a Joint Stock Company in 1993

In 1993, with 51-percent state ownership, Toriy still retained its status as a state-owned enterprise. Management was working on becoming a joint stock company with the objective of obtaining 51-percent ownership by selling shares mostly inside the enterprise. During the country's privatization program, all employees had been given an equal opportunity to purchase shares of the enterprise. Some were not interested in doing so, but management asked employees who acquired shares to keep them within the enterprise, and not sell to outsiders. It was uncertain, however, whether or when this would happen. Management explained that the government was reluctant to allow them to privatize for fear of losing control of a vital R&D and production resource comprised of many enterprises. The government did not want to see such a vital chain broken—one in which Toriy played a crucial role as a unique organization with a monopolistic position. Since the government was also still its major customer, Toriy's management doubted whether status as a joint stock company might ever be allowed.

Toriy is comprised of four organizations: a research institute and two large production plants located in Moscow, as well as a third plant in another city which is an independent legal entity. Prior to the country's economic transition, 10,000 people were employed at Toriy, including 7,000 in the three Moscow facilities. By mid-1993, only 4,500 people were employed there. The staff still included more than ten individuals with doctor of science degrees, and 120 who held candidate of science degrees. Similar staff reductions occurred at Toriy's other location. Under the centrally-planned economy, nine deputies, as determined by the Ministry, had reported to the general director. After the fall of the Soviet Union, Dr. Artiukh reorganized the enterprise, reducing to four the number of deputies who reported directly to him—the chief engineer and first deputy, the chief economist, the deputy for production and plant management, and the deputy for R&D. Five other managers were made assistant deputies. Other departments, such as personnel, remained unchanged, or had some functions combined to reduce the total number of senior managers.

Research Institute

The research institute had nine divisions organized by type of technology. Five were basic research technologies for products such as clystrons, gyrotrons, and magnetrons, and four were applied technologies including machine building applications and medical instruments. Each R&D division had from 200 to 250 employees and was connected to a production unit. Although the R&D divisions did not have independent legal status, each was a separate accounting unit. Dr. Artiukh explained that this structure helped employees feel independent in their scientific work, and made it possible to measure each unit's effectiveness. Divisions were measured on the number of scientific projects, the budget from external and internal sources, suppliers, domestic and foreign customers served, and the volume of products sold. Divisions were treated as profit centers, but how profits were allocated was decided by the central administration. According to the technical director and chief engineer, Dr. Mikhalov, this system made employees feel more connected to the final product, and more accountable for results. He also claimed that measuring R&D performance according to final products introduced and sold to customers was an effective way to measure units. In the past, he explained, enterprises created competition between various R&D units using other less tangible measures. The central management tried to help R&D units in the early stages of important research by managing the money flow among units, and also rewarded units that operated efficiently. Applied technology was given greater emphasis than in the past in order to focus on sales and revenue generation, and each unit was responsible for its own marketing.

Production

Production was fully integrated in that Toriy's operations group made much of the equipment needed for their own use, as well as selling some equipment to other customers. In fact, they produced all operating equipment as well as final products. As a result, Toriy worked with only ten domestic suppliers of raw materials and components. A significant portion of the firm's production still went to fill state orders in 1993. Top management did not welcome this situation, and claimed that dependency on the state as a major customer reduced Toriy's flexibility to redesign some products. This relationship with the state was also an important reason for top management to retain centralized oversight of the enterprise rather than giving more autonomy to the divisions.

Preparing to Operate in the New Market Economy

In the late 1980s, the general director, Dr. Artiukh, and the chief engineer, Dr. Mikhalov, attended an executive management program at the prestigious Academy of the National Economy in Moscow. They found the program useful in learning about market-oriented management, and they also gained some familiarity with the West German economy. Upon returning to Toriy, they set up training programs within the enterprise to give employees basic knowledge of the new accounting and financial practices required for the enterprise to be self-financing. Dr. Mikhalov explained that the situation had started to get more difficult for the enterprise in 1989. By 1990, they estimated that they had delayed changes by a full year, and had taken only small measures toward developing a marketing capability.

Regarding training, the chief engineer believed that people up to age 35 "can swim on their own if you throw them in the water." He added that enterprises could send employees to take marketing and other business courses at an industry training institute. To retain talented people, enterprises paid employees' tuition, and employees contracted to work with their sponsoring enterprise for a specified period upon completion.

STRATEGIC CHANGES IN 1993

Finance

The company's financing system had been changed to measure units as profit centers when the government freed prices in 1992. This change gave greater financial independence to the divisions, but the freeing of prices was not the main reason for the change. More significant was the fact that, in 1993, the government had stopped financing Toriy with subsidies from the state budget. Dr. Artiukh noted that financial issues had become much more important to Toriy, and he held a weekly finance meeting with all division heads to analyze the company's situation. Top management also held many meetings to explain to all employees that everyone needed to find customers and become actively involved in marketing Toriy's products.

Search for Joint Ventures and Other Partnerships

Like many Russian companies at the time, Toriy sought joint ventures with three types of partners: other Russian enterprises, foreign firms, and partners within Toriy itself. The most progress had been made on the third type, which involved creating small enterprises inside the divisions with a separate manager designated to head each internal joint venture. All such enterprises were established as separate legal entities, with their own tax status. Toriy's top management described these arrangements as intellectual joint ventures that were offered only to scientists and engineers as a way of conserving technical competence within the organization. These entrepreneurs, who represented the company's most talented people, had been recognized for their achievements by numerous State awards. The internal joint ventures were designed as opportunities for valuable employees to become owners of their own internal enterprises and have the potential of monetary rewards for their work.

Broadening the Product-Market Strategy

Toriy's top management wanted to exploit the enterprise's traditional areas of expertise and develop new products based on those technologies. For the next five years they wanted to balance consumer products with those for the industrial and defense sectors. For instance, a small unit producing equipment used in drying bricks found a ready market in the booming construction industry, and successfully expanded into that segment.

Another promising marketing effort involved producing power tools for the construction industry. A group of employees identified a strong demand for a new jig saw which they then designed, produced, and sold. Management explained that these employees willingly worked on all aspects of the project and were gratified to receive rewards that were directly tied to the results they themselves had produced.

Management believed that their biggest marketing challenge was to create a sales force and a distribution chain for their products. The enterprise lacked knowledge in these fields, having no employees experienced in sales. As an interim measure, they relied on newly created independent intermediary firms to sell their products, and handle such matters as currency conversion with a Ukrainian customer.

Having been a monopoly under the centrally-planned economy, Toriy still had no direct domestic competitors. Dr. Mikhalov believed that the enterprise's primary concern was finding a "civilized" way of entering foreign markets, and not taking "uncivilized" actions such as selling contraband goods through third countries. One legitimate possibility was to produce as a subcontractor for foreign firms. Some companies had approached Toriy with such proposals, but stipulated that their brand name be used instead of Toriy's.

R&D Strategy

Regarding the enterprise's new R&D strategy, Dr. Artiukh explained that basic and applied research were not contradictory to one another. He noted that there was no real problem getting scientists to do more applied work because they understood that this direction was necessary for the organization's survival as well as their own.

The company sought production joint ventures, but not R&D ventures, with firms in the United States, China, and Ukraine. Targeted products included industrial and medical products such as accelerators and sterilizers used in food production. An important aspect of their plan was to avoid sharing information with potential partners about technology and the technological production process.

Human Resources

Dr. Mikhalov viewed people as Toriy's most valuable resource, and feared losing designers, technologists, and other key scientists. He explained that there was little possibility of bringing in new talent because only a few very committed young people were now attracted to state-owned organizations such as theirs, with most young people opting for the private sector.

Since 1992, 700 people had left Toriy voluntarily, 60 percent of whom were workers, and 40 percent technical personnel. Many left to start their own businesses, or to retrain for new careers, but not a single scientist had left, Dr. Mikhalov recalled. Most of the scientists had worked at Toriy for their entire careers and considered the enterprise their second home. Top management referred to this group as a cohesive team, and noted that the chief designer, for instance, did not want to retrain for another career, but wanted to continue utilizing his specialized knowledge of electronics. The chief engineer echoed these feelings by saying that the electronics industry "is the most prestigious of all in the twentieth century, and the people who work in it are extremely proud of what they do."

He added that he wanted the company to gain the majority of the enterprise shares so scientists could be better rewarded for their accomplishments. A number of benefits were already offered to employees. Employees paid for only 30 percent of the cost of vacation accommodations at the enterprise's resort facilities, and received subsidies for food and medical care. New employee housing was being built using company profits, and employees had the use of garden plots 200 kilometers from Moscow. Consumer goods were also offered, such as those received from a Chinese customer as barter for a major order of clystrons. Employees who had worked on that contract were given priority for these goods.

INVESTMENT AND SUPPLY CHAIN PROBLEMS SLOW PROGRESS IN 1993

Dr. Mikhalov reported that Toriy's most serious obstacle in 1993 was a lack of investment funds. The second major challenge was supply and delivery problems that had resulted from the breakdown in economic relations among former Soviet republics. The unified supply system in the former USSR no longer functioned, and Dr. Mikhalov referred to the government's economic policy as one of destruction, not creation, especially in the area of supply chain management. The drastically reduced salary budgets, as well as delays in receiving funds from the government, were other major obstacles. In June 1993, the enterprise had not yet received its budget for that year, and thus was six months late in paying employees. Changing legislation also posed challenges, but Dr. Mikhalov said they had become more disciplined in responding to such pressures caused by the government.

Despite the drastically reduced funding, the government still considered the electronics sector a high priority, and the Ministry of Electronics was deeply involved in preparing long-term economic plans for the industry. Toriy itself was developing its own enterprise development plan.

Within the enterprise, people had mixed feelings about the future, according to Dr. Mikhalov. Many feared what could be in store and hoped for stability. Individuals expressed feelings of optimism and pessimism at the same time. Overall, employees' attitudes had become more pessimistic when prices and inflation skyrocketed and no tangible improvements in the economy materialized. Even though there was still a demand for television sets, for which Toriy had a monopoly, exorbitant price increases caused by inflation put them out of reach of most Russian consumers. Regardless of how the country was going, Dr. Mikhalov remained optimistic for the enterprise's future, especially if foreign customers could be found. In the past, 90 percent of Toriy's production was for state orders, but by 1993 it had declined to 75 percent.

PROBLEMS RESULT FROM GOVERNMENT ECONOMIC POLICY IN 1995

Financial Woes

From the vantage point of his leadership roles in two major industrial associations, Toriy's general director, Igor Artiukh, had a broad view of government economic policy. In fall 1995, he prefaced his comments about the developments at Toriy with his views on how government policies were affecting his enterprise and thousands of others. He believed that the government's most important task was to understand that enterprises needed funds to invest for the long term. Defense plants especially were in dire straits because many had no orders. Those that did often sold only to the government, which habitually paid late, if at all. For the last year alone, the government owed Toriy 6 billion rubles for shipments. Of this amount, 2.4 billion rubles was owed by the Ministry of Electronics which declined to pay, claiming that Toriy first needed to pay 380 million rubles that it owed to the government. Yet, Toriy could not do so without the government paying them for deliveries. Given this situation, coupled with the fact that Toriy had received no government subsidies during the year, the enterprise's financial position deteriorated badly.

To make matters worse, Toriy, like other enterprises, suffered from the whims of legislators who often passed contradictory and seemingly senseless laws. For instance, the federal energy commission had promised to reduce energy rates, but MosEnergiia, the local regulator, forced Toriy to pay even higher rates. The energy commission also required that estimates of consumption be made one year in advance, and any excess consumption beyond the estimated amount was subject to a penalty of ten times the cost. Energy charges had to be paid in full every month, along with service charges, even if consumption was below the estimated level.

Production Enterprises Suffer

Dr. Artiukh pointed out that the government continued to support Gazprom and other petroleum and mining operations, but not production enterprises whose average output had declined by 24 percent since the beginning of 1995. Although there was a strong demand for consumer goods, a large portion was imported since many Russians saw these as being higher in quality than domestic goods. As a result, domestic production of consumer electronics declined 500 percent from 1993 to 1994, with television sets produced in 1994 being only 21 percent of 1993's output, and VCRs only 23 percent. This was an important product for Toriy, and thus the company suffered greatly from the decline.

Wages were another serious national problem. Dr. Artiukh pointed out, for instance, that a lecturer's monthly salary at a leading university was the equivalent of the cost of a load of sand. Also, many young people wanted to go into business, but lacked starting capital. In such situations, organized crime or "the racket" often got involved and conducted business in "a dirty way," he explained.

Huge capital investment would be needed, Dr. Artiukh noted, for the country to convert successfully from defense production to commercial applications. During voucher privatization, workers received shares of their enterprises, but former communist party committee members and many enterprise directors unethically accumulated shares and power. As a result, the initial capital accumulation was not invested in production, but in import warehouses and other non-production activities. Dr. Artiukh interpreted privatization minister Igor Gaidar's policies of increased taxation and reduced subsidies as ways of limiting the production of poorly performing enterprises. However, Dr. Artiukh believed that the government now needed to change its policy because of the exorbitantly high unemployment that resulted, numbering more than 15 million people according to government statistics for that year. Dr. Artiukh believed the numbers were much higher in reality, since many people had been put on so-called three-month leave, meaning there was no work for them.

Another serious issue facing production enterprises was that raw material prices often exceeded the selling price of finished goods. This situation was another example of the problem of economic laws, according to Dr. Artiukh. He claimed that Gaidar had destroyed the economy with a 2,000-percent increase in prices, yet enterprises' cash was calculated according to the far lower earlier prices. With such hyperinflation, coupled with a 200-percent monthly interest rate, enterprises' funds were woefully inadequate. While banks were free to set unlimited interest rates, government policy prevented state-owned enterprises from making more than a 25-percent profit on their products. In reality, most state enterprises stood virtually no chance of achieving the limit.

Misguided Government Pricing Policies and Customs

Dr. Artiukh noted that leading Russian economists such as Leonid Abalkin and Nikolai Shmelev were familiar with Western economic methods and wanted to apply them in Russia. He himself was also knowledgeable in this field, and had published an article describing how Western and Russian economies differed. In the 1950s, the domestic Russian economy had grown rapidly according to the five-year plans, with citizens being relatively well supplied with food and consumer goods. This growth was the result of Stalin's policy of permitting enterprises to produce 1.48 rubles of goods for every ruble of salaries on their payroll. The economy started to decline when enterprises began producing at higher levels in order to receive more funds from the central ministries, a practice that led to overproduction and wasted resources. Later, when enterprises adopted the *khozraschet* system of cost accounting, they cut both costs and production. These actions led to a tension in the economy because consumers had money to buy goods, but they were often in short supply. During perestroika, Gorbachev's policies for innovation included programs in which many cooperatives could use 50 percent of their profits for any purpose. With money increasingly available, people had "bought everything off the shelves within two years," Dr. Artiukh claimed.

Dr. Artiukh declared that he was a committed socialist. He believed also that it was necessary to "get rid of the unprofessional types in the government." As a supporter of Arkady Volsky's United Industrial Party, Dr. Artiukh believed that the party, which had been founded in 1995, was based on logic and common sense. If Volsky were to become prime minister, he would get rid of the current pricing policies on raw materials and let the market decide the value of commodities such as oil, gas, and wood. He would also revamp the 40-percent customs duty that was currently imposed on many goods. Russian manufacturers were in the difficult position of not being able to afford raw materials, especially from domestic sources. For some resources, such as metals and coal, it was cheaper to purchase from abroad. Dr. Artiukh believed the country needed to stop exporting raw materials until domestic market demand had been satisfied.

Laws were needed to regulate the economy in other areas as well, Dr. Artiukh stated. He believed that defense orders should be paid for promptly by the government, which was frequently not the case. Additionally, he advocated a new economic policy to protect and support domestic producers, claiming that Prime Minister Chernomyrdin and his economic minister, Anatoly Chubais, had miscalculated the volume of foreign investment that would flow into the country. Instead, imports were replacing domestically-produced products, and profits were going abroad. In Moscow, for instance, 60 percent of goods and 70 percent of foodstuffs were imported during the mid-1990s.

Dr. Artiukh also believed that the government, employers, and trade unions should work together to regulate wages. His plan would be to set wages according to qualifications as a way of eliminating huge disparities between jobs in the public and private sectors. In this way, he hoped that qualified employees could be kept in state agencies. For instance, he cited the case of a woman who had been earning 80,000 rubles a month at Toriy, and then left to work at a bank for 2 million rubles a month.

Despite the severity of the country's problems and the extreme difficulties that Toriy was experiencing, Dr. Artiukh remained hopeful about the future. Conceding that the situation would not change quickly, he believed that a key long-term national goal should be to create a strong middle class of professionals, skilled workers, artists, and military officers that could rely on a stable and honest government. He believed that an economic transformation based on production of high quality products was essential to create a critical mass of middle-class citizens, saying: "It's tragic that civilized culture has been destroyed."

In his opinion, the government could take a number of measures to improve Russia's economic prospects. The country's great scientific and technical capability, along with a rich supply of natural resources, were tremendous assets ready to be developed. Dr. Artiukh believed that the government should aggressively address the huge problem of capital flight, stating that an estimated $30 to $80 billion in capital was being sent abroad annually. He claimed that if this money could be repatriated and the outflow stopped, Russia would not need foreign financial assistance. Another policy he advocated was reforming the oppressive tax system that encouraged tax evasion and resulted in lost government revenues. He noted, for example, that it was no longer profitable even to produce vodka, since the heavy taxes on production and sales made it more costly than imported brands.

SURVIVAL STRATEGY IN 1995 INCLUDES NEW PRODUCTS

As part of the government's industrial reorganization in 1995, Toriy was slated to be included among the 100 organizations designated as State Research and Production Enterprises, and would thus remain a state-owned enterprise. Its products in 1995 included microwave communications and television broadcasting equipment, as well as space communications equipment. Some of its products, Dr. Artiukh noted, were similar to those of the French electronics company, Thomson, and Varian Corporation in the US. He was proud of Toriy's products and believed that most of them were world quality. Thus, he was frustrated that some Russian government officials favored foreign products that he considered to be very similar to those of Toriy.

The company had a number of foreign customers, including some in Germany, England, Poland, Ecuador, South Korea, and China, but transactions were not always free of problems. For example, some Chinese customers were six months late in making payments. Because the orders were placed in accordance with government agreements, Toriy was not permitted to go directly to the customer, but was required to go to an international arbitration court.

Dr. Artiukh noted that privatization had changed the business profile of some enterprises, with a former machine tool enterprise now producing caskets, and a former electronics manufacturing plant having been converted to a warehouse for products imported by its new foreign owner. In the same vein, Dr. Artiukh had also become president of RTDS Volvo-Renault, a foreign automobile dealership in Moscow. Toriy was an institutional shareholder of this joint stock company, along with Dr. Artiukh and some other Toriy employees.

One of Toriy's most promising product lines, according to Dr. Artiukh, was acoustic speakers based on a new system of transmitting sound developed by the company's scientists. Because of a lack of resources, the enterprise could produce only small quantities, and needed a strong partner to fund the project, such as Philips of the Netherlands. Dr. Artiukh wanted Toriy to become a partner of the world's third largest competitor in such products. He believed Toriy could help it become number one by utilizing Toriy's technology, which he described as being capable of producing nearly natural sound. In addition to speakers, Toriy now produced highly sensitive high tech microphones designed like the human ear to pick up sounds from all directions.

Medical equipment was another product line that Toriy management hoped would generate additional business. Company representatives and colleagues from Varian Corporation made a proposal to the Pentagon in Washington for funding to help Toriy convert its accelerators to medical applications. However, they were unsuccessful in this attempt, just as they were in trying to obtain funding from US government sources for medical and technical X-ray tube projects.

By late 1995, Toriy's situation had deteriorated badly, and the number of employees had declined over the past two years from 4,500 to 3,200. Dr. Artiukh was unable to create more jobs or invest funds in new production. Yet, he believed he had an ethical responsibility to maintain the technology that had been produced at Toriy under his leadership. He lamented: "The director of a production enterprise can't create paradise for his workers."

QUADRUPLED PRODUCTION IN 1996 DESPITE DIFFICULT GOVERNMENT POLICIES

Government Policies Continue to Suffocate Industry

Many changes occurred in 1996 at Toriy, and despite serious difficulties arising primarily from the country's deteriorating economic situation, the enterprise had quadrupled its production from the prior year. In summarizing his view of recent government policies, Dr. Artiukh explained the main difficulty was that the government was not managing economic and social policies effectively. An energy crisis and nonpayment of debts were still among the most serious problems. He pointed out that the government allowed shareholders to purchase shares in such important industrial sectors as energy, particularly the state gas monopoly Gazprom, and water resources enterprises such as Moscow's water supplier, Mosvodokanal. The new shareholders had begun making their own rules that became onerous for consumers, as well as for the producers of energy. For instance, the price of electricity was set at 243 rubles, but cost only 43 rubles to produce. This six-fold margin apparently did not benefit electricity producers, but generated large profits for shareholders who were not inclined to reinvest in the producing enterprises.

Regarding nonpayment of debt, Dr. Artiukh explained how the government's policy of limiting the money in circulation in order to curb inflation was causing hardships for industry. Because the economy was operating on debts using promissory notes, delays were incurred in payments for wages, products, and raw materials such as electricity. Aggravating the situation for enterprises, the government repaid its own late debts without interest, yet charged other organizations fines for late payments. For instance, Mosvodokanal, a municipal organization of the Moscow city government, imposed a 2-percent fine for each day that Toriy delayed payment, amounting to an annual interest rate of 730 percent.

In 1994, Toriy produced 2.7 billion rubles of products, but was not paid for them. Dr. Artiukh borrowed some money from banks and, "as a result, in 1995 these debts prevented me at times from paying salaries." Also, as a result of the government's widespread use of promissory notes, Toriy received in July 1996 what it should have been paid in April 1995, with no interest added. Thus, by September 1996, Dr. Artiukh had paid salaries only up to April of that year. He claimed that if Toriy were to receive payment for all the debts that it was owed, employees "would be able to live and work very easily." And most debts, he noted, were due from government agencies.

Dr. Artiukh emphasized his major concern regarding government policy:

> There is such unfair and unofficial pressure on industry that companies, instead of functioning normally, are suffocating.

His position and that of his colleagues in the Association of Entrepreneurs and Industrialists was that investors' fears of investing in the production sector had to be overcome:

> Production simply requires more money to be given directly to enterprises. Money exists as a roof among enterprises, and if you give my enterprise money, or better still, give it directly to the people who buy our products, then we can function.

Protectionism was another policy that Dr. Artiukh wanted the government to adopt. He believed that when foreign currency was allowed to circulate in Russia, it provided jobs abroad rather than in Russia. He noted that "the free market, which our troubled managers consider to be a fairy tale, is unregulated and is unlike anywhere else in the world." He related the case of Russian producers being prohibited from exporting chickens to America because when they tried to do so, "it created a scandal in America." Dr. Artiukh strongly advocated a new government policy to remedy the situation:

> The government must defend its own producers. Unfortunately, we do not have this in Russia, yet it is essential.

Unstable and constantly rising prices continued to be a serious obstacle for Toriy and other industrial enterprises. Because prices of raw materials, electricity, and other inputs were rising constantly, Toriy's working capital was completely inadequate, and the company could not estimate profit on the products it manufactured. Dr. Artiukh believed that "what we really need would be to once again have the shock treatment that Gaidar gave us in 1991."

Dramatic Shift to Commercial and Consumer Markets

Dr. Artiukh explained how the product mix had changed in 1996: "Every year the situation changes and we now have divided up our production, with 70 percent devoted to consumer products and 30 percent to military products." As a national research and production enterprise and scientific center, Toriy continued to work on a number of communications systems. For example, Toriy scientists were developing satellite communications applications for new networks and communication systems. The enterprise's commercial satellite communication systems had been purchased by organizations in Russia and South Africa, and were also used in the United States during the tracking of Haley's comet. One of Toriy's satellite stations was in use at the Russian Institute of Space Research, and another in the United States. Work was also continuing on aircraft landing and control systems.

High quality acoustic speakers continued to be a promising consumer product. Toriy was actively seeking an experienced foreign partner to help it become "the world leader in acoustics" through joint production and marketing. Toriy had already created a joint stock company for its speaker operations and had accepted investment in the form of shares from some investors. Toriy's scientists had developed a technology, patented in 12 countries, which produced an extremely high level of sound clarity, and could be manufactured on a simple assembly basis. The innovation consisted of the ability to expand or extend stereo sound. Only prototypes had been created, but once the system was perfected, Toriy hoped to produce the speakers in large quantities. Models that Toriy currently manufactured included three types of acoustic speakers at the 112-decibel level. The 110-decibel level was considered the standard for digital recording to obtain a full dynamic range, and Toriy technology had capacity for twice that level.

The company also produced medical equipment such as electro-nitro-stimulators, SVCh scalpels, and accelerators for sale to medical centers. The scalpels were an improvement over earlier versions used around the world. In early models, scalpels used heat to stop blood flow from an incision. These were replaced by laser scalpels that stopped blood flow, but burnt skin tissue because of the intensity of the laser. In contrast, Toriy's new scalpel made incisions and used microwave radiation to heat the blood, thereby causing it to coagulate and stop flowing.

Accelerators were another medical product that the firm was currently producing. One was utilized on site at Toriy to sterilize needles, syringes, and other medical instruments for health organizations that were Toriy customers. The company had also recently begun experimenting with accelerators to disinfect mattresses, and found that method more effective than using steam. Toriy was negotiating to install its accelerators in five railroad stations to sanitize mattresses from sleeping cars.

Clystrons, which are television transmitters that emit light and sound, remained an important product line for Toriy. The enterprise still had a monopoly for this product in Russia, Ukraine, and Belarus, and exported to other countries as well. Dr. Artiukh claimed that Toriy's clystrons were developed using special parts that made them about 15 years more advanced than competitive models. He explained that Toriy had been developing this technology since the early 1970s, and was one of the first organizations in Russia to introduce radial clystrons and electronic beams. According to Dr. Artiukh, the clystron that Toriy had developed for the MIG29 aircraft in 1978 had been studied by NATO as late as 1995. The German government had ordered four airplanes equipped with the device, and it was also used in Russian F16s and some MIG29s. Foreign companies, including Thomson of France and Hughes of the US, had begun making products similar to Toriy's clystrons, a product area in which Dr. Artiukh and his colleagues had recently received a state prize for their work.

Scientists Remain Loyal and Create Intrapreneurships

Similar to 1995's situation, 3,000 people were employed at the institute and factory in Moscow, but 500 of them, according to Dr. Artiukh, were essentially unemployed. The latter included women on maternity and childcare leave who continued to be paid. Employment had declined dramatically from the 7,000 who had worked in the Moscow facilities "in the best times." Yet, Dr. Artiukh emphasized:

> Not a single scientist has left our enterprise. We have all grown up here together in this enterprise from our childhood, so to speak, when we graduated from the Moscow Physics and Technical Institute. I, for example, graduated from the Institute in 1967 and never changed my job, and the same is true for the chief designer, as well as for our physics technologist.

Besides friendship and loyalty, another motivation for scientists to remain at Toriy was the entrepreneurial opportunities that were available to them within the enterprise. Dr. Artiukh elaborated on the internal firms that had been created as partnerships:

> Designers, developers, and all of those who are able to create work without depending on large volume equipment can develop a project simply by working with their own personal talents. We sign agreements with them, help these groups to survive, and directly support them. They themselves look for projects, and they also attract production orders, such as for acoustic speakers, for the benefit of the entire enterprise.

Dr. Artiukh emphasized that such small intrapreneurships "as a rule are created for us to survive during this time. The transformation we are making on an economic level is more profitable than the limitations that we had been experiencing." He added that Toriy's management understood the value of the intrapreneurships, and that the company needed to restructure its organization. He affirmed that Toriy had considerable flexibility to create new units and close older ones. Still, he emphasized that it was essential for the country to retain large enterprises to effectively use technology in order to achieve economies of scale and high productivity. While acknowledging that industry needed to be restructured in Russia, he regretted that the process had been so dramatic: industry was in effect being destroyed, masses of people had lost their jobs, and business people had resorted to operating on a barter system.

Dr. Artiukh's Dreams

When asked about his plans for the future, Dr. Artiukh replied: "Let me tell you my dreams." He felt confident about his plans because he had already fulfilled most of his prior year's goal, which was to produce four times more output in 1996 than in 1995. He also had hopes for developing various systems that would find applications around the world, including new generations of communication stations, and new acoustic speakers that he believed could provide a very large return from a relatively small investment.

Another major initiative involved plans to create a scientific and educational center on site, in collaboration with the Moscow Physics and Technical Institute where Dr. Artiukh was a department head, and another institute with which he also had an affiliation. At the proposed training center, Toriy employees would receive technical training in physics, electronics, and other scientific subjects in order to develop expertise and generate ideas in new areas. Dr. Artiukh explained that the training center was seen as a way of dealing with the serious problem of attracting qualified scientists to the state sector:

> Very few of the students we train in organizations such as the Physics and Technical Institute want to work in state-owned enterprises. We hope that the government will begin to understand that private industry must be supported by state research and development, and that money that has been earned must be returned to the enterprises that generated it. Here we hope that our productive collaboration in creating the new educational center will be an example for managers. But, as the saying goes, 'you can't be a prophet in your own country.'

Dr. Artiukh confirmed his serious intentions for the proposed center: "We plan to operate the scientific and educational center and award diplomas regardless of the difficulty in supporting it."

Happy to be State-Owned

By 1996, in a change of heart from his earlier views, Dr. Artiukh recognized many advantages in remaining state-owned. He was now convinced that it was the most appropriate status for advancing Toriy's scientific mission:

> We are a state enterprise, and we are happy about that. We are the only organization left in our field. In my opinion, to give this enterprise to shareholders would immediately mean that we would stop doing scientific research. Scientific research requires funding by the government. No other sponsors would be able to carry out such projects as making nuclear reactors, developing energy from water, or launching rockets to the sun. We have transformed ourselves into a state-owned scientific center. We have a substantial scientific base, as well as special facilities, and a great deal of unique equipment that we do not want to see destroyed. In addition, we train specialists. If we want this enterprise to remain as a scientific institution and to work in the interests of the country and the world, then it must remain state-owned.

Dr. Artiukh's dreams, however, were never fulfilled. His untimely death was reported in early 1999.

PART THREE

Hybrid Companies

5. Mikromashina

BEGINNINGS AS A STATE CONSUMER APPLIANCES PRODUCER

Mikromashina is a manufacturer of small electrical consumer appliances including shavers, hair clippers, hair dryers, fans, and coffee grinders. A former state-owned enterprise, it became a private stock company in 1993 under the government's privatization program, with the majority of shares passing to the company's managers and workers and some outside private owners. Operations continued under the long-time director. Mikromashina was founded in the 1960s and enjoyed a prime location in the northern part of Moscow. It had been a very successful enterprise under the centrally-planned economy, primarily because it reported for many years to the prestigious and well-financed aviation industry ministry. A major advantage of this relationship was that high-quality raw materials were relatively easy to obtain. The company had a reputation for producing attractive and reliable products. In recognition of this achievement, it had been awarded the Red Banner and the Badge of Honor by the USSR Council of Ministers, and was admitted to the All Union Board of Honor of the USSR.

Originally, the enterprise was part of a consumer products industry group. In the 1980s, when that group became large and unwieldy, enterprises were reassigned to other ministries, with Mikromashina transferred to the Ministry of the Aviation Industry. Another structural change occurred in 1991 when many industries were brought under the newly created Ministry of Industries. With the advent of privatization in 1992, most industrial ministries were disbanded and Mikromashina subsequently reported to the Committee for the Defense Industry.

In 1982, Mikromashina constructed a new 20,000 square-meter building. The government invested $1.5 million to upgrade the production equipment, providing 40 plastic injection-molding machines and various types of metalworking equipment. Raw materials such as plastic and steel tapes for shaver foils were obtained from more than 800 suppliers. As a hedge against shortages or supply delays, the company kept large inventories of essential materials, including 40 tons of raw plastic. Management's philosophy was to be as self-sufficient as possible and, consequently, the enterprise produced virtually all the parts for its products. The organization included a technical department that designed and produced molds for plastic components, an injection molding shop that produced plastic parts, a metalworking department that cut metal tapes into perforated shaving foils and produced other small metal parts, an electroplating shop, several assembly lines, and a manufacturing department that developed improvements in products, machinery, and production operations.

A number of services were provided on the premises free of charge to employees including a medical and dental clinic, day care center, kindergarten, cafeteria, and recreation areas. Employees also had access to children's summer camps and vacation resorts at no cost or at a nominal charge.

As late as 1992, Mikromashina operated at virtually full capacity. The company was able to retain its work force of 1,700 employees, and financed operations from cash flow and government subsidies. Several production lines assembled products, with subassembly lines providing parts manufactured in other departments. Lines were semi-automated and staffed by teams of workers who were eligible for team bonuses as well as individual wages. The production lines were supported by two adjacent rows of 30 women conducting subassembly and testing at their workstations. The premises were clean and orderly, and workers were fully engaged in their activities during a 1993 site visit.

The company's electrical products were highly desirable in the shortage-ridden Russian economy. They were often rationed by the aviation industry ministry according to social need, with preference given to orphanages and other needy institutions. Seventy percent of output was shipped to a major distributor in Moscow, while much of the remainder went to the company's joint venture with its Swiss and American partners.

THE JOINT VENTURE AND ITS IMPACT ON MIKROMASHINA

In 1989, Mikromashina entered into a joint venture called Miro with Thielmann Rotel AG of Switzerland. Mikromashina owned 60 percent of Miro, whose name was created from the first two letters of each partner. Rotel manufactured electric motors and household appliances that were distributed throughout Europe and the Middle East. The company contributed modern machinery in return for its share of the joint venture, while Mikromashina provided workers, equipment, and space in its building. By 1992, the joint venture employed 45 people.

The joint venture was among the earliest to be signed under the 1988 joint venture law because the two firms had been jointly producing shavers for eight years prior to the agreement. During this time, Mikromashina's shavers had been modified to meet European standards, resulting in 20 percent of production being exported to Western European countries including Italy, West Germany, and Switzerland, as well as Eastern Europe and Syria. At that time, hard currency from exports provided 60 percent of the JV's profits. As 60-percent owner, Mikromashina utilized these profits to help finance its own operations as well as those of the joint venture, and invested in new product development and upgraded equipment. Continuous product quality improvements were also made to meet the requirements of the Swiss partner and overseas customers.

In 1990, Nypro Inc., an American company headquartered in Clinton, Massachusetts, purchased half of Rotel's ownership, becoming a 20-percent partner in the joint venture. Mikromashina retained 60-percent ownership, with its proportional claim to the JV's profits. Nypro was a world-class plastic injection molding company with sales of over $100 million. It had many plants located around the world operating as joint ventures. The company brought to the JV expertise in manufacturing and assembling precision plastic components, and planned to provide engineering, tooling, and injection molding technology. Nypro planned to build a new plant according to its own specifications adjacent to Mikromashina's facility and install advanced high technology equipment, such as process-controlled plastic injection molding machines. \

STILL PROFITABLE IN 1993, BUT PROBLEMS DEVELOP

Things began to change for the worse for Mikromashina in 1993 with the country's increasingly rapid move toward a market economy. Despite growing problems, Mikromashina remained profitable, earning over one million rubles in 1993. Rampant inflation caused prices for the company's raw materials to skyrocket, and imported products posed fierce competition when Mikromashina raised its prices. Inflation also took its toll on consumers' purchasing power. Many could no longer afford Mikromashina's products, which were considered luxuries in comparison to food and other essentials. Sales of shavers weakened, with the price rising from 25 rubles in the late 1980s to 1,700 in 1993. Coffee grinders had almost no market, yet demand for hair clippers and hair dryers remained relatively strong.

In spite of these problems, Mikromashina was able to survive reasonably well by relying on its diversified product line, export market, and the joint venture. Although production had begun to slow, product quality was still at a high level due to successful improvement efforts that began in the 1980s. The company had also kept current with new technologies and processes. They were thus able to continue offering a reasonable combination of product, price, and quality, although it was becoming more difficult to do so.

In 1993, the government reduced its subsidies and the company's financial position weakened. Layoffs had become unavoidable, and the work force was cut by 400 to 1,300 employees. To maintain employment, work was increasingly performed manually rather than utilizing more efficient equipment. Viktor Levintan, who was the chief engineer and one of the initiators of new incentives, explained:

> Our major motivation now is to pay according to contribution, for instance, two to three times more for important jobs like those at the end of a production line with high responsibility for quality. Some people are paid by units produced, some by time worked, and some by both. We have a system of bonuses now, which rewards people depending upon their production. Seeing others unemployed is also a big motivator for people.

Yet, in a period of hyperinflation, wages were not sufficient to maintain motivation, and productivity suffered as the year progressed. For example, two engineers and one production supervisor resigned in order to make more money in private business. Mikromashina had difficulty providing support to the JV, and began utilizing some of its JV profits to maintain its own work force. One promising development in the JV was that construction began on the JV's new building adjacent to Mikromashina's facilities.

In discussing Mikromashina's profitable operations in 1993, Viktor Levintan acknowledged that profit was hard to calculate due to constant inflation and advance payments made to suppliers to ensure delivery. Adding to financial pressures, the company was required to make quarterly tax payments on estimated annual profits of 32 percent. Thus, 8 percent of the estimate was due each quarter. To improve financial prospects, Viktor began discussions with a number of potential foreign partners to find additional exporting opportunities.

Most long-term company managers and workers, including chief engineer Viktor Levintan, wanted Mikromashina to continue as a producer of small electrical consumer appliances. They feared, however, that some newer managers were seeking a quick payoff from the company's newly privatized status. Viktor explained that company managers and workers obtained 51 percent of shares earlier in the year. The government retained 49 percent, a portion of which was to be made available to the public at money or voucher auctions. Mr. Levintan hoped that the government would retain a substantial percentage to keep large blocks of ownership from falling into unfriendly hands. He and his supporters sought to maintain control and continue to lead the company in the direction they had established.

SALES DROP DRAMATICALLY IN 1994

Problems mounted through 1994, with sales dropping 60 percent compared to the prior year due to continuing competitive pressure from imports. In March, Viktor Levintan was promoted from his long-time position of chief engineer to acting director until an election could be held at a shareholders' meeting as mandated under privatization legislation. He explained the company's financing dilemma:

> How to find financing and thinking about the future are our biggest worries now. Even if we were able to produce more products for our major distributor and other customers, we would not receive payment in the foreseeable future.

Bartering and Delayed Payments Used as Stopgap Measures

The company's problem was similar to that of thousands of other enterprises since the nonpayment of debts among companies had reached an estimated $10 billion by the middle of the year. Like the others, Mikromashina was unable to pay suppliers or utilities, and delayed wage payments by several months. To make matters worse, the government had begun to impose penalties for nonpayment of taxes and mandatory contributions to the employee pension fund.

Mikromashina's sales deteriorated dramatically as its markets evaporated. Only 20 percent of production was now shipped to the company's major distributor. Viktor explained that living standards in the country had plummeted, and that inflation had become rampant. The price of bread, for example, had increased 2,400 percent from 25 kopecks to 600 rubles after the government freed prices in 1992. At the same time, the company was able to raise its prices only about 500 percent due to increasing competition. Foreign products were especially prized by consumers even though they sometimes sold at prices four or five times higher than Mikromashina's. Viktor had explored exporting, but realized they could not do so profitably because their products often could not compete with lower-priced ones. Their coffee grinders, for instance, sold profitably in Russia for $10, but could bring only $7 in England and $5 in Iran.

During the year, managers had taken several measures to deal with the financial problems. They resorted to bartering with customers and suppliers, such as paying suppliers with the coffee grinders they produced as well as grain and other materials received from customers. Discounts were offered to customers who paid in advance or on delivery. Space in the company's building was rented to other businesses, including a computer firm and a soft drink company. Viktor was afraid that the company had not raised its prices fast enough to counter inflated costs. Noting that marketing was very important, he explained that the company could not afford to hire a marketing expert since such specialists were paid from $500 to $1,500 per month. He had considered sharing a marketing person with another company, but was not convinced this strategy would solve Mikromashina's serious problems.

Meanwhile, the situation continued to worsen for the company and for Viktor personally. Fear, uncertainty, and personal ambition led some managers to challenge Viktor's leadership before the year's end. Some employees feared that the company would be destroyed by opportunists who would line their own pockets. This national trend involved shares being consolidated into few hands, usually directors, other senior managers, and favored outsiders. Viktor was being pressured to hold the first shareholders' meeting by those he called "The Young Boys." These managers had threatened court action to force the issue, but Viktor viewed their behavior as a self-serving push for power. He noted: "They think a new *barin* will be the answer," referring to the term for powerful paternalistic landlords in Tsarist times.

Nypro Buys More of the Joint Venture and a Stake in Mikromashina

In 1994 Nypro increased its share of Miro, the joint venture, to 33 percent with purchases from its partners. Mikromashina retained a 50-percent share and Rotel, 17 percent. The joint venture was still healthy and was producing a reasonable profit in rubles. However, Mikromashina continued spending more of its share of profits to alleviate its own cash crisis, rather than reinvesting in Miro. The lack of financial support for the JV contributed to a slowdown in construction of the new plant. Increased costs of construction materials were also an inhibiting factor, estimated to be 2,500 percent higher than before the government freed prices in January 1992. Also, the Western partners hesitated to invest more in a plant until legislation on land ownership became clearer. Such provisions were not included under the share ownership of the newly privatized enterprises.

Despite the partners' reluctance to invest in a new plant, Nypro approached Mikromashina during the year with an offer to purchase its share of the joint venture. Nypro's objective was to establish itself more firmly in Russia as part of its overall global strategy of having plants in key areas of the world. Gordon Lankton, Nypro's president, was optimistic enough about Russia's future to purchase 10 percent of Mikromashina itself in mid-1994. Although Viktor Levintan admired Gordon Lankton, he still wanted Mikromashina to remain independent: "We are not happy if a big papa will swallow us fully, not even a nice papa," referring affectionately to his friend.

Nypro's interest in Mikromashina was due in part to its desire to ensure the availability of components needed for the joint venture. Lankton visualized the joint venture becoming a supplier to the many foreign multinational corporations doing business in Russia, while continuing to export. He also admired Viktor and enjoyed their working relationship. Viktor felt the same, but was somewhat reluctant to have the American company gain even more ownership in the still quite profitable JV. Nevertheless, he was highly cognizant of Mikromashina's precarious situation, and knew that an additional cash infusion from Nypro would help. Referring to Mikromashina and the joint venture respectively, he remarked: "The mother is ill, but the daughter is healthier."

MOUNTING DEBTS AND TOP MANAGEMENT CHANGES IN 1995

Search for New Business Opportunities

The company's many problems resulted in a desperate financial situation by 1995. Its debts early in the year totaled around $500,000, including over $120,000 in unpaid taxes and $170,000 in late penalties and overdue employee pension fund contributions. An additional $80,000 was owed to employees for unpaid wages. Sales had continued to decline precipitously to an average monthly level of only $55,000. Nonetheless, Viktor Levintan believed that the company would not go bankrupt in the near future. Its building was estimated to be valued at more than $7 million, and would be very attractive to foreign companies due to its condition, location, and the shortage of such facilities in Moscow. He also noted that the company's receivables from sales were $400,000, and that most state-owned and newly privatized companies were in situations even worse than Mikromashina's.

All of 1994's problems continued into 1995 with few positive developments. The country's unstable governmental and economic environments, and the lack of a solid business infrastructure, continued to plague companies like Mikromashina. One positive development was the slowing of inflation, but the lack of business prospects caused even more layoffs in the company, such that the employment level was about 700 early in the year.

Despite the troubles, Viktor met his goal of producing some products every day, although at a drastically reduced level. He explained: "We must keep operating to maintain a future for the company and also the work force. I am not happy to see our equipment stopped." Viktor was especially concerned about the continuous layoffs that forced long-term employees into very uncertain futures. As acting general director, he felt a personal responsibility to maintain a high level of employment.

With the objective of maintaining continuous operations, Viktor investigated opportunities to engage in joint production with foreign companies and to produce parts for others. He had held discussions with many companies, including Gillette's Braun of Germany, and Kenwood of the

United Kingdom. He had proposed to Braun that they produce two product lines together, with the Braun product to be sold at a higher price and with higher quality than Mikromashina's product. Braun, however, was interested only in its own brand and would effectively have relegated Mikromashina to the role of subcontractor. Although not his objective, Viktor realized that subcontracting might be Mikromashina's only viable alternative with foreign companies. He was also investigating the possibility of a new environmentally-safe technology that would cost over $1.5 million. Although the Russian government had expressed some interest, Viktor realized that the probability of obtaining funding for such projects was low. He retained some hope, however, that the government would continue to subsidize companies like Mikromashina, although this was counter to stated government policy.

Nypro Increases Ownership of Joint Venture and Mikromashina

Several events of major importance to the company occurred during 1995. First, Nypro purchased for cash Mikromashina's 50 percent share of the joint venture, increasing its ownership to 83 percent, while 17 percent remained with Rotel. The joint venture by this time had been converted to a joint stock company because tax and other advantages for joint ventures had essentially disappeared. Legislation now permitted joint stock companies and allowed 100-percent foreign ownership of such businesses.

The second important event was an agreement between Mikromashina and Nypro negotiated by Viktor Levintan and Gordon Lankton. Negotiations that had been ongoing since early 1994 resulted in Nypro increasing its ownership of Mikromashina to 25 percent from the 10 percent it had acquired earlier. Gordon Lankton said at the time: "Viktor is the key player now and he wants this to happen." Lankton also hoped to purchase an additional 20 percent of Mikromashina from the Russian government under the privatization program, in return for investing $300,000 directly into Mikromashina as well as making a small payment to the government. An outside investor, the Moscow Investment Fund, owned an additional 15 percent, while another investor owned 5 percent. Company managers and employees, who had originally received 51 percent at the time of privatization, held most of the remaining shares. Lankton was quite optimistic that Nypro could increase its share in Mikromashina to at least 45 percent.

The third major event was the mid-year ouster of Viktor Levintan as acting director of Mikromashina and his replacement by one of his rivals, Sergei Molchanov. The new general director was one of the group of disgruntled managers who had become serious adversaries to Viktor, whom he referred to as "The Young Boys." They were especially upset that he had not called the first shareholders' meeting at which a general director would be elected. Viktor had hoped to remain as general director since he was only a few years from retirement. Moreover, he did not want to see drastic changes that would threaten the employment of loyal, long-term employees who had no realistic opportunities for employment elsewhere.

NEW MANAGEMENT FACED WITH OLD PROBLEMS IN 1996 AND 1997

During 1996 and 1997, Mikromashina's troubles continued, but the joint venture remained profitable. Continuing negotiations with Nypro were carried on by the new top management team that had come into power, and Viktor Levintan returned to his former position of chief engineer. Nypro's global strategy resulted in record annual revenues of over $200 million and unprecedented profits. It expanded operations in North America, Europe, Latin America, and Asia, conducting most as joint ventures with local partners. Gordon Lankton firmly believed that such cooperation was essential for successful operations abroad, and helpful even in the United States.

In spite of difficulties in dealing with the Russian government and other shareholders, Lankton was intent on increasing Nypro's stake in Mikromashina. Negotiations progressed with the company management, but the Russian government delayed approving Nypro's plan to increase ownership of Mikromashina. Additionally, according to Lankton, outside shareholders had a highly inflated estimate of Mikromashina's value. Still, in 1997, Nypro built the most modern cleanroom molding assembly facility in Russia on Mikromashina's site, modeled after Nypro's worldclass facilities · elsewhere. One molding machine was installed to begin operations.

Throughout 1996 and 1997, Mikromashina's situation worsened, and its value continued to decrease. The company laid off more workers and looked for new sources of income. Revenues came primarily from leasing space to other firms, and conducting business as a trading company that imported and distributed parts from China. A minor amount of production of its traditional electrical consumer appliances was carried out to meet the small demand from some older Russian consumers. The company also supplied tail light parts for Lada automobiles, but Lada failed to pay for them. General Director Sergei Molchanov negotiated a deal whereby Mikromashina took title to a number of Lada's street sweeping machines for which the Moscow city government had not paid Lada. He then leased the machines back to the Moscow city government. Molchanov's creative solution created a positive cash flow for Mikromashina, and satisfied both Lada and the city government.

NEW OPPORTUNITIES EMERGE IN 1998'S POST-CRISIS PERIOD

Things changed little for Mikromashina in 1998 until the country's mid-year financial crisis, which ironically helped the company's sales. The dramatic devaluation of the ruble made imports too expensive for most Russians, and demand for some of the company's products began to increase. Its coffee grinders, hair clippers, and shavers became more popular, but had to be reengineered to meet the increased quality many Russian consumers had come to expect. The company's plastic molding capacity, however, was seldom utilized after the crisis. Employment dropped to under 200 people, and leveled off at 140 by mid-1999. Even more space had been leased to 15 small businesses, including software companies and R&D facilities. Some were run by employees or former employees, one of whom was a member of Mikromashina's board of directors.

In 1998, Nypro became the largest shareholder of Mikromashina, owning nearly 50 percent of the company by buying out shares of some employees including those of Viktor Levintan and the joint venture's general manager. The Russian government still owned 20 percent, with the remainder owned primarily by Mikromashina employees and former employees including two major building tenants. Lankton continued to be interested in purchasing the government's shares, but negotiations had become extremely complicated.

By mid-1998, the joint venture, Miro, virtually ceased to exist as Nypro bought out all of its assets by paying overdue taxes and penalties. Nypro became a 100-percent owner of the entity, which had become little more than a shell organization. Nypro then created a new organization, Nypro Moscow, as its wholly-owned Russian subsidiary. In exchange for making Miro's tax payments, Nypro took title to the former JV's four high quality German-made molding machines which were installed in its cleanroom facility. This brought its machine total to five, and Nypro planned to install three additional machines by late 1999 to meet increasing product demand.

Sensing the need for new leadership, Gordon Lankton made the decision to appoint a new general director for the new company, rather than employ the director of the former joint venture. He selected Tanya Dreval, a long-term JV employee and its former sales manager. She spoke fluent English, and was the person who had first contacted Lankton about becoming involved with Mikromashina and its joint venture. She fired former managers and others who she realized had been dealing under the table, taking salaries while not working, and hiding the fact that the company was not paying taxes. A senior Nypro executive spoke very highly of the appointment:

> Tanya cleaned house at Miro. She knew where the problems were and who the unproductive people were who had forgotten how to work. She knew that they had been pulling the wool over our eyes.

Tanya Dreval developed additional business for the new company, which currently produced only for firms in the Russian market. She brought contracts from Russian water and soft drink bottling companies for whom Nypro Moscow produced plastic bottle closures. Nypro Moscow also entered a new business of repackaging imported consumer products for Colgate-Palmolive, Procter & Gamble, and other multinationals. Additionally, the new company began molding plastic telephone parts for Beeline Communications, a growing Russian telecommunications firm which produced handheld digital electronic cordless phones. Beeline had started out as a distributor for Nokia of Finland before establishing its production operations. Ms. Dreval developed a new technical team by promoting the best young people from the former joint venture. She was also supported by a small administrative team, including an experienced controller who had worked for a major US auditing firm in Moscow. He also served as her bodyguard.

With the demise of the joint venture, Nypro and Mikromashina had ended their operating relationship. Ironically, Nypro Moscow became one of Mikromashina's tenants when Tanya negotiated a lease for space in Mikromashina's building for Nypro's plastic injection molding cleanroom. Nypro had explored possibilities with other companies and other buildings, but did not find a more optimal situation than what existed at Mikromashina. Like all tenants, Nypro Moscow had to negotiate with Mikromashina's General Director, Sergei Molchanov, for its allocation of energy. Like most enterprises in Moscow, Mikromashina and its tenants were required to forecast their energy use. If Nypro underestimated its energy requirement, it had to renegotiate with Mikromashina.

A Nypro US senior executive explained one reason for staying in Mikromashina's building: "We knew the people at Mikromashina." And not overlooked by Nypro officials was the fact that Nypro US owned nearly 50 percent of Mikromashina, and wanted to help that company survive. They also believed that Sergei Molchanov was doing a fine job, not only in developing creative survival strategies for Mikromashina, but also in redirecting the company back to its basic business of producing small consumer appliances. One senior Nypro manager felt that if the political environment stabilized, Mikromashina could have a promising future, as could Nypro Moscow. The latter company was continuing to invest in its operations solely from its own revenues, supplemented by funds from its American parent. The operation was not yet profitable, but was described by one US executive involved in the operation as approaching profitability. He emphasized that Gordon Lankton remained committed to the company's Moscow operations. Lankton not only took a long-term view of the business operations, but also believed that good business relationships with international partners can contribute to harmonious international political relations.

6.   Tonar

COMPANY WITH A SOCIAL MISSION

The Tonar group of companies was started in early 1988, and was formally founded in September 1990. The company's name is an abbreviation of Russian words meaning "goods for the people," and was founded by two scientist-executives, Chairman of the Board of Directors and General Director, Vadim Vadimovich Andronov, and Chief Scientific Advisor, Konstantin Vladimirovich Ananichev. Tonar began as a state-owned organization, but the senior managers foresaw the coming of privatization and included provisions for privatizing in their charter.

Still, company leaders expected to remain partially owned by the government because the large-scale projects they envisioned required coordination with the state. Dr. Andronov explained:

> Reconstruction of the market meets a lot of difficulties along the way: it resembles an old Russian road with pits and stones. For people who were proud of Russian accomplishments only a decade ago, perestroika was a painful experience. It was difficult to see disintegration of the total system. The system had its ills, but it was a working system that was bringing tangible results to the Russian people. It is better to be both state and private because some state ownership will always be important in Russia's future. We don't want a 'Chinese wall' between state and private enterprises, but should make use of both state and private money.

Continuing his Chinese analogy, he described himself as a fan of the Chinese method of privatization, adding, "Russia's has been too fast and too wild." He noted that China's use of strong state-private relationships in combination with thriving entrepreneurships was a model that Tonar attempted to follow.

The original company objectives reflect the name chosen for the organization, and also the social conscience of the founders. Dr. Andronov explained that their approach was "to do business ethically and for the long term, and to welcome foreign participation with like-minded partners." Reflecting the social and ethical orientation of the firm, the board of directors included the Moscow Metropolitan of the Russian Orthodox Church. Tonar's executives recognized that a large unfulfilled need for consumer goods existed throughout Russia, and their primary objective was to provide a means for making consumer goods accessible across the country. Another objective with a strong social mission was to help victims of the 1986 Chernobyl nuclear disaster find jobs and housing.

A third goal was to develop ways to best utilize the high-technology potential of enterprises as they converted from the defense to the consumer and industrial sectors, as well as save workers' jobs in those organizations. Management discussed, for instance, the possibility of applying biotechnology developments from their laboratories to assist in the clean-up of the Chernobyl area. Managers also wanted to create jobs and planned to bring raw materials from other republics to the Moscow area to be processed by local workers. The fourth objective was to assume a role in developing and financing small businesses. Dr. Andronov and his colleagues saw Tonar as "a bridge between small businesses and larger organizations that could provide various types of support to the start-ups."

The two founders had a wealth of scientific and managerial experience which they had gained in senior positions in the centrally-planned economy, as well as in assignments abroad. Dr. Vadim Andronov, Tonar's Chairman and CEO, had held numerous managerial and scientific positions. He was a doctor of science, spoke fluent English, and graduated from the Sloan Fellows Program at the Massachusetts Institute of Technology in 1978. Dr. Konstantin Ananichev, who also held a doctor of science degree and spoke excellent English, was educated as a mechanical engineer and a technologist. He was 62 years old when he co-founded Tonar in 1988. After holding various positions in technology management for Soviet design bureaus and factories, he spent four years in England as chief inspector of critical machinery to be exported to the USSR. Dr. Ananichev had held a series of important positions in both the Ministry for External Affairs and the Energy Ministry. In these positions, he spent substantial time abroad, including in Iraq where he was an industrial development planner for the Middle East. He also had responsibility for building power plants in Syria, India, Czechoslovakia, and Finland, as well as at the Aswan Dam in Egypt. He had written a well-known book on practical ecology which addressed issues such as municipal waste, edited a monthly technological research journal, and taught courses in his specialty. He had also served as the head of the USSR State Committee for Science and Technology for English-speaking countries and Japan, and led the Committee's exchange program with the Massachusetts Institute of Technology in the US. He noted with little exaggeration: "I have had 200 titles in my life."

PROGRESS AS A PRIVATE SECTOR-STATE PARTNERSHIP IN 1993

By 1993, Tonar was a stock company with 52-percent private and 48-percent state ownership, as had been planned in the original charter. Dr. Andronov expressed pride in being a public stock company, but also noted management's reasons for desiring partial state ownership:

> The State needs a private approach to help manage projects like revitalizing Chernobyl. As a stock company, our personal interests are looked after. There are three of us who are doctors of science and Tonar directors. We get a state salary and fringe benefits such as medical care and food, as our scientists also do. In addition, as directors we were able to buy our shares at a nominal price.

Dr. Andronov believed that, without the availability of bank credit, all future projects would be in jeopardy, and thus Tonar established a commercial bank within its organizational complex. Eventually, he expected the state ownership to decrease to 25 percent, in favor of private shareholders' interest in the business. Reflecting the company's interest in private stock companies, Tonar became one of the founders of the Russian Commodity Stock Exchange. In mid-1993, Dr. Andronov explained:

> Only in recent weeks have we in Russia started to work in a civilized way. Earlier, things were more wild, but now people are beginning to think about ideas like the social responsibility of business. The State and the people have little money, so now entrepreneurs must do real business.

Tonar thus hoped to utilize the government as a venture capitalist for entrepreneurs, with Tonar acting as the facilitator or bridge. Dr. Andronov noted that many Russian entrepreneurs were importing goods from abroad and selling them profitably, but he disapproved of their activities in general: "This does not help the economy, there is no value added. It is more negative to continue this type of business."

Objectives and Organizational Structure

Tonar's long-term objective was to operate as a modern high technology corporation. Another goal was to provide cash to finance these longer-term developments. Dr. Andronov described Tonar's primary asset as being "intellectual property, that is, the skill, knowledge, experience, and know-how of our people." Most employees were in their early thirties, with five to ten years of practical scientific experience. Many had been trained in exchange programs abroad, including the Massachusetts Institute of Technology. Tonar's technical philosophy was to operate with a pragmatic and applied approach in order to commercialize technology relatively rapidly.

Tonar directly employed 2,200 people in corporate functions and the management of its decentralized daughter companies. Of the 32 people who held executive management positions, all had graduate degrees, and eight spoke English fluently. The group included managers over and under age 40—a distribution that the senior executives felt offered Tonar an excellent combination of experience, knowledge, and skills needed to develop and implement large, complex projects. Three levels of managers ran Tonar's operations, and each level had its own remuneration scheme. Higher level managers' rewards depended more upon company profits than did those at lower levels. Half of Tonar's employees were women, including a good percentage of company managers.

In addition to its central Moscow headquarters, the company had offices in five cities throughout Russia, and was investigating the possibility of opening offices in some European countries. Dr. Andronov felt, however, that a major problem would be finding reliable partners in these countries as well as in Russia. Nonetheless, they hoped to find Swedish, Italian, German, American, and Russian companies to become partners in Tonar's Russian projects such as converting solid waste into usable materials.

Tonar employed approximately 20,000 people in the companies in which it was a shareholder. Its 20 diverse companies employed scientist-managers who possessed a wide range of experience and talents. Along with high intellect and professionalism, Tonar looked for people with an entrepreneurial spirit who were capable of reacting quickly to Russia's constantly changing circumstances. The average age of new employees was around 30, and many had work experience in the West. Most of these Tonar "daughter enterprises" of five to ten people were technical operations in which Tonar owned the technical process in partnership with the scientist-entrepreneurs. This arrangement was in contrast to owning the product or real estate such as plants, although Tonar did have controlling shareholder interest in some of its plants. Arrangements called for Tonar to receive a share of profits from these companies. Dr. Andronov elaborated:

> We create these smaller companies for scientists and give them independence. We help start them up and let them fly. We provide them with salaries, management know-how, and financial assistance. The scientist-managers run their own companies, but remain in the total Tonar organization. We feel that this has a very good effect on their morale. A person should not look for a quiet life, but needs to have some interest in life that will motivate him to desire more. This can be travel, money, science, or anything else. If I know what motivates a person, I know how to work with him.

To motivate these managers, Tonar offered them 10 percent of their individual company if justified by their performance each year. It was thus possible for these entrepreneurs to own their own companies after 10 years. Dr. Andronov added:

We also want them to have further training, and are trying to arrange exchange programs with business schools in the West. We try to operate like a Western company utilizing modern management. We have adapted Western experience to our own conditions, and we haven't gone bankrupt.

Problems in the Environment and the Organization

Despite efforts to improve company performance, Tonar was experiencing various problems in 1993. After the government's 1992 policy of freeing prices created hyperinflation, many scientists sought better paying opportunities in business and trade. Another problem was the lack of state regulations for intellectual property, "which makes it difficult to manage this type of company," Dr. Andronov noted. Extremely high taxes and the lack of credit at reasonable rates were additional barriers to effective company operations. The government's method and pace of privatization, executives felt, were also a problem. The system was too bureaucratic, and changes were necessary to facilitate and clarify the privatization process for enterprises.

Referring to Tonar's internal issues, Dr. Andronov believed that they had decentralized too fast, were using the wrong processes, and had too much bureaucracy. Acknowledging the need for a more effective organizational structure, he added that their managers needed more training, and that he and other top managers also needed help in creating "an atmosphere of trust among business people" in order to conduct business on a mutually ethical basis. He added:

> There are too many unfulfilled promises in Russia. And there are also many broken promises on the part of foreign people dealing with Russians.

Business Strategy

Although Tonar had developed some large projects to provide cash flow, its fundamental business strategy was to act as a bridge to help small businesses obtain advantages from large businesses and the State. Dr. Andronov stated: "There is euphoria about small businesses in Russia, but they need help." Tonar executives often selected areas of activity by analyzing the structure of industries such as polymer producers and metal processors, both of which were prevalent in the Moscow area. Additionally, Tonar tried to facilitate cooperative efforts among industry groups in order to gain economies of scale, while still ensuring that firms remain small entrepreneurships. By providing such management guidance, Tonar executives hoped to develop entrepreneurs, but recognized the value of leveraging their combined capabilities. Tonar also assisted these groups in obtaining financing for their operations.

In fulfilling its social mission, Tonar worked with larger enterprises such as power electronics companies. Their goal in this case was to help rebuild and modernize this industry which included ten companies in Moscow and other regions. Specific objectives were to save jobs, provide economic development, and increase production of consumer electronics that had been produced in these plants alongside the defense and military products. Although the Moscow polymer and metals activities were a regional initiative, the power electronics activities represented an interregional program. Another plan for interregional development was in the area of telecommunications systems, and Tonar executives were negotiating with U.S. telecommunications companies for joint projects.

A third group, special projects, was under the direct management of Dr. Andronov, and included very large projects in plastics and oil. Tonar operated a major polypropylene production operation in southern Russia, and participated in a joint project with a large chemical plant in Siberia. Additionally, the company had won a competitive bid to operate an oil refinery in Kaliningrad in the westernmost part of Russia. Dr. Andronov reiterated the philosophy that guided their actions: "It is necessary for domestic businesses to grow, rather than continuing to import foreign products and export raw materials that are needed here." He cited the example of exports of scrap metals to Europe, with the result that Russian companies had none to use in their own businesses. Yet he emphasized that Tonar welcomed foreign participation in its programs, and noted that they already had partners from the US in a venture to help Russian farmers.

Such projects produced earnings for Tonar to help finance its high technology operations. The company received orders from the State Food Committee, for instance, to send food to northern regions utilizing the distribution network that Tonar had established. The company also received government contracts to produce consumer goods in its polypropylene operations, such as plastic for greenhouses and dishes. In essence, Tonar operated as a holding company employing a portfolio strategy at the corporate level. At the business unit level, the firm operated large cash-producing operations and projects, as well as smaller embryonic technological start-up companies.

CONTINUED SUCCESS IN 1994 DESPITE OBSTACLES

Tonar continued its successful growth throughout 1993, and by 1994 had become one of the leading companies in Russia according to the CEO, Dr. Andronov. Tonar had become known for its large-scale projects and operations, and for its scientific and technological accomplishments. Based on these strengths and its expertise in various scientific areas, the company was able to secure contracts and funding from numerous organizations. At the end of 1994, the company had assets of 285 billion rubles, and investment in new production totaled 26 billion rubles. Dr. Andronov explained why they were so successful:

> We correctly determined our resources and strengths, and recognized our people as our most valuable asset. We united three generations of people in our company and used the oldest generation's strengths very well, and trained and developed younger people. This is not a typical strategy in Russia, but we felt it was key to our survival.

The company seemed to be well financed. In addition to its profitable operations, Tonar received continuous contracts and assistance from various governmental bodies such as the Moscow city and regional governments. The company had a special license that entitled it to bid on government projects.

Many Tonar activities were performed under short-term contracts with companies, which generated continuous cash flows to cover day-to-day requirements of the business. Many organizations, according to Dr. Andronov, saw great potential in Tonar, and provided favorable contracts and terms to the company. For instance, the large enterprise, Interneftgaz, had signed a contract to lease Tonar's new polypropylene factory which was nearing completion. Additionally, since its return on investment was rising, more shares of the company were sold, including many to foreign investors. Tonar's own bank, the Russian Food Commodity Bank, provided extensive credit and discount loans. With regard to customers and clients, company management reported few problems in collecting receivables in a timely fashion. They reported that government tax policies had improved somewhat, but were still a major problem. Managers did not expect the situation to brighten very much, and as Dr. Andronov said: "We don't expect miracles."

In addition to its reputation and performance, much of Tonar's success was due to the broad network of relationships that the senior executives had developed, building upon their leadership positions in scientific projects in the centrally-planned economy. Dr. Andronov explained that "it looks very much like lobbying in the US, but it's a little different and more difficult since people lobby much more openly here." He cited the difficulty of lobbying government organizations that did not appreciate the importance of high technology in Russia's future. He was confident, however, that Tonar's executives would be able to work under any government administration, regardless of its political orientation. During 1994, he felt that Tonar's executives had developed even stronger contacts with government agencies. One manifestation of their influence was their success in convincing the government agencies to reduce their ownership of Tonar to 24 percent.

The company's success, however, did not come without personal cost to the executives. Both Dr. Andronov and Dr. Ananichev suffered heart attacks during the year. This was the second one for Dr. Andronov, who affirmed: "Work is my life and means everything to me."

Company Culture and Management Philosophy

Under the leadership of Dr. Andronov and Dr. Ananichev, Tonar had developed a management team and utilized more and more group decision making. Because they had a highly educated staff, they encouraged trust and openness in deliberations. Dr. Andronov stated: "The question of power is a very difficult one, but I think we have enough authority to manage this organization."

As additional motivators, they promoted employees on the basis of performance, and were considering issuing shares to deserving employees. Following their policy of annually rewarding successful entrepreneurs with ten percent of the shares in their companies, Tonar distributed such ownership to four entrepreneurs in 1994. With some smaller companies, Tonar supplied products at a discount, thereby allowing the small firms to resell them at a profit. It did not concern Dr. Andronov whether those companies sold other merchandise: "I accept it, and there is really no point in asking, since I will not get a straight answer anyway."

Senior executives recognized the importance of treating employees with respect and dignity, realizing that the company had to earn their support and loyalty. Tonar employees were fortunate to receive their salaries on time, in contrast to many other organizations. Additionally, they received medical care, insurance, meals, vacations at company-rented dachas, and opportunities to study abroad. Even though there was some downsizing when individual projects did not materialize, personnel were usually moved to other areas of the company. As a result, although salaries were average, turnover was extremely low and senior executives reported no major personnel problems. To avoid layoffs, scientists were often hired for various individual projects on fixed-term contracts ranging from three months to one year.

Mission and Strategy

Tonar retained the central focus of its mission, which was to initiate and participate in socially beneficial projects. The company continued to develop projects to alleviate unemployment and help economic development in various regions of Russia. Emphasizing their commitment to conduct business in an ethical manner, the senior executives noted that a major recurring problem was that foreign firms deceived them and broke their promises. For instance, according to Dr. Andronov, a major European food company had misled them in their attempts to develop a food distribution system.

The company's corporate and business strategies remained unchanged. At the corporate level Tonar retained its holding company structure, and senior executives continued to believe that they needed a relationship with the government, rather than becoming a 100-percent private stock company. The corporate portfolio strategy remained a positive feature, with Dr. Andronov crediting it with providing stability: "Diversification helps us with our balance sheet since we can take funds from one organization for use in another. It also provides a more favorable tax status and spreads our risk." To illustrate the effects of hyperinflation, he noted that they had invested 100 million rubles in their operations in the Tomsk oil region in 1990, but total corporate investment there had risen to 15 billion devalued rubles by late 1994.

By showing consistency in their business strategy, Tonar was able to engage in longer-term projects and gain financing for these activities. The company had built a reputation for expertise and performance that could come only with a consistent strategy. Dr. Andronov clarified that their primary strategic direction was projects for developing raw materials as well as other activities to help revitalize Russia's crumbling infrastructure. As an example, Dr. Andronov pointed to the huge polypropylene plant they had built in the Stavropol region in southern Russia. Producing 100,000 tons of polypropylene per year, including 20,000 tons designated as superior quality, the plant was one of the largest in the Russian Federation. The company had acted as its own general contractor in this venture, and to ensure quality and timely construction, had hired a Turkish firm for the actual construction. A large investment was made in technology and machinery imported from England, Japan, and the US. Dr. Andronov explained it was necessary to utilize foreign contractors and equipment because Russian companies could not yet provide the level of technology and construction quality required.

Company leaders had the strong support of the Moscow regional government since output from the polypropylene plant would be utilized as raw material in numerous plastic operations around Moscow. Tonar had hired a marketing research firm to study the needs for polypropylene in the Moscow region before embarking on the construction project. The marketing consultant concluded that many food packaging, consumer goods, and other companies were unable to operate effectively due to the lack of polypropylene materials. Dr. Andronov believed that "investing in production like this is quite unique in Russia today." In doing so, the company had provided employment, economic development, and Russian-made consumer and industrial products. Plastic products included pipes utilized in gas pipelines, construction materials, and automotive parts. Dr. Andronov attributed much of Tonar's success in such projects to the solid and extensive relationships the company had created in recent years with government, commercial, and other private organizations.

An illustration of this network can be seen in the financing of a $300 million plant, which upon completion was to be leased by Interneftgaz. Tonar had the support of the Department of Construction and the Department of Energy. Also, Tonar had sold shares in the operation to Montazhstroi, a leading construction company, and Menatep Energy, part of a major conglomerate. Dr. Andronov stated that Tonar was able to attract such strong partners while retaining a major financial interest in the project.

The firm's ability to attract partners is also evident in another venture where a Finnish firm and Samsung of Korea cooperated with Tonar in building a new plant to produce integrated circuits. The project, Dr. Andronov felt, would help in the conversion from defense production to commercial applications. On a smaller scale, some daughter companies, cooperating with former military plants, were developing new electronics applications as well as microgenerators for producing electric power. Tonar, with the support of the Russian Academy of Sciences, was working with the Moscow city and regional governments, and seeking foreign investors to apply these technologies to Moscow's water system and power supply. Another Tonar company was negotiating with a Korean firm to license technology know-how.

Tonar had also made progress in another socially important project, creating a wholesale market distribution network for food products based on European standards for warehouses and other features. In what Dr. Andronov described as a fantastic project, Tonar had partnered with a Dutch company, and had links with retail stores to complete the distribution system. In its efforts to help Russian farmers, the company was assisted by a former communist party secretary of agriculture who was an expert in what Dr. Andronov referred to as long-forgotten methods. Tonar would add modern management techniques to make these methods more efficient and effective. The project was important to the Moscow city and regional governments because the infrastructure and networks of the former Soviet period that had provided food for the Moscow area had been dismantled. A new system was needed, Dr. Andronov explained, to prevent food shortages and possibly social unrest in Moscow, a situation the governments clearly wanted to avoid.

Reflecting the ecologically responsible values of senior managers, the company was developing a solid waste processing and recycling facility near Noginsk in the Moscow region. Dr. Andronov noted that Moscow's Mayor Luzhkov had ranked environmental issues as Russia's third or fourth most important problem, but Moscow's most serious problem after crime. The facility employing a biological, non-thermal process would convert one-half million tons of waste products per year into useful materials for industrial and consumer goods. Half of the waste treated was to be newly generated waste that would be hauled to the plant, while the second half would be taken from existing dumping locations. Material presently in waste dumps had to be treated because it already constituted a major environmental hazard. The Timokhovo location, for instance, was the largest in Europe, with 32 million tons of waste already on site.

In the new facility, little fuel would be required because the needed energy would be a by-product of the technological processes used in waste conversion. Tonar itself had provided some of the technology and equipment from its factories in Budennovsk and Tomsk. The Noginsk plant, developed by Tonar, constituted only one project of its ecological program. The company also wanted to work on industrial smog reduction and water purification projects. It was also planning to build a hazardous waste recycling plant in Timokhovo. Dr. Andronov, being an ecologist, headed the ecological operations which employed 20 people, primarily technical experts, and a governmental deputy minister was also deeply involved. The company cooperated with government agencies in determining short- and long-term objectives to be met through Tonar projects. For instance, before undertaking the Noginsk project, Tonar's scientists had conducted three years of research on recycling, focusing on development of building materials such as building blocks and corrugated roofing materials from processed waste.

A second project in which Tonar provided ecologically friendly technologies was the modernization of a chemical factory near the Moscow regional town of Kupavna, which produced industrial applications of rubber. Tonar's technological contributions were utilized to prevent pollution from poisonous substances in the plant's processes which could harm the area's population.

At the close of 1994, Tonar was a successful, diversified, socially responsible organization, owned 76 percent by private shareholders and 24 percent by various government bodies. The company employed nearly 20,000 people in its corporate holding company and 20 daughter companies, and had built and operated numerous large projects, as well as engaging in new high technology developments. It operated its own commercial bank, established numerous partnerships with various government organizations and foreign companies, and had succeeded in attracting substantial funds for its ambitious capital investment program. The company had made substantial progress toward fulfilling its mission of providing goods for the people, as well as employment and economic development in various regions of the country. Dr. Andronov concluded: "I am looking to the future with careful optimism. I don't know what it will bring, since the country has so many problems beyond our control."

FAST, DYNAMIC GROWTH IN 1995

Dr. Vadim Andronov, CEO of the now five-year-old Tonar Group, described the company in late 1995 as a "dynamic, fast-growing enterprise which has attained very positive results." He believed that they and their associates had worked very hard in building their open stock company with governmental partners, the city of Moscow and the Moscow regional government. Their mission and strategy remained unchanged, and they foresaw continued development as a financial-industrial holding company. However, they recognized that they would have to continually raise funds for their many projects, but had often organized them as separate entities enpowered to raise their own funds. Dr. Andronov declared:

> We love our work and our firm. We are working better and more efficiently this year because we have developed strong ties with many banks and other financial institutions.

Tonar had continued its close relationship with various governmental bodies that owned approximately 20 percent of the company. Tonar executives retained controlling interest of 41 percent through their bank, The Russian Food Commodity Bank. The ownership was distributed among other private shareholders as follows: 20 percent held by Renaissance Bank, five percent by Unikom Bank, five percent by Mezhregionkom Bank, five percent by Roschemneft, a major chemical and oil corporation, and four percent by Zarubezhneftegazstroi, a large international oil and gas construction corporation. Dr. Andronov stated that their strategic goal was to remain as owners and manage their own properties. He explained that the second phase of the country's privatization program in 1994, which was intended to attract new capital into enterprises, had little effect on them since they continued to be well financed by both government and private investors, and they operated profitably in this partnership.

Problems Amid Prosperity

Elaborating on the privatization process, Dr. Ananichev, the second-ranking Tonar executive, described the situation as resembling the "wild law of the jungle. The old Soviet group is still working and has de facto power in many former state-owned organizations." He noted that the biggest problem for Tonar was attracting key people for its decentralized organization, and that this resource was becoming even scarcer. Another problem was securing enough foreign and Russian investments for its major projects. He spoke passionately about the company's philosophy, its motto of goods for the people, and its objective of being an incubator for start-up R&D entrepreneurships. A third set of problems was the primitive stage of both the market system and a supporting infrastructure in which to conduct business, as well as widespread unethical business practices. He summarized:

> Tonar's objective is to introduce a social consciousness and concern for the people into the new culture of Russian enterprise.

Management and Organizational Structure

As a private stock company, Tonar was managed by a board of directors. Its eight members were not all shareholders, but included associates and supporters of the enterprise and its executives, including the chairman, Dr. Andronov, and Dr. Ananichev. At the corporate level, a nine-member executive committee headed by Dr. Andronov made decisions on all major areas of company activity. A Works Programs Committee, headed by Dr. Ananichev, decided which projects Tonar would undertake. Five other corporate committees were responsible for financial policy, investments, key personnel appointments, small business development, and major areas of consumer need. These seven committees oversaw the general management functions of Tonar, and ensured that the decentralized entities, including daughter companies and major projects, would operate consistently with Tonar's philosophy and objectives. This involved activities that would result in consumer goods and services offered at reasonable prices to the public. Corporate oversight of unit managers was necessary since Dr. Ananichev believed there was a need to retrain many of them and change their economic mentality. In general, he believed there was a lack of management talent with the skills needed to operate in a dynamic market-oriented environment. Partially in recognition of this failing, Tonar no longer provided the opportunity for the small-company entrepreneurs to earn an annual ten-percent ownership stake in their companies. Instead, these individuals were offered a stock purchase plan in Tonar itself.

The company's organizational structure consisted of three primary divisions, each of which was subdivided into two departments as follows: (1) Industrial Development and Construction Division consisting of the Petrochemical Production Department and the Construction and Renovation Department, (2) Engineering and Scientific Research Division with its Engineering Ecology Department and the Department of Science and Technology and Special Programs, and (3) Agriculture, Wholesale Trade, and Interregional Logistical Networks Division which consisted of two departments that were developing a regional network of food production and distribution. In exercising corporate control, Tonar's corporate management utilized planning and control systems, including financial planning. Corporate itself directly managed only its own budget for corporate activities, and received a management fee from the projects it oversaw. Each unit had its own budget and operated quite independently, but within the planning and control guidelines from corporate management. Tonar Holding Group had share ownership control of all operating units.

Financing Decentralized Operations Through Outside Investors

Tonar's financing strategy was to create individual companies around each major project, and finance each separately. Although Tonar executives had earlier attempted to retain controlling interest in projects, partners were now brought in. Dr. Andronov stated that Tonar executives' shareholdings in the company had cost between $2 and $3 million, but the real value could be measured in the tens of millions. Yet, the company's need for cash was great, and required continuous dilution of their ownership position.

The practice of financing projects, such as polypropylene plants and the proposed solid waste conversion plant, as independent companies allowed Tonar to leverage its own financial resources, as well as to diversify its risk. "This will be our financial mechanism to complete plants," Dr. Andronov said. Tonar's developing strategic approach was aimed more at creating and managing businesses than owning a majority share as in the past. This change resulted primarily from the large capital needs involved in the projects undertaken by the company, as well as the relative scarcity of funding.

For instance, the projects ordered by the Moscow city or regional governments would be financed by those bodies, while the national government would fund projects related to its areas of interest. Government auditors scrutinized carefully where Tonar invested government funds, and the company therefore kept detailed records of its spending. The ecologically friendly solid waste conversion and recycling plant was financed primarily by the Moscow city government. Another large project, the second polypropylene plant, would be approximately 50-percent owned by private investors including chemical and oil companies. The central government would secure ownership, and Tonar would sell blocks of its remaining shares to new investors in order to finance completion of the project. The plant was being built in Budennovsk near Chechnya. Plans called for construction to be completed in 1996, but the Chechnian war had delayed progress. The government's interest was in the plant's capability to produce processed oil utilizing some of the country's enormous raw crude reserves.

The projects became the responsibility of various Tonar divisions. The new chemical plant, for instance, was managed by the Petrochemical Production Department of the Industrial Development and Construction Division. The same was true of Tonar's polypropylene plant, which Dr. Andronov described as being very successful in 1995 despite problems with construction and financing. The construction of the waste conversion and recycling plants, as well as their future operations, would be the responsibility of the Engineering Ecology Department of the Engineering and Scientific Research Division. Tonar's third division, Agriculture, Wholesale Trade and Interregional Logistical Networks, was responsible for developing wholesale warehouses and distribution systems. The objective of this project was to distribute food to various regions of Russia outside Moscow, which was the best supplied city in the country.

After being disappointed by a Dutch partner, Tonar managers had begun working with a US firm to develop a modern distribution system that would be one of the first in Russia. Dr. Andronov elaborated:

> Russia's previous distribution system, especially for foodstuffs, was destroyed, and nothing has yet replaced it. Today, people trade in Russia using small vendors on street corners. There is no distribution system, and chaos is dominating all over the country. Our task, as a socially responsible organization, is to create perestroika in the distribution system and reorganize it into a structured one.

He described this undertaking as a very big project, which would begin in Moscow, and radiate throughout the Moscow region before being extended into other areas. One reason for this sequence was the willingness of the Moscow city government to provide substantial funds for the project because of its importance in filling a crucial infrastructure need.

In total, ten large shareholder groups would be involved in the project in addition to several smaller and medium-sized businesses. Tonar would, as usual, attempt to maintain control through its shareholdings, but operationally each of the initial four wholesale centers would be independent and have its own budget. Dr. Andronov explained that each would operate as a separate enterprise with small firms inside such as transportation, processing, packaging, as well as product areas like meat, dairy, and produce businesses. The objective was to develop small companies under the umbrella of a large enterprise in accordance with Tonar's mission of bringing quality food to the public at a reasonable price.

The Tonar group of companies enjoyed another successful year in 1995 as they increased their assets and funding, and some plants began operations. Clear plans were being implemented in constructing new facilities, and research and development of an applied nature continued in the company's technical division. Although problems persisted with construction, financing, and partners, Tonar utilized numerous partners successfully in all of these areas. Senior management realized that it needed a large network of partners with various interests to facilitate the company's progress. Management had clearly shown the ability to adapt to the newly developing needs of a transitioning economy, and not become immobilized by a bureaucratic and centralized approach to their business. Perhaps most importantly, Tonar's founders had retained a consistent set of values and beliefs that they translated into a social mission, and operationalized through the company's projects and plans. Dr. Andronov summed up his views of 1995:

> How would I evaluate this year? Tonar is a fast-paced corporation in terms of developing new subsidiaries and related businesses. Our first years were

focused on creating a structure and developing new leadership. Now we are concentrating on real business.

REFOCUSING AND CONSOLIDATION IN 1996

Decreased Activities in Small Business Development

In late 1996, the company had become more focused. Management reduced diversification and concentrated on the large projects which had received funding and which were intended to be self-financing. Less emphasis was placed upon developing small technological companies within Tonar, and plans called instead for developing smaller companies within the umbrella organizations expected to result from Tonar's major projects. Dr. Andronov stated bluntly: "Diversification in our company failed."

Tonar's board of directors re-evaluated their goals regarding small businesses, and concluded that the corporation had to develop even stronger ties with big businesses in order to support development of small businesses. Dr. Andronov explained:

> Small businesses don't shape the face of the country. Only the development of major industry can launch us to a new level of economic development. We understand that technological progress cannot be achieved on the basis of small businesses. Large organizational structures are needed to produce major technological achievements.

Limited financing was one of the reasons for their shift in strategy, but Dr. Andronov added that many of their small-company scientists had a narrow view of innovation, considering it to encompass only advanced technology:

> They seemed interested only in the long-run payoffs, which leads to great uncertainties. Lots of them have good ideas and desire to produce something original and new, but these novelties aren't paying off in the short term. This is not the way to plan. We had hoped to find men and women who had a wider vision of what innovation means, one that started with customers and moved backward to products and then technology.

An additional problem was retaining the very best of the small-company entrepreneurs. Dr. Andronov noted: "Every good manager wants to start his own business after working here for some time. He comes to learn the ropes and then leaves us to start his own enterprise." He also acknowledged that many talented managers and scientists had left for the West. The combination of financial limitations, too few market-oriented entrepreneurs, inability to retain the best entrepreneurs, and the need to focus on large projects led Tonar to decrease its activities in small business development.

Refocusing on Three Large Projects

Another reason for reducing diversification, according to Dr. Andronov, was that "our economy is still running on inertia from the past. When new people try to do things as they are done in the US or Europe, they often fail because there is no understanding of such approaches, and therefore no support." Tonar's response was to limit its involvement to a few large projects. The first and most successful continued to be the polypropylene plant which Tonar had built in the Stavropol region. A second plant with state-of-the-art equipment located next to the existing plant was expected to be completed in 1997. The endeavor was successful primarily due to strong industry demand for products in food packaging and automotive parts.

Tonar's second major project, a wholesale distribution network, had run into problems and delays, but Dr. Andronov stated:

> We will do the project, we are sure of it. We want the same type of centers as in the US and Europe to attract foreign companies and to educate Russian citizens and companies in the right way to do this. We want to base our plans for this infrastructure on small, independent businesses, which would also provide the opportunity for individual farmers and collective farmers to sell their products.

Problems had occurred when their American partner backed out of the agreement, as had a Dutch partner some time earlier. Dr. Andronov explained:

> The American partnership died when the company was unable to find the necessary investment, and told us, 'Sorry.' The Dutch party had offered to build a pilot distribution center, but probably spent too much money in the preparation stage, and backed out of the project.

Capital needs were extremely high and Tonar was unable to raise the required funds by late 1996. Managers were in negotiations with new potential partners, however, and the Moscow city and regional governments were still very supportive of the project. Tonar had invested some of its own money as well as that of the Moscow governments in purchasing land and materials for two of the four planned food distribution warehouses in the Moscow region. The first, to be located in Dolgoprudny, would consist of a major refrigeration storage building surrounded by smaller buildings in which wholesalers could package their products for retail distributors. Dr. Andronov acknowledged the threat of criminal activity:

> In Russia today, most businesses are controlled by or threatened by criminals. But we're not afraid of such activity because we're tied in with the Moscow city and regional governments as shareholders.

Regarding their third major project, solid waste treatment, Dr. Andronov noted that 20 million of Russia's 150 million people lived in the Moscow region, and that 20 percent of the country's GDP came from the area. Consequently, a solution was needed to the three million tons of solid waste that was being dumped annually at more than 20 locations in the Moscow area. Tonar had been designated by the governmental bodies as the general developer for a solid waste disposal and recycling plant, for which the company had a unique non-thermal technology requiring no external energy source. Site preparation had begun with funds from the city and regional governments as well as Tonar, and construction was to start in early 1997.

Dr. Andronov felt that these governments would likely become majority shareholders rather than retaining the usual 25 percent. Estimated to cost $225 million, the project was very capital intensive and finding private shareholders was difficult. But Tonar was negotiating with a strategic investor whose equipment would be installed in the plant. Dr. Andronov said that British and Italian banks were ready to provide credit to be used in building the first plant. Tonar itself would build only one plant, and then would offer its consulting services and contracting to other Russian cities after successfully launching the venture. In keeping with the company's strategy, Tonar would own only the system at the heart of the plant's operation, and would license the system to others. Tonar's ecologically responsible philosophy, technical ability to meet a major municipal need, strong network of relationships, and relatively consistent strategy all played a part in the company's successful involvement in the project.

New Service Team Structure

Tonar's organization structure was little changed from earlier years, except that there was less activity in the R&D incubator start-ups. One organizational innovation was the service teams in each division. Once a project was funded, a service team was created that was responsible for all aspects of the project. Each team operated independently and followed a project through its stages to completion. In late 1996, three service teams worked with Tonar's three large projects, one located in each division.

Tonar's executives recognized the need for managerial training. Dr. Andronov remarked:

> The main drawback of many present managers is their narrow scope of knowledge, while Tonar needs people with a diverse understanding of commercial and financial aspects of business, as well as an understanding of the profit motive. We cannot find such people, so we'll have to train them, possibly sending some of them abroad.

Training for a number of other managers was to be conducted by manufacturers whose equipment was or would be installed in the polypropylene and solid waste conversion plants. Managers who would run the food distribution system and its components were to be sent to Holland for training in specialized logistics, but plans to do so were being deferred until more progress was made on the project.

Plans also called for the members of service teams to move from Tonar into the various shareholding companies that were to be established once the projects were completed. This tactic provided team members with the opportunity to become managers of ongoing enterprises which Tonar executives believed was motivation for them to perform well during the project. With the employment level remaining at approximately 2,000 people, headquarters included only 20 managers and staff, and 5 to 10 managers provided the leadership of each division. Most other employees were involved in the construction or operation of Tonar's major projects, while some were involved in the company's incubator activities.

True to Strategy Despite Difficulties

The year 1996 saw a decrease in the diversity of Tonar's activities, and a resulting focus on a few large projects, one in each of the company's three divisions. Continuing difficulties with some partners, as well as problems in raising capital for large-scale capital-intensive projects, slowed the pace of company progress. The difficult economic and political environment of the country took its toll on Tonar, foreign investment was very slow to materialize, and investment from domestic sources was scarce. Tonar's bank, The Russian Food Commodity Bank, through which Tonar controlled some companies, was experiencing severe difficulties, and executives were thinking of selling some assets to raise additional funds for the bank.

Tonar's strength continued to be its clear mission and strategy to engage in projects providing needed goods and services of real value to the Russian people. This approach resulted in its continuing close association with the Moscow city and regional governments, which provided much of the funding required to undertake large-scale projects. Although problems were mounting for the company, Dr. Andronov concluded: "We have told you the whole story. Tonar is our child and we want it to grow up and be successful."

NEW LEADERSHIP IN 1999

The mounting difficulties of the post-crisis period took their toll not only on the company, but also on its two founders. In early 1999, the deaths of both Dr. Andronov and Dr. Ananichev were reported. They had built an important socially-conscious business organization, but did not have the opportunity to see their "child grow up and be successful." Dr. Andronov's son took over leadership of Tonar, and continued to follow the strategic directions set by the founders. Although difficulties in financing continued to reduce the scope of the company's projects, Tonar maintained a website describing its projects and expressing interest in finding partners. The country's improving economic situation in the first half of 1999 provided additional hope to the new managers that the founders' objectives might be ultimately achieved.

7. Ekip

ORIGINS AS A SCIENTIFIC AND INDUSTRIAL COOPERATIVE

As Russia moved toward a market economy in the early 1990s, many scientists became involved in attempting to commercialize the abundant technology that had been developed during the Soviet era. Many did so within the framework of state-owned enterprises, while others took advantage of the new opportunities of the times. One of these scientists was Dr. Anatoly Savitsky who started the firm, Ekip Scientific and Industrial Commercial Company, as a cooperative in the late 1980s. The company's name, Ekip, was an abbreviation for ecology and progress. The diversified entrepreneurship's first financing was a 10-million ruble loan from Promstroitelnyi Bank to finance a number of research centers. The bank required no collateral from Dr. Savitsky, and the loan was repaid within two years.

With the coming of privatization, in the early 1990s, Dr. Savitsky became the major shareholder when Ekip evolved into a closed stock company with an investment of 50 million rubles. As a scientist turned entrepreneur, Dr. Savitsky's mission was to commercialize technologies that would be more effective and more environmentally friendly than traditional ones. Moreover, he was fond of stating: "Business contacts are a way to peace." The company's motto, "Don't be held captive by unfulfilled hopes," reflected its progressive mission. In summing up his personal philosophy, Dr. Savitsky said: "I am not today's Russian, I am tomorrow's."

As his projects increased in number, Dr. Savitsky entered into partnerships with other firms and individuals to secure financial and other resources. For instance, he joined with other scientists and production facilities as partners in an aircraft project. Later, he and some colleagues formed other firms such as Ecotechmash, a closed joint stock company which specialized in the production of equipment for reclaiming and recycling oil from drilling and production sites. As the company diversified, Dr. Savitsky created additional firms in partnership with other individuals and institutions to gain the resources needed for growth.

Anatoly Savitsky was a graduate of the Moscow Energy Institute, and had worked for many years as a research scientist specializing in new energy sources. In his mid-forties when he founded Ekip, Dr. Savitsky hoped his personal values and concerns for the environment would be reflected in the broader Russian business context. He valued ecology and the environment and saw them as key ethical issues as Russia evolved to a market economy. He believed that many New Russians placed little value on these and other ethical issues in their decision making. Yet, he was dedicated to such values for himself, and hoped to influence others to adopt a similar view.

Thus, besides being a dedicated scientist, Dr. Savitsky believed that he could be influential in business by following an ethically-oriented and ecologically responsible path in his own firm. In the introduction to his ecological encyclopedia, he discussed what he believed to be the moral factors that should guide the activities and decisions of business people. He also demonstrated his values by participating as a speaker at a major international conference on business ethics in Moscow in 1993 which was sponsored by the Academy of the National Economy.

EKIP AND ITS PROJECTS IN 1993

Holding Company Structure

Dr. Savitsky believed that privatization was good for him and his colleagues, since they could become owners of enterprises rather than government-employed scientists. He added, though, that it was often difficult to divide shares among stockholders and managers, and that conflicts sometimes could result. He described Ekip as a holding company with a number of operating companies in which Ekip owned varying percentages, and in which he himself had varying amounts of managerial involvement.

Ekip's headquarters consisted of 20 people including several of Dr. Savitsky's family members. His sister was the chief financial officer. His brother, who had been a Foreign Service diplomat and spoke fluent French, had valuable skills in international marketing and raising capital from foreign investors whom Ekip was approaching to help finance future large-scale operations. Dr. Savitsky's son was employed in one of Ekip's operating companies, and installed insulation in buildings. Other key headquarters people included the commercial director and the chief accountant.

Overview of Projects

The company's long-term strategy was to develop ecologically friendly technologies and products based on energy conservation and nonpolluting materials and techniques. All of these products required large capital investments which the firm could not sustain without major funding from external sources. Ekip's management had thus undertaken shorter-term projects to generate sufficient cash flow to continue developing long-term projects and to pay current expenses.

In 1993, most products of the various operating firms were in the developmental stage, although some had progressed through prototype testing and others were in the early operating stages. Long-term product plans were primarily in the areas of aviation and water transportation, oil reclamation equipment and processes, and power generators. Shorter-term cash-generating projects were also ecologically-oriented, such as production of an environmentally friendly insulation material for the construction industry.

Longer-Term Project: Flying Saucer

The project which Dr. Savitsky believed held the most promise for the long-term success of the company was an advanced aircraft designed in the shape of a flying saucer. He had selected the flying saucer as the company's first project because of the very poor transportation infrastructure and largely obsolete aircraft operating in Russia. He estimated the project would take about 10 years to achieve profitable operations. The aircraft, called The Ekip, was initially funded by the Russian defense budget. Development was carried out by the private stock company, Ekip Aircraft Concern, of which Dr. Savitsky was vice-chairman. His own company, Ekip Corporation, was a 25-percent shareholder, as was the highly regarded Saratov Aviation Plant. Its general director, Dr. Aleksandr Yermishin, was the chairman of Ekip Aircraft Concern. The firm's chief designer and one of Russia's best-known aircraft and space scientists, Dr. Lev Shukin, owned 50 percent of Ekip Aircraft Concern, having been involved with the design of this type of aircraft since 1978. In December 1993, *Inter Press Services* reported that Dr. Savitsky described the aircraft as having a diameter of 25 meters with an estimated cost to build of over $70 million. The craft was also reported to be very fuel efficient and quiet, and was virtually undetectable by radar because it flew below radar screens.

A larger version, the Ekip L-3, was slightly smaller than a Boeing 767 and could carry 400 people or 40 tons of cargo at a speed of up to 400 miles per hour. According to the chief designer, Lev Shukin, the vehicle's take-off and landing could be performed on almost any surface using a hovercraft-type cushion of air. Thus, no major changes would be required at existing airports to accommodate the aircraft.

In a July 1993 report, The BBC of the UK quoted Dr. Yermishin as saying that, while many scientists were leaving Russian companies for better opportunities, Ekip "managed to retain them, promising to include in the plant's program the unique flying apparatus of the Ekip firm." He believed that the exciting nature of the project provided the necessary motivation to retain the best scientists.

Longer-Term Project: Electro-Gas Dynamic Generator

Ekip was developing a unique type of generator that was said to have substantial advantages over competing products, especially for the Russian market. The company had obtained one million ecus from the European Community to help finance the project. Some of the funds were used to register the patents which had been obtained from the inventor, along with exclusive rights to all the technical designs. In mid-1993, Dr. Savitsky and other family members were deeply involved in the project, which was staffed by 10 people in Moscow, including two marketing specialists. Another 20 were located in Saratov where Ekip was producing equipment prototypes. Financing was not a problem at this stage, according to Dr. Savitsky, since many people were interested in becoming partners in the project. At the time, he was deciding which companies would produce the products, and which ones would become partners.

The advantages of the generator stemmed from its design, which did not use a conventional rotor, and involved virtually no moving parts. It was thus highly efficient, subject to little deterioration, and required low maintenance. Another advantage of the generator was that it could be utilized in locations which had limited energy sources since it recaptured and recirculated its fuel gas, thereby greatly reducing the amount of energy required. A good deal of interest had been shown by energy suppliers from remote locations in Russia which had problems providing adequate energy service to customers. Dr. Savitsky claimed that most of the pollution usually associated with generators was eliminated, including an 80-percent reduction in carbon dioxide and nitrous oxide emissions.

A smaller version of the compressor based on the same principles was being tested for refrigerators at the company's Saratov plant. The advantages stemming from the lack of moving parts included durability, low maintenance, and noiseless operation.

Medium-Term Project: Clay Absorption Process

In the late 1980s, Dr. Savitsky obtained from a professor-inventor the rights to a clay absorption process which could potentially be used to manage ecologically dangerous situations as well as conserve water. The process had been patented in Russia, the US, and other countries. Until 1990, the Russian government allowed production of the material only for state use, while prohibiting its sale to others. Ekip entered a joint venture with a Greek trading company that had invested funds to build a small plant in Greece in 1994.

After signing the agreement, Dr. Savitsky learned that the Greek partner was not a production company, and was acting primarily as an investor rather than as a production partner. In response, he said: "We are protecting ourselves by keeping the technology secret, and only disclosing how to use the material and not how to produce it." The joint venture hoped to have other firms produce the material under license, but again, intended to keep the basic technology secret.

Dr. Savitsky explained the properties of the clay absorption process which produced a previously unknown clay-like material. Upon contact with water, the material expanded approximately 50 times in size, forming a gel that could be used as an opaque barrier. One primary use would be for storing hazardous waste in the ground, potentially helping to solve a major ecological problem in Russia and elsewhere. Other uses would be for in-ground water storage for agricultural purposes such as on the bottoms and walls of ponds and irrigation canals. The technology could also be used to prevent water loss in sandy areas by making sand virtually opaque upon being mixed with this material. Still another use was as a fire retardant, by becoming a smothering agent when applied to burning materials due to its rapid expansion properties.

A number of potential customers had shown high interest in the process, and demand already outstripped the production capacity of the single smaller plant in Uzbekistan, which produced less than 5,000 tons per year. The Greek plant scheduled to open in 1994 was expected to double the company's capacity for the material. To dramatize the lack of capacity, Dr. Savitsky referred to a hazardous situation at a Russian atomic power station. An adjacent pond used for cooling water from the reactor had radioactive bottom sediment estimated to be 400 million cubic meters. The government wanted to create a virtual grave for the sediment since there was no other way to solve the problem. Dr. Savitsky estimated that 480,000 tons of clay material was needed to supply this one job. However, he noted that many potential Russian customers did not have enough money to pay for the material.

Still, the need for more production capacity prompted Dr. Savitsky to pursue opportunities to license production to others. He described the process as very profitable, with the finished product selling for around $1,000 per ton, while production costs were approximately $120 per ton. The Greek joint venture partner was responsible for marketing and distribution of the material worldwide, as well as for selling licenses for the process. In addition to scarce financing, another problem was obtaining materials to produce the substance. The scarcity of supplies resulted from two specific political problems—the non-cooperation between the Russian and Uzbekistan governments due to disputes over oil, and the civil war in Armenia. Dr. Savitsky noted that Ekip had taken steps to solve the supply problems outside government channels by utilizing the company's connections.

Medium-Term Project: Wave Mover

One of the main projects financed by Dr. Savitsky's firm was an environmentally friendly wave mover for installation on the bows of medium-sized oceangoing craft such as commercial fishing boats. Dr. Savitsky's company had obtained exclusive rights for this technology, and profits were to be split 50-50 between Ekip and the inventor. A number of distinguished scientific research institutes had been involved in designing the device, including the Mechanical Engineering Department at Moscow State University, as well as various institutes in St. Petersburg and Kaliningrad, including the Krylov Institute. Production and testing were to be conducted at the Almaz Shipyard in St. Petersburg, a leading military facility undergoing conversion to commercial operations. Following successful development and testing, Dr. Savitsky planned to reinvest profits in Ekip, and to subcontract production of the device to other companies to conserve cash.

The project had received substantial government support because of its potential importance to transportation and the fishing industry. Ekip had received 4 million rubles, for instance, to produce working models of the apparatus. Dr. Savitsky explained that support for projects of this type was often difficult to obtain. Progress on the wave mover was made possible by strong support from the Ministries of Science and Technological Planning as well as approval from an advisor to President Yeltsin. Dr. Savitsky also noted that Ekip could help potential purchasers get government loans to buy the wave mover. The cost was approximately 20 percent of a boat, with a payback of about one year.

The wave mover acted on the principle of wave energy being transmitted to the vessel and providing a supplementary source of propulsion. The mechanism looked like underwater wings when attached to a ship's bow, and allowed a vessel, with its motor turned off, to proceed against the waves at a speed of 6 to 7 knots per hour. The company estimated that fishing boats utilizing the device could save up to 30 percent of the fuel that would normally be used. Additionally, the wave mover provided a stabilizing effect, which reduced the rolling motion caused by waves, and improved fishing catches by being less invasive. The wave mover project was in its final stage of development in late 1993. Research and development and prototype testing had been conducted by scientists in an artificial waterway laboratory at Moscow State University. A test was planned at the Almaz Shipyard in St. Petersburg before the end of 1993, and an open ocean trial was scheduled in the Baltic Sea in 1994.

Technology for using wave energy was not new. Theory development had begun as early as the 1930s, and the first device had been patented in Britain in 1985. During that year, the Norwegian firm, Veritec, had conducted a test in which it reported energy savings of 20 percent. Veritec was convinced that wave movers could save 42 percent of a ship's energy source when operated at speeds of around 15 knots. Also in 1985, a relatively small Japanese firm, Hitachi Zosen, with annual sales of $27 million, had successfully tested a wave mover on a 600-ton ship. The various technologies and their associated benefits were the theme of a conference at University College London in 1985. Yet, no technology or product had gained acceptance in commercial markets such as fishing vessels.

Short-Term Cash-Generating Project: Ecological Encyclopedia

Another way in which Dr. Savitsky and his colleagues demonstrated their support for ecological issues was by producing an eight-volume encyclopedia of ecology in Russia. The first printing was 5,000 copies and a second edition was planned. Among the authors were Dr. Savitsky and Russia's deputy minister of ecology. Ekip also advertised its environmental products and services in the encyclopedia.

Guarded Optimism

In late 1993, Dr. Savitsky concluded: "Ekip is moving forward, but not as fast as we would like." To finance the continuing cash-flow needs of the business, he leased out space in a Moscow apartment building that he owned, and raised additional capital from friends. He was also attempting to sell a seat he owned on the Moscow Stock Exchange, but was having difficulty finding a buyer. Dr. Savitsky also emphasized the poor investment climate in Russia for scientific projects: "People with money don't want to invest in science due to the risk and the long payback period."

PROJECTS AND PROGRESS IN 1994

Longer-Term Project: Flying Saucer

Dr. Savitsky noted that the project to build Ekip Aircraft Concern's flying saucer, The Ekip, was continuing, and that by late 1994 the company had received loans from the Russian government totaling one billion rubles. He described The Ekip as a huge project that would need billions of additional rubles in investment to complete:

> Foreign competitors such as Boeing and Airbus are tracking our moves, and if we seem to succeed, then maybe they'll be willing to invest. We are staying with the project, but money will dictate our progress.

He added that he had not invested additional funds because he did not have a controlling interest, but his firm, Ekip, retained 25 percent ownership.

The project had received a great deal of international attention, including substantial coverage in the Western press. An April 1994 article in the *Toronto Star* noted that a small remote-controlled prototype had been successfully tested at the Saratov complex, and that a larger version was to be tested in the summer. A May 1994 *London Times* article described the craft's versatility, as well as its low operating expenses and construction costs. For instance, it was reported that a passenger version could be developed for 2 billion pounds in Russia, as opposed to 10 billion in the West. Another advantage was that the aircraft required a take-off distance of only 500 yards, much less than that of conventional aircraft. The article also reported on another unconventional Russian aircraft:

> The Russians have another unusual aircraft dubbed 'The Caspian Sea Monster.' It looks like a flying boat but can skim over the sea under radar or fly high in the sky like a conventional airliner, and 28 of them are presently operating in Russia.

The point was that, although The Ekip was an unconventional aircraft, other unusual aircraft had been developed in Russia that had proven to be successes.

The *Times* article also stated that the company was developing an international consortium to carry the project forward into the commercial production phase scheduled to begin in 1997. The article noted, however, that the program still faced many obstacles:

> The future of the Russian flying saucers and other technologies hidden during the Cold War is uncertain. The Russian government's financial commitment is in doubt. Foreign companies may be able to provide backing, but they face several obstacles. They have to be sure that the designs will be commercially viable and there is an image problem to overcome. Westerners see Russian-built aircraft as unsafe and unreliable. Furthermore, Russian engineers may be unwilling to share their technology with outsiders.

A June 1994 *London Times* article reported that "more than 80 American companies have expressed an interest, and Yermishin [chairman of Ekip Aircraft Concern] spent last week negotiating with Lockheed Missiles and Space Corporation in California." In mid-1994, the company was continuing to promote its program, and had exhibited its aircraft at a major commercial exhibition in London. An August 1994 article in *Komsomolskaya Pravda* highlighted the company's increasingly difficult financial situation. The firm's deputy executive director was quoted as saying that the project was running out of funds, and that $10 million was needed annually for the next several years to continue trials and begin production. He added that the engineers had not been paid in several months, and had been supporting themselves by working on construction projects for cottages.

Ekip Aircraft Concern was continuing development of the larger saucer, the L-3, and had carried out ground take-off tests of a large radio-controlled model during the summer of 1994. Water take-off tests were also conducted during the fall. Two larger models were being built to ground test and air test the aircraft's systems and flying ability. Because of the project's complexity, more than 20 organizations were involved in the research, development, and testing activities. All were Russian enterprises in the process of converting from defense to commercial operations. Project participants included the Saratov Aircraft Plant, the Scientific Manufacturing Associations Energy and Saturn, the Kuibishev Motor Plant, and Geodesia Scientific Research Institute.

Longer-Term Project: Small Passenger Airplane

Dr. Savitsky described a second project of Ekip Aircraft Concern, a 20-seat airplane with a more conventional design. The craft was called Ibis, after a bird that lives near the water, because the plane was capable of landing on water as well as land. The project was less ambitious than the flying saucer project, with much smaller capital needs. At this point, the company was limiting its activity to design work, and planned only ground testing in the foreseeable future in order to conserve funds. If sufficient investment capital could be found, the aircraft would be produced in a former military plant.

A New Longer-Term Project: Oil Reclamation Equipment

A new venture that began in early 1994 was a program to develop equipment to carry out the Russian government's project for the environmental security of Russia. This business involved developing specialized equipment to reclaim oil from sludge which forms during oil drilling activities and oil and petrochemical processing. Oil sludges also form during tank car washing and treatment of municipal sewerage systems, and often become sludge ponds near enterprises. Company records noted that more than 1.5 million tons of oil sludge had accumulated in the country by 1994, and the figure was increasing rapidly. The devastating effects of such accumulations, and the related gases which sometimes flared into flash fires, were recognized as a very serious problem in many regions.

The venture was actually a restart-up of activity begun in the early 1990s under the name of Rotech. The operation had received special credits from the government, but Rotech's president at the time misused those funds, according to Dr. Savitsky. He described the president as "an unqualified and unethical person who over-promised and failed to deliver." As a result, Rotech was dissolved, and the new firm, Ecotechmash, was created in early 1994. Dr.

Savitsky appointed himself as the audit committee of Ecotechmash in order to stay close to the financial situation.

The twofold objective of the new company was to develop equipment that could reclaim usable oil from sludge locations, thereby cleaning up the environment, as well as to reclaim natural resources for domestic use and export. In the latter case, the company had obtained a rare and valuable license to export reclaimed oil. Management also intended to develop oil products to be produced by the company or its partners.

The techniques and equipment created by Ecotechmash's scientists had been patented in Russia. Company literature noted that more than 100 employees were among the leading specialists in the field of oil sludge processing in the CIS, and they had been the leading specialists of the former state enterprises in the fields of processing, utilization, and decontamination of waste oil. The company described itself in promotional material as "the only firm in the countries of the Former Soviet Union which is able to ensure the complex solutions to the problem of gathering, processing, and utilizing oil sludge and contaminated soil." In 1993, the company had manufactured two sets of specialized equipment for gathering and processing oil sludge, at a reported cost of $1.16 million each. The equipment was installed at oil processing and extracting sites of the Russian petrochemical company, Ufaneftekhim, and the oil products company, Permnefteproduct. The profits from these operations were being utilized to build additional equipment for these and other customers.

The need for such equipment in Russia was undeniable, but market demand was highly uncertain because of the inability of Russian companies to pay for environmental clean-up projects. The devastation caused by decades of unrestrained industrial pollution made the entire country a potentially large market for equipment from Ecotechmash and other companies. Around 1994, some projects to modernize privatized enterprises or construct new manufacturing operations contained provisions for clean-up of polluted sites. In some cases, financing by international agencies such as The World Bank required the reclamation of polluted sites as a condition for loans and grants. Although implementation of projects would have required new clean-up equipment, funding still remained a problem in most cases, as did the unfamiliarity of many Russian managers with the need for pollution clean-up.

Competition from major European and American global companies was formidable. According to Dr. Savitsky, these included Alfa-Laval of Sweden, Kloecher Humboldt Deutz AG of Germany, and Baker Oil Tools, a division of Baker Hughes Inc. of the US. These firms were well-established in Russia, having sold a wide range of equipment there for many years. Their worldwide reputations gave them a substantial competitive advantage over Ecotechmash. Additionally, Baker Oil Tools established a joint venture in 1994 with

Sidanco, a Siberian oil company, to clean up Western Siberian oil sites utilizing Baker Oil Tools' equipment.

According to Dr. Savitsky, Ecotechmash's equipment was much less expensive than competitors', which he reported to be priced between $3 and $5.5 million. He believed that his company's equipment was superior in its simplicity of operation and reliability, allowing it to be operated by relatively unskilled and low-paid workers. He explained that foreign equipment had been known to fail when operated by such workers. Still, Ecotechmash was negotiating with Alfa-Laval of Sweden, Bogart of the US, and a German company to act as a distributor for these companies' products and offer a fuller line to Russian customers.

The company's detailed prospectus for fundraising contained a feasibility study developed at the Saratov oil-processing plant. In 1994, the company was attempting to raise $82 million to carry out major projects of cleaning, processing, and reclaiming oil sludge at several oil drilling and refining sites. The funds would be used to finance equipment and to pay for related expenses in the site clean-up. Additionally, management was seeking funding from the European Community organization, TACIS, which supported ecological projects in the Former Soviet Union.

Over a four-year period, Ecotechmash expected to reclaim 1.8 million tons of oil. Utilizing its export license, the company expected to sell the oil on the world market at a total price of $164 million, realizing an annual profit of over $10 million. Management hoped to continue with similar profitable projects involving the clean-up of areas polluted by oil sludge.

Other equipment and technologies were also aimed at remedying the environmental damage caused by the petroleum industry. Equipment was being developed for liquidating oil products and accidental spills, cleaning oil and oil-product storage tanks, treating ballast water, cleaning and reclaiming oil drilling mud, cleaning and reclaiming used oils and synthetic cooling liquids, and processing and reclaiming waste oil and associated gases produced during extracting and processing. Manufacture, commercialization, and utilization of this equipment were extremely costly, and the company was thus unable to go beyond the development stage simultaneously with their ongoing project.

Medium-Term Project: Wave Mover

In fall 1994, the wave mover apparatus was installed on a fishing trawler at the Almaz shipyard in St. Petersburg for sea trials. Dr. Savitsky felt fortunate for the attention given by the shipyard's chief engineer, since this was a very small project for the shipyard. A senior government official also sent a letter to the shipyard clearing the way for the test. There had been some problems because the yard usually worked on large military vessels, and the test vessel was considerably smaller. Preparations for the trials were reported in an October 1994 issue of *Izvestiia*. Dr. Savitsky stated that the project would require at least $20 million in investment to begin production, and expected to obtain those funds in the near future. To bring the project into full operation in a number of plants, he believed that a total of $100 million would be required.

Shorter-Term Cash-Generating Project: Insulation Material

Production of insulation material started in 1993 in cooperation with another firm, and was undertaken primarily for short-term profit to help finance Ekip's other businesses. Activities approached profitability by the end of that year, and became quite profitable during 1994. The project was different from most of Ekip's businesses because the company did not hold the patent or have exclusive rights to produce and sell the product. Dr. Savitsky's partners held the patents, which they had licensed to Ekip in exchange for 10 percent of profits. Other investors would receive approximately 40 percent, while Dr. Savitsky and other partners would receive 50 percent.

The project was compatible with Ekip's business philosophy because it was a more environmentally safe method of insulating buildings than the polyurethane material commonly used in Russia. Dr. Savitsky explained that polyurethane was highly toxic and flammable while their own material was not. He added that good insulation conserves natural resources since it reduces the amount of energy needed for heating and cooling. Ekip's material was said to be more economical to produce, and a good market existed for it to insulate dachas in the countryside as well as new homes in the Moscow suburbs. Other applications included storage buildings for agricultural products and industrial applications such as electric power stations.

A related activity was production of a concrete foam for construction projects, which was substantially cheaper than competitive polyurethane materials. A plant was being built with an expected opening by mid-1994. Potential customers ranged from individuals to large construction organizations, and some construction firms and private individuals had invested in the project. This capital, as well as borrowed funds, were being invested in the plant, and the company was in the process of buying equipment and training personnel.

Short-Term Cash-Generating Project: Ecological Encyclopedia

The highlight of the encyclopedia project in 1994 was discussions with the American company, Continental Resources Corporation, concerning English translation rights. Any income generated was to be invested in Ekip's long-term projects.

Financial Squeeze

It became apparent during 1994 that many projects were developing slowly due to lack of sufficient funding. In spite of attempts to generate cash flow through a number of fundraising and business endeavors, the many projects requiring large amounts of capital could not be sustained without major investments. Dr. Savitsky stated, for instance, that although there was considerable interest in England and the US in the flying saucer project, no money had been forthcoming. He added: "Such scientific projects are our business and we continue to depend upon government funding to sustain development efforts."

To supplement his income and to learn more about management, Dr. Savitsky had taken a position as a vice-president of the Russian branch of the British trading company, Roditi. The firm was one of Russia's largest entrepreneurial companies, and was a wholesale distributor of consumer products and foodstuffs. It had a large warehouse as well as a number of retail stores. The Russian operation was being operated as a separate open stock company with some of its own shares sold publicly. Dr. Savitsky saw this organization as one in which he could learn more about managing in the market economy, while still remaining involved in Ekip and its operating companies.

REFOCUSING IN 1995

By mid-1995, Ekip was having difficulty making progress on its portfolio of projects. Dr. Savitsky said: "Because of the lack of financing, work is going slowly on most projects." The situation required him to make decisions about how he spent his time and which activities to focus on. He concluded that his time would be better spent working closely on Ekip's projects, and decided to leave Roditi. He felt, however, that the experience had some positive aspects:

> I think that in the near future I will concentrate my efforts on scientific-production activities, and not be involved any longer with Roditi. I joined Roditi in the hope of gaining additional capital to invest in Ekip. But now consumers don't have much money for consumer goods, and trading companies like Roditi aren't making many profits. Nevertheless, I learned some good lessons about life while I was at Roditi.

Longer-Term Flying Saucer Project on Hold

Although financial constraints prevented making much progress on the development of the flying saucer aircraft, it still received substantial attention in the foreign press as well as in Russia. For instance, a quote from the chief designer of the Ekip aircraft, Dr. Lev Shukin, appeared in the spring 1995 issue of *Samolet/Aviation* magazine. He described many features and advantages of the craft, and discussed the many obstacles encountered in moving the new aircraft's design to a true project stage. Dr. Shukin also acknowledged Dr. Savitsky's stature in the technical community: "Then there appeared a man who backed up a project of an aircraft of this type, A.I. Savitsky, a great enthusiast and expert who offered his assistance to a group of scientists and designers in developing a flying wing." His admiration for Dr. Savitsky's contributions to the project was evident from this tribute. Dr. Shukin also expressed regret that lack of financing had prevented much progress in the project.

Long-Term Clay Absorption Project is Dropped

Because of the continuing difficulties in obtaining raw materials for production, as well as the company's cash constraints, the clay absorption project was dropped from Ekip's portfolio.

Wave Mover Becomes a Longer-Term Project

One of the changes in project priorities caused by the lack of financing was redesignating the wave mover to a longer-term project. Yet, like the aircraft, this apparatus continued to receive substantial publicity after a successful open-sea test in the Baltic Sea in November 1994. Dr. Savitsky and two designers of the wave mover claimed in an April 1995 issue of *Sudostroenie-Shipbuilding* that this was the world's first successful test conducted on a working fishing trawler. In mid-1995, Dr. Savitsky stated: "In the next one or two months, I plan to modernize the current wave mover for trawlers and also to conduct new trials in the Baltic Sea." Thus, in spite of financial constraints, the project was proceeding, but at a slower pace.

Progress Continues on the Electro-Gas Dynamic Generator Project

Regarding energy-related technologies, Dr. Savitsky stated:

> A lot of my technologies are not being used right now, but I know that energy issues will always exist. I also know that next month the price of energy will double, and this will be a shot in the arm for my sector. People will need to find new technologies, and some of these will include my energy-saving technologies, which will soon be used in the gas, energy, and oil industries. In the past year, considerable positive developments have occurred related to the electro-gas dynamic generator technology. We became part of a program of the Committee for Science and Technology on the use of this technology in automobiles. This program involves working with the gas industry which is interested in improving the environment with gas-powered vehicles.

The company was successful in adapting this technology to gasoline tank pumps, which needed to be hermetic like vacuums to ensure durability. Dr. Savitsky added:

> Since our pumps don't have moving parts, they are very suitable for this use, and people in the gas industry have shown a lot of interest in this. Now we have a good contract with the gas people, and that money will be used for research in our electro-gas dynamic technology. I think that our success in this field will be rather remarkable. Now, we are looking at different applications like pumping oil, and have had lots of interest from people in the oil industry.

Insulation Material Business a Shorter-Term Cash-Generator

During 1995, progress continued in production of the company's environmentally-friendly insulation material. A very positive development for the company occurred in January 1995 when the Russian government banned the use of polyurethane insulation. By doing so, the material that had been the major competitor for Ekip's product was eliminated from the market.

Selecting Opportunities and Setting New Priorities

In summing up his views on conducting business in Russia in 1995, he emphasized the need to be extremely flexible given the scarcity of financial resources. When opportunities arose, often through contacts within his extensive network, Dr. Savitsky was ready to react. Regarding his involvement in so many projects, Dr. Savitsky explained:

> You need to know how to do a lot of different things to succeed in Russia. The only collateral we have is our technology and our word, so we need to rely on our personal contacts to accomplish things.

FROM QUICK PAYBACK PROJECTS TO LONG-TERM ONES IN 1996

Mission, Strategy, and Business Environment

In a press release in March 1996, Dr. Savitsky summarized Ekip's mission as well as the business environment of early 1996. The statement also revealed how Ekip's strategy was reflected in the priorities assigned to projects, which in turn were related to the company's financial strategy. The statement began with the company's mission:

> The employees of Ekip and myself as general director believe that the future is not in getting rich from trading and other such commercial activities. Rather, it

lies in discovering and bringing to market the potential of the Russian scientific intelligentsia. The directions of the firm are to develop new types of transportation vehicles as well as energy-saving and environmentally-safe equipment, and new environmentally-friendly materials for the energy, construction, and transportation sectors.

He went on to describe the business environment as being "wild capitalism." He referred to the huge profits being made in banking and real estate, as well as in the petroleum and gas industries. Moreover, he explained that in the background of these profitable activities, his firm and others were encountering extraordinary difficulties in financing and running their businesses. Among their problems were the government's oppressive tax policies and low consumer purchasing power. He added: "And the crisis in the country's financial system affects our work since state agencies can give us only small amounts of funding for our projects." Dr. Savitsky concluded that, in spite of these difficulties, "the opportunities for developing private initiatives fill us with optimism and great hopes for the future."

The company's strategy had evolved in recognition of both the external conditions and the company's resources. Dr. Savitsky explained: "We are trying to combine our scientific and production activities with others that are purely commercial." The press release went on to describe his view that the possibilities for the company were due both to the country's new economic conditions and the long experience that he and his colleagues had gained working on their technological innovations.

He stated: "Our basic strategy can be expressed by the phrase: From quick payback projects to long-term ones." He identified three categories of projects: those producing immediate cash flows, those with a 1- to 3-year payback, and those with a long-term payback period of 5 to 15 years. Two projects were included in the immediate cash-flow category, the ecological encyclopedia and the company's participation in various opportunistic trading projects. The medium-term projects included the company's insulation material business, the electro-gas dynamic technology equipment, and the oil reclamation equipment. The wave mover and aircraft innovations were designated as long-term projects.

Dr. Savitsky elaborated on his strategy for Ekip:

> We are not going into any completely new activities but are concentrating on a few projects that we really believe will bring us a payback in a relatively short time. Some projects I'm interested in are moving along fine. In some directions, I expect to see more success than in such projects as the flying saucer or the wave mover. The most promising project is related to introducing the technology of electro-gas dynamics in various industries such as gas, automobile, and power generation. Another promising direction is related to our equipment used in ecological procedures to separate oil from water in the soil.

Small Investments in the Flying Saucer Project

Although the long-term projects were generally receiving little investment during this period, some advances occurred in the flying saucer project. An October 1996 article in the popular magazine, *Ogonek*, noted that a radio-controlled flight of a test model had been held in Nizhnii Novgorod, and broadcast in the UK by BBC television. The article also reported that the State Forestry Service had expressed interest in ordering 300 small saucers, which would be designed specially for firefighting. Finally, the article quoted the chief designer as expressing readiness to begin production of flying saucer aircraft as soon as financing became available.

Electro-Gas Dynamic Generator Becomes Ekip's Major Project

In 1996, Ekip's major project had become its electro-gas dynamic generator technology and equipment. To help finance its development, Dr. Savitsky had been successful in obtaining nearly $200,000 from TACIS, the European Community organization dedicated to environmental projects in Eastern Europe. The project was called Ekip Mostransgaz, and funds were used to buy equipment and hire experts for about a year and a half to develop the technology. Dr. Savitsky stated: "I was able to hire quite a few highly capable scientists because their salary level was not very high." Ekip did not employ these experts directly and their salaries were paid by TACIS.

Dr. Savitsky described the Ekip Mostransgaz project:

> When natural gas is extracted and transported for heating and other purposes, there are problems with pressures and compressors. A lot of exhaust gases are given off and a lot of heat is wasted. This is a valuable resource, but when it is wasted, it is also harmful to the environment.

Ekip was working with the firm, Kriakor, which was using two Ekip turbines to produce electrical energy. Dr. Savitsky reported that the company had saved over 80 million kilowatts of energy in one year at this single power station.

Ekip was developing a business plan with a partner organization, Gazinterservice, to expand the project further. This company was involved in introducing new and different technologies into Mostransgaz's system. The partner provided data on the stations. Ekip's scientists used the information to calculate how much energy the entire Mostransgaz system was losing at its various stations, how Ekip's technologies could help, and what kind of equipment was needed to solve their problems. Dr. Savitsky added: "As soon as I show Mostransgaz the way out of their crisis, I am sure I will be called upon by Gazprom and other industrial conglomerates, and our technologies will grow quickly."

Dr. Savitsky was aware that a business plan was necessary for Ekip Mostransgaz, but added: "This is poorly developed here, and it's one of the gaps I am trying to overcome with the help of the TACIS program." He knew that a plan would have to contain the economic and financial aspects of the project, including what financial losses were being incurred by Mostransgaz, and what the cost would be to remedy the situation. In developing the business plan, he had involved his son and daughter, both in their early twenties. His son was a computer programmer who developed computer programs containing the information to calculate the power station's potential. His daughter, an energy economist, planned to transform this information into financial and economic analyses. She was to receive specialized training in England to prepare for this assignment. Dr. Savitsky felt that if his daughter learned how to combine an economic and technical base in a business plan, this would be a unique opportunity for her, and she would become a rare specialist in Russia. He explained his views of having his children involved in the business:

> So I built a kind of chain in which my son is interested and gets a salary of approximately one million rubles a month ($200) for what he does. My daughter also will receive a salary, and this combines the pleasant with the useful for all of us. Therefore, I see a good future for my children in that economic analysis will go forward together with science and technology. If this is confirmed in a business plan, money will quickly be found for investment, and there will be a real payback. Therefore, I feel comfortable about the future for myself, my wife, and my children. We are making a definite investment in knowledge in the development of our children in the field of economic education.

Dr. Savitsky elaborated further on his strategy for the electro-gas dynamic generator project. Regarding production facilities for the equipment, Dr. Savitsky stated:

> In the near future I would like to strengthen my branch in Saratov which is becoming a fine production facility. Right now we are producing test models, but we will make our own equipment in the factory and introduce our latest technology. However, this must go on in parallel with the patent process, because to expose the patent too early would give our competitors an opportunity to produce a similar product. To protect against this, we are now working on a cheaper technology of our own invention which we will patent. We will keep this product inexpensive so that it's better for our competitors or anybody else to buy from us rather than to make it themselves. Right now, we are upgrading our technological facility and completing work on the patents which is expensive. We already have practical working models in use, and I believe next year will be more financially interesting.

Dr. Savitsky went on to explain that his business had bought 30 percent of the shares of the factory. The director of the Ekip Aircraft Concern, Dr.

Yermishin, had come to him with a request to help him obtain the controlling packet of shares owned by the Saratov factory, arguing that he could attract investments and move projects faster if he had controlling interest. Dr. Savitsky hesitated to do so, stating:

> Not having heard about a concrete investor or a concrete investment project, I decided not to hurry with permission allowing him personally to gain the controlling packet. I believe it's much better for the factory to be in control than a strong individual. The individual exists today, but tomorrow may not be there, and then what becomes of the rest of us? Therefore, there must be a ready investor who will invest real money before I would agree. So, I have to be tough sometimes, and not meet good people half way.

Oil Reclamation Processes and Equipment Show Promise

Dr. Savitsky believed that oil reclamation processes and equipment continued to be a promising direction for the company. The company now had equipment installed at two sites, one in Bashkiria and the other in Tatarstan. He explained that the company planned to develop some new technology that would do an even better job of separating oil from water and soil by literally sucking the oil from these substances. The technology was based on that used in the electro-gas dynamic generators, exemplifying a cost-effective approach to technology development. The project was moving fairly slowly because, as Dr. Savitsky explained: "Again, we need a lot of money to really get this going."

Insulation Material Continues Profitably

Dr. Savitsky noted that the building industry was continuing to show interest in the company's material and that it still produced a profit. The company continued to develop facilities to produce its own type of plastic foam or penoplast, which was a superior product. Unlike competitive materials, it was noncombustible. The company continued to work with partners in the building industry.

Some Progress With the Wave Mover

Dr. Savitsky noted: "Ekip continues to make progress with this project, attracting investment that I don't have to pay off with shares or patents or other such assets." Various organizations had become interested in the project because of its potential benefits. Ekip still had the support of the State Committee for Science and Technology as well as the departments of machine building and transport. Dr. Savitsky expressed his gratitude to all of these government organizations:

It is prestigious for us that they support our work. They're like partners that I can trust without fearing that they will seize my knowledge. The Committee for Science and Technology has already given our company about 260 million for this project.

Dr. Savitsky had recently met with a group from the Japanese Ministry of Science. They had selected his wave mover project from among many others to highlight at an exhibition in November 1996. He expected to travel to Japan to participate in the exhibition.

Sources of Financing Include Veksels

As noted earlier, Dr. Savitsky was very skilled at attracting funds from various state sources in Russia, from the European Community organization, TACIS, and from partners who participated in the company's projects. Additionally, he continued to operate several cash-producing operations such as the ecological encyclopedia and the insulation materials business. He was exploring the possibility of getting very low-interest loans which were sometimes available for developing environmentally-clean technologies, but as yet the company had not received any such credits.

Dr. Savitsky continued to look for new sources of funds. He explained a vehicle called "veksel" that, although likely only a temporary phenomenon, might produce some short-term cash. The term arose due to the cash shortage among companies that had grown to very serious proportions through the mid-1990s. Companies unable to generate cash payments for their products and services began exchanging IOUs among themselves. These IOUs became somewhat of a commodity that traded at a discount, and Dr. Savitsky believed that, given his network of associates, he could bring together parties for mutual benefit, and make a profit in the process. Some, who had valuable IOUs from energy companies, for instance, could be matched with others who owed IOUs to those energy companies. This area was important because energy companies were able to withhold electricity and fuel from debtors, and thus paying these bills was critical for companies. Although not related to his businesses, Dr. Savitsky continued to explore various avenues to secure cash to invest in his projects.

Looking Ahead

Dr. Savitsky emphasized his new focus and priorities as he looked ahead:

I believe that the time of hard financial problems is coming to an end. I now see a lot of people who are ready to invest money in my business. I am already starting to choose them not just as capable partners, but am considering those who are interesting to me and who want to be involved in things that interest me. I am not trying to discover new directions, but am concentrating my efforts on those activities that are crystallizing. For the most part, I am going to devote most of my efforts in the direction of new technologies in the energy sector.

CONTINUED FOCUS ON ENERGY TECHNOLOGIES IN 1997 AND 1998

Ekip's overall strategy did not change during 1997 and 1998. The company continued development work on projects that were likely to produce cash in the short and medium terms. Their fundamental business continued to be developing equipment and materials that would be environmentally safe, and that were improvements over presently utilized techniques.

The company's primary objective was to focus on development of energy-efficient technologies, which would be applied specifically in heat pump systems. Company technologists wrote a number of articles and made presentations and speeches at various organizations including government agencies. Ekip took the lead in founding a large scientific-production association devoted to promoting heat pump technology.

Ekip's management directed a major effort at the Moscow city government to convince decision makers there of the importance of environmentally safe energy-saving technology. Beyond this specific thrust, the company was involved in developing preliminary plans, test models, and marketing activities for various projects. Activities centered on the development of scientifically-based products that could be produced domestically.

The company also continued work on an experimental model of the electro-gas dynamic compressor, or EGD, for use in household refrigerators. During most of the period, the company received support from the Ministry of Science and Technology. Ekip was also successful in gaining the support of Iurii Luzhkov, the powerful mayor of Moscow, for continuing its developmental activities on the Ekip aircraft. The company also continued to work with TACIS, which sponsored a three-month internship in France for Ekip's deputy general director.

On the negative side, the company was not able to begin manufacturing new equipment due to lack of financial support from the government scientific agency, NIOKR. Probably due to similar problems in gaining financing, competitors did not seem to be particularly active in the market. Ekip was, however, able to avoid additional pressures on its financial situation in that management successfully defended the company against claims from tax authorities. On balance, Dr. Savitsky viewed the company's financial situation as being reasonable under the circumstances.

During this period, no changes occurred in the company's ownership, top management team, or organizational structure. Managers did, however, place more emphasis on merit and productivity in their motivation and reward systems.

The August 1998 Crisis

Dr. Savitsky noted in December 1998 that the country's financial crisis had substantially decreased funding for scientific research and development. He acknowledged that it was difficult to make progress in the type of work in which Ekip was primarily involved. He noted, however, that the support of the Moscow city government for Ekip's aircraft development work continued after the August crisis. Dr. Savitsky emphasized that, in spite of the difficulties, including the company's difficult financial situation, Ekip was managing to continue its activities, albeit at a reduced pace. In speaking of the country's economic difficulties, he anticipated a period of financial stabilization occurring by the second half of 1999. He emphasized that the company continued to pursue its goals and follow the strategy that had been established during the preceding years.

PART FOUR

Entrepreneurships

8.   Premier Bank

ONE OF THE EARLIEST COMMERCIAL BANKS

Premier Bank was founded in August 1988, shortly after the law on cooperatives was passed, and was registered as one of the first three commercial banks in the USSR. In fact, Premier was assigned the first registration number in the government's records. The founder, Dr. David Moseevich Kruk, was a highly regarded professor of finance and department chair at the prestigious Moscow Finance Institute. In his late sixties at the time he founded the bank, the energetic and innovative scholar believed that the law on cooperatives could actually provide conditions to launch a successful private business venture. As a result, Dr. Kruk and the rector of the Institute, while keeping their academic positions, established Premier Bank. Dr. Kruk's longer-term plan was to hand the management of the bank over to his son, Aleksandr, who had graduate business degrees from Moscow State University and Northeastern University in Boston.

Economic Environment up to 1993

Starting a private bank in a country where none had existed before was a challenging task. The early days were very difficult, Dr. Kruk acknowledged, because the government offered no help, taking a "sink or swim" attitude toward private enterprise. Dr. Kruk had included banking as one of the diversified businesses in the charter of his cooperative, thus giving him the legal basis for starting his bank. At the time he founded Premier, banks were required to have a minimum founding capital of 5,000 rubles, a relatively modest sum. With no help from the government, he obtained founding capital from several companies he had worked with in the past. Among the founding shareholders were four bankers including the president of the large Sotsbank. One cooperative contributed 400,000 rubles, and another 200,000, with total founding capital amounting to one million rubles. Dr. Kruk controlled 60 percent of the shares, including those he held in trust for silent partners, and as president, he made the final decisions in the company.

Dr. Kruk explained that new commercial banks like his feared giving credit to enterprises that had no cash to pay their debts. Much of the cash crunch in the early 1990s stemmed from the government's failure to pay its debts to enterprises, and as a result, they were unable to pay debts owed to one another. The problem was exacerbated by the "gigantomania" of the former Soviet economy in which each enterprise was linked logistically with hundreds of other organizations. For instance, Dr. Kruk noted that a manufacturer of vans in Lithuania was virtually shut down after the collapse of the USSR because it had continued to rely only on engines from Russia.

PROFITABLE IN 1993 DESPITE INFLATION AND REGULATION

Strategy for Profitability

Premier Bank's revenues came from four activities. One was from giving credit to domestic companies. The bank counted among its clients more than 500 private companies, as well as small state enterprises, and social organizations such as the Social Democratic Party, the Chess Federation of Russia, and several Christian missions. The bank had a policy of not giving credit to large state enterprises, Dr. Kruk explained, "because of their instability, and because we don't want to be blamed for closing state enterprises and laying off thousands of workers." A second source of income was investing in businesses owned by clients. Premier Bank held shares in some of its clients' businesses, a practice that is generally legal in Europe, but prohibited in US banking. A third way of generating revenues was by converting rubles into hard currency on the currency market, and taking profits on the rate fluctuations.

The bank's fourth way of making money was working with foreign clients. One proposal being considered was to buy several companies in Spain and Italy to create a small consortium of firms interested in exporting to Russia. Dr. Kruk explained: "If these firms have difficulties, we're prepared to run them for a few months. We'll try to make them viable and then keep them as an investment or sell them at a profit." His preferred way of working with foreign firms, as he had done with a half dozen companies, was to lend to importers only if they had secure contracts with Russian buyers. Loans were needed to pay customs duties and transportation charges, which could amount to 25 percent of the transaction as in the case of imported plywood. The goods themselves became collateral for the loan.

Dr. Kruk's plans and policies were based on a one-year time horizon. He was prepared to invest only in ventures that would pay off in one year because of the risk of hyperinflation. As a result of the systemic breakdown in the supplier-customer chain, banks were reluctant to make loans for fear of not being repaid. This left few alternatives in which banks could invest their funds, with the result, according to Dr. Kruk, that 80 percent of banks were in trouble by 1993. He himself, in 1991, had stopped making loans secured by finished production, and gave credit only in exchange for hard currency deposits. He acknowledged that it was paradoxical that borrowers needed to give money to get money, but noted that such a system could actually be beneficial for both borrowers and lenders. In 1993, the annual interest rate charged by banks ranged from 160 to 240 percent, or roughly 13 to 20 percent per month. At the same time, monthly inflation was 30 to 35 percent. Dr. Kruk gave loans, based on companies' sales, for three-month periods, resulting in four annual turnovers of the loan funds. This policy assured the bank of a return that substantially exceeded inflation.

The Government's Economic Policies in 1993

As an expert on finance, Dr. Kruk had strong and informed opinions about the government's economic and financial policies. He credited Gorbachev with having taken the first step from totalitarianism to a market economy, and believed that no country could change without inflation and unemployment. He believed that these economic conditions were "more an unpredictable psychological issue than an economic one, because the Russian people have had a constitutional right to work. You can't fire 25 million people at one time, so individuals can't understand why they themselves might lose their jobs." Many struggling enterprises tried to ease workers' unemployment by providing part-time work or a token wage to keep them technically employed. The depressed defense sector was hit particularly hard, he noted, and many workers were angry that their relatively secure positions and lifestyles had seriously eroded.

Dr. Kruk explained that inflation was due primarily to the government's policies toward the money supply. The money supply was supposed to equal the total price of goods. However, production output was declining, while the money supply was growing. Every month, the Central Bank added one trillion rubles to the money supply so the prices of goods rose, and inflation accelerated in a geometric progression.

While hard currency was substantially more stable than the ruble, Dr. Kruk noted that no objective indicators supported the ruble-hard currency exchange rates. The government announced the dollar conversion rate four days each week, and the deutsche mark rate on the fifth day. In mid-June 1993, Dr. Kruk was optimistic that the dollar-ruble exchange rate would improve in the ruble's favor.

He was not so sanguine, however, about the heavy hand the Central Bank had in regulating activities of Premier Bank and all other commercial banks:

"My main headache is the Central Bank. It interferes in every aspect of my bank." Commercial banks were prohibited from dealing directly among themselves, and were required by law to have an account with the Central Bank and to process all non-cash transactions through that institution. The Central Bank often took a long time to process transactions, and tied up the funds of individual banks, while keeping interest earned on their money.

The Central Bank monitored each bank's monthly performance using 20 indicators, and imposed fines amounting to 20 percent of assets if a bank failed to meet the targets. The fine had increased tenfold from the 1991 level of two percent of assets. Premier Bank rated very well on the indicators. However, a more serious problem was that the Central Bank kept 20 percent of each bank's assets on reserve to cover potential fines, thereby severely restricting the funds that banks had available to lend or invest. Premier Bank and other commercial banks could not keep much cash on hand since so much of it had to be deposited with the Central Bank. Compounding the problem for commercial banks, the Central Bank could and did freeze accounts virtually at will.

Premier Bank was one of many banks that suffered losses caused by the 300 million rubles in counterfeit currency that had circulated through the Central Bank in 1993. The Central Bank had deducted money from Premier's account, claiming that some transactions had been paid with counterfeit money. Although Dr. Kruk and other bankers eventually won a legal dispute over the Central Bank's unjustified action, he was never repaid by the Central Bank. Nevertheless, Dr. Kruk realized he was more fortunate than another commercial banker he knew who, besides not being repaid, had his bank's license revoked by the Central Bank and was forced to close. "The Central Bank has full rights, but little accountability toward its clients," Dr. Kruk concluded.

In another attempt to control the banking system, the Central Bank had proposed a law in 1993 to close banks having less than 50 million rubles in assets. Dr. Kruk pointed out that of the 1,750 commercial banks in the country, 70 percent fell below this asset minimum. If the government had passed such a law, the commercial banking sector would have been virtually destroyed, the country would have returned to a tightly controlled central banking system, and the developing market economy would have been dealt a serious blow. Summarizing his frustrations with the unpredictable environment, Dr. Kruk stated: "I run a reliable bank, but who can guarantee that I won't get new directives tomorrow?"

Other Problems with Legislation and Corruption

The law on private property was another obstacle for the banking industry, Dr. Kruk explained. He had wanted to expand the bank's operations into making loans to finance real estate and land transactions, but legislation on land ownership was too uncertain: "If we had a real law on private property, then we could deal in real estate and land. And furthermore, people need to learn to respect the law so that land can be taken from people who don't pay their debts."

Dealing with local authorities in Moscow was another frequent annoyance. For instance, city government officials had tried unsuccessfully for four years to force Dr. Kruk to move from his desirable downtown office location, since its proximity to the Kremlin made it an especially attractive site for government offices. Officials' tactics included forcing him to re-register the firm, and fining him for petty infractions such as not having a pail of sand available in case of fire. "Everything in this regard seems to work on who you know, not by the law," he lamented.

The banking industry itself was another source of concern for Dr. Kruk. Although he considered the top five banks and their branches to have capable people and to generally operate like normal banks, he was alarmed by the practices of the vast majority of banks. He feared that many were engaged in risky and sometimes corrupt practices that violated internationally accepted banking practices.

Profitable in a Chaotic Environment

Despite the problems in the country and the banking industry during the twelve months ending June 1993, Premier Bank earned a 650-percent return on investment before taxes, several times the rate of inflation. Regarding the country's situation. Dr. Kruk was of two minds: "We're in an abyss, and we need to have shock therapy like Poland. And the privatization process will take time." Yet, despite the government's many serious problems, Dr. Kruk was relatively hopeful about the country's leadership: "President Yeltsin has his faults, but he's our only hope for now."

GREATER CENTRAL BANK CONTROL AND INDUSTRY COMPETITION IN 1994

By the fall of 1994, Dr. Kruk was no longer working at the Institute of Finance, and was fully involved in Premier Bank. He believed that the complexities of the banking environment had increased due to macroeconomic instability and the government's focus on taxation and fiscal issues rather than industrial restructuring. He was especially concerned about the erratic and oppressive tax policies: "Taxes don't stimulate investment, which is what banking is all about."

Dr. Kruk's Assessment of the 1994 Economic Environment

In describing Russia's economic environment in the fall of 1994, Dr. Kruk cited several key indicators. According to government data, the country's production output had declined 26 percent in 1993-94, compared to an 18-percent decline in 1992-93. Unemployment was officially reported to be seven percent in 1994, up from one percent in 1993. Unofficially, unemployment in 1994 was estimated at 10 percent, with 4.5 million workers unemployed, and another four million only partly employed. Inflation was pervasive and prices of many Russian goods were moving toward world levels, but low quality made them uncompetitive in export markets. Inflation also caused production costs to rise steeply. Above all, Dr. Kruk believed "the most dangerous thing is the nonpayment crisis." He stated that of all credit issued, 75 percent was not repaid. Debts owed among suppliers totaled 31 trillion rubles, payments owed to the state budget were nine trillion, and four trillion rubles in unpaid salaries were owed to state workers.

Control of the Banking System Tightened Further by the Central Bank

Dr. Kruk believed that the government was tightening its control of the economy even more, and that its main target was the banking system. He explained that the Central Bank had 400 offices in Russia to monitor commercial banking activities, and to collect the 20 percent of assets that every bank had to keep on reserve with the Central Bank. He noted: "The Central Bank is at the center, and it has extensive rights. For instance, it takes away licenses and removes managers without any apparent reason, and disregards the terms stated in bank charters." He acknowledged, however, that many banks were poorly managed and needed to be reformed or closed.

To manage the money supply, the Central Bank sold at auction every two weeks some of the 20 percent of commercial bank reserves that it held. In fall 1994, the annual interest rate charged by the Central Bank to most commercial banks was 210 percent, but the rate was doubled to 420 percent for late payments. These rates applied even after seven consecutive months in which the Central Bank had reduced the stated interest rate in proportion to the declining inflation rate. An additional frustration for many bankers was that some banks received preferential treatment. Dr. Kruk noted that "some growing, prosperous banks receive government help in the form of subsidies and cheap credits. For instance, Mosbizbank obtained credit from the Central Bank at a 15- to 20-percent annual rate, rather than the typical 210 percent."

Some of the operations of the Central Bank in 1994, Dr. Kruk explained, included establishment of a money market in Russia, which was operating in an orderly fashion by the fall of that year. Transactions involved the relatively conservative short-term treasury bonds known as GKOs. These securities had expiration dates of three and six months, and were sold twice monthly by the Ministry of Finance. Additionally, the Ministry participated in the secondary market by selling currency papers and securities called *veksel* through the four branches of the Moscow Interbank Stock Exchange.

A third function of the Central Bank was controlling the ruble exchange rate. In 1993, it allocated $1.5 billion to support the ruble, but with little success. By 1994, most money had been diverted from currency exchange dealings and reallocated to domestic financial markets. The Central Bank and the Ministry of Finance, by that time, had begun to work together to try to manage both the securities market and the exchange rate. In the fall, responding to a lobbying effort by exporters who preferred a weaker ruble, the Central Bank set the dollar-ruble exchange rate equal to the inflation rate, which was more favorable to exporters than the previous policy. Monthly inflation dropped to five to seven percent in the summer of 1994 according to official statistics, but was expected to rise to at least 12 to 15 percent in the fall.

Four Major Business Activities in 1994

Premier Bank's charter capital increased 5.5 times by the fall of 1994, and profits were 700 percent of charter capital. By that time, Premier Bank served 800 private enterprises, half of which were active customers. Dr. Kruk considered only a relatively small number of these clients to have strong performance, specifically those involved in exporting raw materials such as oil, aluminum, steel, and other metals. Some importing firms were also doing well, but they had to be clever in reporting their taxes in order to retain any profits. "If firms tried to obey all the tax laws, they couldn't possibly survive," Dr. Kruk said. He added that corporate taxes claimed around 85 percent of profits, with the remaining 15 percent lost to bribery and corruption. He believed that most enterprises were hoping to survive until the government changed its policies and created a climate more favorable to profitable operations.

In its quest to be profitable, Premier Bank in 1994 was involved in four major activities: currency transactions, financing commercial operations, factoring activities, and real estate financing. Currency transactions were the bank's most profitable business and involved daily trading of dollars, rubles, and soft currencies of former Soviet republics such as Ukraine and Kazakstan. Trades were also made on the dollar-deutsche mark exchange rate, with the deutsche mark costing more in Moscow than in Frankfurt. The bank's objective was to take timely profits on the spreads between various currencies.

Financing commercial operations for clients was a second activity. For instance, the bank had financed the sale of plywood exported to Russia by a Miami entrepreneur, as well as the sale of lumber, diesel oil, and metals for a large Taiwanese firm. An example of the bank's third activity, factoring operations, involved a clothing manufacturer. Premier Bank paid the firm's expenses to display and sell clothing at an exhibition in Moscow in exchange for a percentage of the profits, using the firm's receivables as collateral. The fourth activity, real estate, was managed by Dr. Kruk's son, Aleksandr. He financed hard-currency mortgages for private apartments, which was becoming an increasingly profitable business.

Competition had increased in all areas of banking during 1994. "There's a fight for clients now, whereas last year banks had niches," Dr. Kruk explained. Currency transactions were still Premier Bank's most profitable business, but had become less profitable because of heavy competition. "There are three times more exchange kiosks in Moscow than bakeries," Dr. Kruk claimed half-seriously. He added that the Central Bank favored large banks, and had passed a law that was to take effect on January 1, 1995 requiring banks to have a minimum of five million ECUs of capital. Such requirements would surely limit the number of commercial banks since the total charter capital of Russian banks was six trillion rubles, while their total assets were 100 trillion rubles. Dr. Kruk believed that many banks were not adverse to upsizing because of the resulting economies of scale, but he predicted that some large banks would fail if they were to stop receiving government help. In contrast, he noted that "mid-size banks like Premier have experience in surviving without such help, and we plan to quadruple our charter capital next year to two billion rubles."

NONPAYMENT CRISIS AND BANKING SHAKE-OUT IN 1995

Dr. Kruk's Analysis of the 1995 Economic Environment

In the fall of 1995, Dr. Kruk said that the main problem in the economy continued to be nonpayment of debts by the government and enterprises. This situation helped trigger a banking crisis since many outstanding loans were not repaid, resulting in a lack of liquidity among banks. The nonpayment stalemate was in its third year and constituted a systemic problem in the economy, with more than 90 percent of enterprises saddled with unpaid credits. Some firms survived by bartering or paying cash directly to one another rather than using the banking system. Such practices were useful to avoid evidence of transactions that could be taxed. With only a few kopeks remaining for each ruble of income after taxes, firms found inventive ways to avoid paying taxes. Dr. Kruk recalled how the general director of a large state enterprise had wanted to deposit money in Premier Bank. Dr. Kruk refused because he suspected that the manager sought a reliable bank in which to hide funds from government tax authorities. Such questionable behavior on the part of some managers was yet another reason why Dr. Kruk continued his policy of not dealing with large state enterprises.

In an attempt to stabilize the country's currency, the government had created a ruble corridor such that the Central Bank would intervene if the ruble went outside the range of 4,400 and 4,900 to the dollar. Dr. Kruk said that "banks aren't concerned because the market keeps the ruble within this range." However, exporters had become worried when the ruble increased in value, making exports more expensive and reducing exporters' profits.

Another event affecting the banking industry was the government's announcement that after 1995 it would no longer issue government bonds, or *obligatsii*. This action was taken in response to the World Bank's policy of not issuing credits to Russia if such bonds were in circulation. Additional government bonds would increase the M2 money supply, thereby undermining the ruble's value and further destabilizing the economy. The World Bank also looked unfavorably on promissory notes or *veksel*, which had repayment dates and interest obligations, because these could be sold on the financial markets. The problem with these notes was that anybody could sell them, but by remaining in circulation, they perpetuated the circle of debt since the obligation remained outstanding.

More problems arose because the government's relatively optimistic inflation forecasts were not met during the year, and Dr. Kruk expected that the two-percent monthly level promised by year-end would likely be closer to 10 percent. He added that inflation was one of the reasons that economic reforms could not be carried out, and predicted: "Overall, the government's 1995 reforms will turn out just like those in 1994. Nothing is happening to improve the economy."

Dr. Kruk believed that a monthly inflation rate of around two percent would be required to stabilize the economy and attract Western investors. He noted that risk-tolerant firms were the ones most likely to invest in the current environment, and that even they were unwilling to invest in more than 50 percent of any project. He described how his bank was negotiating with two small American firms, one in oil and the other in building construction, but had not reached an agreement since the US firms wanted Russian banks to invest first. He claimed that banks needed to invest funds in the production sphere rather than services, but that the 50-percent decline in the country's production output since 1990 was a deterrent to such investment. He added that exports had fallen to 12 percent of the 1990 level, and that production was shifting to a colonial mode of exploiting natural resources and semi-processing goods, rather than manufacturing finished products.

Banking Crisis

In 1995, the growing number of negative economic and regulatory developments resulted in a banking crisis. The liquid assets of banks had been greatly reduced by the requirement that they keep 20 percent of their funds on reserve with the Central Bank, as well as 1.5 percent of their foreign currency. In one instance, Premier was required to put on reserve 70 percent of the funds it had received from a large bank. Furthermore, the Central Bank accelerated the payment schedule of reserve funds, from one payment at the end of each month, to more frequent payments. "These regulations hurt banks badly. The Central Bank continues to be the commercial banks' worst enemy," Dr. Kruk complained.

Further exacerbating the banking crisis, in August 1995 banks stopped making payments on debts they owed each other. Dr. Kruk predicted that the situation could not be resolved easily nor in isolation from other systemic problems in the economy. He believed that the best solution would be for the government to take action to stabilize the economic and financial situation.

Concentration of the banking industry was still a serious possibility. Of the country's 2,500 banks, one-third were located in Moscow due largely to the fact that 70 percent of the country's foreign currency was held there. According to Dr. Kruk, the government wanted to gain tighter control over commercial banking in general, and of the 50 largest banks in particular. He claimed that large banks helped the government by transferring state budget funds to enterprises, as well as non-budget funds, in ways that were advantageous to the government. In return, the government provided cheap credits to these banks.

Although some banks had fared well during the year, Dr. Kruk pointed out that three of the top 30 had gone bankrupt, while some other banks had their licenses withdrawn by the government. The bankruptcy of one leading bank in the spring of 1995 hurt nearly a dozen others, and was clear testimony to the fragility of the system due to the interconnectedness of the country's banks. During the year, the government's rating system showed a marked decline in the rankings of many banks.

Still Profitable in 1995

Premier Bank ranked among the top 100 banks, and while not large, was profitable. The bank continued to be involved in a variety of activities aimed at generating income. Currency transactions were still profitable since, if the dollar sold on the currency exchange for 25 rubles more than it did in transactions between banks, Premier Bank made a profit. The bank was also involved in financing short-term government bonds against which loans were typically made for one to two weeks, and seldom for more than two months because of volatile government policies. Credit was also issued to those who put up their homes as collateral. Dr. Kruk stated that he did not favor this line of business, but that his partners did.

The bank also continued to finance transactions among firms, often overseeing their activities from start to finish. For instance, Premier provided financing for three Russian oil companies, including the large Siberneftegaz, and helped them negotiate an oil-exporting contract with foreign firms. The foreign purchasers were required to pay 30 percent in advance to cover transportation, pipeline charges, customs duties, and VAT, with the remaining 70 percent due on delivery. The bank advanced 15 percent of these transaction costs to finance half of the initial 30-percent requirement.

OPERATIONS PASSED TO KRUK'S SON IN 1996

By the fall of 1996, Dr. Kruk had passed the management of Premier Bank to his 30-year-old son, Aleksandr. He was well versed in Russian and Western banking and financial practices, having earned graduate degrees in management from Moscow State University and in international finance from Northeastern University in Boston. He also had several years of experience at Merck Corporation, the pharmaceutical multinational, as well as several years at his father's bank. In his new role, Aleksandr described economic conditions and the banking industry during 1996, as well as Premier Bank's activities for that year.

Activities of Russian Banks

Many banks had prospered in 1995 and early 1996, with more than 200 banks meeting the requirement imposed by international agencies to have capital in excess of $5 million. In 1994, only about 30 banks were reported to have this level of capital. Aleksandr explained that "many banks made fortunes in 1995 and 1996 by dealing in government bonds or GKOs, and other instruments such as government treasury tax write-off certificates called KNOs." The government bonds were similar to U.S. treasury bills and were generally considered "normal by world standards," except for their extraordinarily high interest rates. Annual rates had been as high as 150 to 200 percent in early 1996, but by autumn had dropped to 50 percent.

Tax write-off certificates were notes purchased from the government, which gave holders the right to reduce their taxes by the amount of the certificate. Aleksandr explained that the total amount represented by the certificates was three to five times higher than that of government bonds. This action was seen by the International Monetary Fund as an inflationary measure because enterprises could pay their taxes using these certificates, rather than cash which would reduce the government's deficit. Banks made profits by charging enterprises and individuals as much as 30 percent to cash their treasury bills and notes. Those with a large capital base had the best opportunity to engage in such transactions and make huge profits in the process.

Deepening Crisis in the Banking Industry

The banking crisis of 1995 had resulted in many bank failures. Aleksandr recounted:

> There was a serious interbank crisis in Russia. After this, many banks went bankrupt. Others survived, but the situation was still bad. Some banks covered their losses through high yields on short-term government bonds with one-month expiration terms. The most lucrative market for Russian banks is municipal bonds, especially state bonds, but it is also the most shaky and volatile market.

Russian banks, according to Aleksandr, could be classified into two main groups, one being large banks, the other comprised of small and medium-sized banks. The large banks, roughly the top 30 to 50, had substantial volumes of loans outstanding, with Inkom Bank, for instance, reported to have over $1 billion. Such banks suffered tremendous losses since bad loans were estimated to be at least 30 percent of loans issued in Russia, in contrast to less than 10 percent in the US. Aleksandr explained: "So in Russia, it's not good to say you have $1 billion in loans. It means that you eat the money of your stakeholders." During the summer of 1996, three large banks went bankrupt: the tenth largest, the seventeenth, and the thirty-first. Small and medium-sized banks, in contrast, fared better, according to Aleksandr:

> The strength of the small and medium-sized banks was their scale. They could not afford to give big credits to enterprises. They had bad loans too, but not as significant an amount. Because of the high yield of government bonds, they were able to increase their capital base and earnings significantly in 1996.

Large banks were widely known to have strong political connections whereby influential government officials gave them preferential credit terms, and also directed business to them. In return, some banks supported various political parties, as Aleksandr explained:

> Big banks are making their profits on government money. They are not paying any interest, or just symbolic interest like 18 percent in rubles, while inflation in the last year has been 200 percent. So now there is a big battle among them to get government accounts, such as the Moscow city government and various state-owned enterprises, as clients. They are struggling for these clients and are using their political connections and all other means of attracting these accounts.

The banking industry was headed for more upheaval, Aleksandr predicted:

> I think a crisis is deepening because the banking industry cannot be healthier than the economy as a whole. It can be for a short period, but then the situation will be equalized. The large banks say that nothing is wrong, that industry is in good shape. But official statistics show that more than half the banks are in a loss position. Only about a third are doing well, while two-thirds need some restructuring, and one-half of those will cease to exist.

Many large banks had invested heavily in enterprises, Aleksandr explained, by buying shares in them. The leading bankers, called oligarchs, created industrial groups of investment funds, factories, oil refineries, and other enterprises. Examples included Ex-Im Bank, whose capital was estimated at one trillion rubles or $200 million. Ex-Im created the industrial group, Interros, which employed more than one million people. The bank had purchased the world's largest metal factory for 170 million rubles, and advanced the enterprise an additional 300 million rubles in credits. Other holdings included a large oil company and metallurgical factories purchased for approximately 500 million rubles, far less than the real value of these enterprises.

Serious problems, however, developed as a result of these banks investing heavily in industrial enterprises. Aleksandr explained:

> At first it was good for banks because they could buy enterprises cheaply. And since all the enterprise's money was handled through the bank, enterprises were not paid interest on their deposits because the bank was the owner. But, on the other hand, the banks had to give them credits so they could operate. Otherwise, if it's a large factory, the director goes to the government or the municipal authorities and complains that 'these Robber Barons are drinking our blood. We have nothing, yet they drive Mercedes.' But the management of such enterprises was usually not very good, and the enterprises often failed.

Aleksandr added that large banks still sought corporate clients rather than individuals. The plan was to buy enterprises and replace Soviet-era managers with new and more effective ones. In reality, however, this seldom occurred.

Another well-known banking situation was that of Mikro Odin, which got its start by accumulating a large amount of capital through buying and selling raw materials when the government freed prices in 1992. Mikro Odin became one of the top 100 Russian banks and began acquiring stakes in large industrial enterprises. It bought 50 factories, including the huge Zil Truck Plant in Moscow. After pouring $50 to $100 million of credits into the ailing truck factory, Mikro Odin accumulated $100 to $300 million in debt and went bankrupt. Ex-Im Bank stepped in as a strategic investor and bought the bank and its assets. Ex-Im Bank then sold Zil to the Moscow city government for $6 million, in what amounted to a renationalization of the bankrupt factory.

The renationalization process was also occurring within the banking industry itself. Some large banks asked the government to buy them back because they had accumulated excessively high levels of debt. The government did purchase a number of banks including Agrikombank, one of the largest, and it also bought a 10-percent stake in Menatep, whose 60 industrial enterprises employed over half a million people.

In these dire circumstances, a number of well-publicized scandals had rocked the banking industry. For instance, Ex-Im's president was also Russia's First Deputy Prime Minister, and a scandal had erupted over accusations that government officials had illegally used government money to help the bank. Another scandal involved the multibillion-dollar Stolichnyi Savings Bank, which had been founded with the help of the head of the country's banking system. This influential official was reputed to have obtained money from the Moscow city government's budget to help the bank.

Aleksandr unequivocally stated his views of the banking system: "Yes, the banking system is in crisis. But the government and the financial leaders, such as the finance and privatization ministers, are always saying that the situation is good, and that we should just wait one more month. Then it's one more year." Aleksandr offered a number of reasons for the crisis:

> It's very risky to give credits in this country. You have to know your clients very well. Banks do have a lot of bad debts. They offset them with profits from other instruments such as government bonds. But now the bond yields are down. Inflation is around 30 percent and yields on these bonds are down to around 50 percent. It's necessary and healthy for the country that banks earn more money to cover their losses. The fear is that if the government stops paying the banks against these bond issues, all the banks will be crushed. The financial system and enterprises will be crushed. But I don't expect such a disastrous crisis.

Implementation of sound government policies could stave off a crisis of such monumental proportions, Aleksandr believed. One possibility was to devalue the ruble by half, thereby reducing the country's internal debt by half. However, this measure could not be undertaken without a return to high inflation and the government printing more money. The consequences would be that enterprises would not have current assets to run their operations, but banks holding large debts would have their debts reduced by inflation and would regain partial health.

Another government policy option to avert the collapse of the financial system, Aleksandr noted, would be to reform the tax system:

> One way is to improve tax collection. But the tax system is complicated and there are too many taxes. The only way for an enterprise to survive is to not pay taxes, and companies do so by conducting transactions in cash rather than through banks, or they use the barter system. Otherwise, they can't exist.

144

IMPRESSIVE GROWTH IN 1996 AND 1997

During 1996, Premier Bank's assets quadrupled to about $10 million, and its capital base increased by seven times. This growth occurred with no increases in the 25 full-time and 30 part-time staff members. Premier ranked within the top 20 percent of Russia's 2,000 banks. Aleksandr elaborated:

> I increased the asset base, and of course, the capital base then goes up. There is a shortage of resources, so you have to find ways of getting them. In the US, the thing is to make the right investment on loans. But the most difficult thing here in Russia is assets, or resources.

Aleksandr summarized the economic environment and Premier Bank's situation in fall 1996:

> Competition is rising, but it is not really a competitive environment overall. It is not even a market economy. Yet, for the banking and financial sectors, it is the most competitive market for sure. Competition is toughest for the large banks because the bigger the scale, the scarcer the resources and the big projects. Russia has small and medium-sized banks that will remain the newcomers in the industry for the next five years. Many will die, and many will merge with others.

Increasing the asset base was the bank's major project in 1996 and 1997. Not only was this Premier's most successful project for these two years but, as Aleksandr pointed out, it was achieved at a time when the banking industry as a whole was experiencing a decrease in its asset and capital base. Aleksandr accomplished his goal by increasing the number of working clients, primarily by getting about 100 friends to deposit their money in his bank.

> We have a very wide circle of people who put their deposits in our bank. We have about 800 clients, but 650 to 700 have had no transactions in at least a year. Now we have about 140 active companies. These include about 50 product and service companies that were started from scratch and are operating, making money, and growing. Quite a few of these are run by my friends who do their projects through Premier.

One client, Modeltelekom, was started in 1994 with a $1 million investment by a friend of Aleksandr's. By 1996, it had become the second largest paging company in Moscow with monthly sales of about $2 million, and the company's growth continued through 1997. Aleksandr pointed out that another successful client, Kambelga Telekom, had $25 million in sales in its first two years of operation. The company had transferred half its account from other banks to Premier. These companies exemplified the clients that Premier sought.

Our clients are prosperous and legal businesses that have liquid money. Big banks are popular in our country because they get money from the government's budget, and most enterprises don't have money to invest. But small banks like ours don't have access to government funds, so we look for enterprises that are solid and have money.

Not all of Premier's clients were successful, however. The bank had given credit to a construction company to build cottages in the Moscow region, but the venture did not succeed and the client failed to repay the loan. Aleksandr emphasized: "If we work with industry, we need to have better control. If we don't have control, we lose money. That's why big banks want to acquire large enterprises, because they want to control the credits they give to them."

Money market transactions in the financial markets were still Premier's main activity, with major investments in government securities, or GKOs. Transactions included corporate stocks, government and municipal bonds, and interim bank credits. Aleksandr elaborated:

I would prefer to work on Wall Street with our assets because transactions are easier when visible. Our corporate markets, on the other hand, are speculative. According to my experience, many people make a fortune on these markets. But 90 percent of the money that circulates in this market is from Western international aid funds and is dominated by Western players. The Russian market is not as developed as Wall Street. A year from now, maybe we will operate in capital markets, but now it's too early. Bond and financial markets give small but stable profits, more predictable profits that can be forecasted.

During 1996 and 1997, Premier invested depositors' funds primarily in government and municipal bonds and interim corporate short-term notes. Aleksandr explained the process: "We deal in interim notes among reliable banks which we know. Two weeks maximum, normally two or three days, or overnight. For the bond market, maybe six months, but no more. One year is a long, long strategy. The situation is changing very rapidly."

Premier also wanted to engage in other transactions such as making more loans, but did not have enough assets to do so. Such transactions were done primarily by large banks, such as MDM Bank in Moscow. Aleksandr described how MDM had been founded by three young people, one educated in the West, with an initial investment of $100,000. Within two years, they had become the 69th largest bank, with a capital base around $60 million and assets close to $1 billion. The uncle of one of the founders was Viktor Gerashchenko, then the head of the Central Bank. "The connection helped," Aleksandr confirmed.

By 1996, Premier's involvement in starting up real estate companies had slowed. Aleksandr explained:

Two years ago it was very active because I bought in a rising market. Now the market is declining. Our other businesses include reselling and distributing pharmaceuticals for Western firms. We also work with some trading companies, have an oil agreement, and some one-shot deals. Of course, as a bank, we participate in lots of financing projects as well.

As for Premier Bank, Aleksandr explained his strategy for the foreseeable future:

Our strategy is to stay small now and grow slowly by increasing our assets and capital base. We are not trying to be a market leader. Maybe we will find a Western bank to be a partner. We're not a company that goes bankrupt by reaching $50 million of turnover and dealing in large credits. We are the oldest Russian bank, eight years old, and have always met our obligations. It was not a bad start.

1998 AND THE AUGUST CRISIS

In early 1999, Aleksandr Kruk reviewed the changes that had occurred in the bank's situation during 1998. He assessed the first half of 1998 as being comparatively acceptable for the bank. It had gradually increased its capital and paid annual dividends to shareholders in full—25 percent for common stock, and 75 percent for preferred stock. The number of clients opening accounts with the bank had also increased. The only change in the bank's management throughout its existence was Aleksandr Kruk replacing his father as CEO in 1996.

In spite of the uncertain situation in the country, economic indicators had stabilized to some extent by the beginning of 1998. Thus, the decision had been made not to cut back sharply on investments in short-term government bonds which carried the government's assurance of unconditional reliability. However, lending to clients continued to be limited, with credit lines, if approved, being well secured.

Like his father who founded Premier, Aleksandr was critical of the Central Bank's policies toward the country's commercial banks:

We think the Central Bank has taken a wrong policy approach, which negatively affects these banks. Such policies include the sharp increase in the bank reserve requirement. The Central Bank seems now to have taken a position that runs against the interests of large and all other banks. The course of the Central Bank toward breaking up small and medium-sized banks has become apparent. Given Russia's vast size, combined with its federal mode of governing, these policies can only lead to negative consequences.

The government and the Central Bank, he believed, had taken even more steps in the wrong direction regarding banks. These actions were exacerbated by the incessant assurances of the federal government that everything was going well and would become even better. This was contrary to reality, and tension began to mount in the economy. In spite of this negative situation, Premier Bank, as well as many other financial institutions, placed their hopes on the development of the economy. Aleksandr explained:

> We believed this was a reasonable position, even in mid-August of 1998, since we remained a fully liquid bank. Our GKO holdings alone covered in full all our liabilities to clients. Given our positive situation, we believed that most of the August 17 decisions made by the government and the Central Bank were not simply misguided—they were completely wrong.

Aleksandr believed that the basic problem was the simultaneous devaluation of the ruble by three and a half times, and the freezing of GKOs and OFZs. The freezing of these securities, which amounted to tens of billions of dollars, deprived banks and their clients of working capital. Aleksandr remarked:

> The declaration of a default was, to say the least, an adventurous move, if not an act of crime against the nation. It threw the country into a deep pitfall, out of which we will be pulling ourselves for years. And that would succeed only if more well-qualified and determined leaders come to power than the ones who caused these problems and who continue to be in charge of the economy today.

He qualified his criticism somewhat, stating:

> We did agree with one point, however, that the ruble had to be brought to its true value in relation to the dollar exchange rate since it had obviously been kept artificially above its real value. Even in 1996, we believed, and shared our opinions in the newspaper, that reducing inflation to 8 or 9 percent in that period was an erroneous economic policy. What would have been a justified measure would be having an annual inflation rate of 25 to 30 percent resulting from new currency issues. However, the additional monetary supply should not have been used for covering budget debt, but for investing in industries that were capable of developing solvency over a period of six months.

In spite of the economic catastrophe the country found itself in after August 17, 1998, Premier Bank continued to provide services to its clients, though not without extreme efforts, since most of its assets were frozen. The bank was also forced to cut salaries by 40 percent, but tried not to lay off employees. Aleksandr Kruk noted that some structural changes and redistribution of responsibilities encompassing the whole organization had taken place twice after August 17, and additional changes were being introduced on an ongoing basis in response to external circumstances.

Before August 17, management's plans centered on growing the bank. After that date, Aleksandr stated that his strategy was aimed at only one objective— to hold out until its frozen GKOs had been released. On January 18, 1999, the government began releasing some of the frozen GKOs, but on a gradual basis. And to make matters even worse for banks like Premier, the government's reorganization of its debt called for repaying only one ruble for each ten represented by a GKO. Aleksandr explained that it would take five years for the bank to receive even these reduced payments from the government. He also pointed out that if the country were to be shaken by high inflation in 1999, the bank would be unable to return even partial payment of funds to its clients, which is what it had been doing during early 1999. He added: "And although Russian citizens have already become used to being lied to by the government at every step, banking clients make insistent demands upon their banks for return of their funds."

Aleksandr Kruk concluded that Premier Bank would try to remain self-sufficient through the crisis:

> We believe that the overall economic situation and the state of our bank are difficult, but not hopeless. After August 17, it became even clearer to us that in our business we can only rely on ourselves. We are not expecting to be helped out by the government, the Central Bank, or the federal assembly. We are expecting long-term obstacles from them. Now, we want to find the right direction. Whether we'll succeed is hard to say, but we are not considering terminating business operations by our own accord. We are doing, and will continue to do, everything possible that is under our control.

9.   BusinessLink

BUILDING A BUSINESS WITH WESTERN CONTACTS

BusinessLink, a diversified business services company in St. Petersburg, began operations in May 1991 as a limited partnership (TOO) of four senior faculty-administrators from St. Petersburg State University. The partners had numerous personal contacts with Westerners that materialized into business relationships when Russia began its transition to a market economy. Operating informally at first, the partners became more formalized in their business approach when they began working with Procter & Gamble Corporation, their first major client. They advised the American company about market entry strategies, conducted marketing research, and recruited Russian employees for them. Coca-Cola became BusinessLink's second major client on a referral from P&G. Building on their early success and developing reputation with leading Western companies, the partners decided to focus on this segment as their initial strategy, and to offer additional services such as advertising and public relations. As partner Dr. Yurii Molchanov explained: "In creating services, we followed our clients."

Dr. Molchanov received his Ph.D. in physics in 1978 from Leningrad State University, which was later renamed St. Petersburg State University. Like his partners, he had taught and conducted research at the University before founding BusinessLink. Dr. Molchanov continued his work as vice-rector for international relations, and spent time at the University nearly every day. His high visibility and interactions with international academics and managers were extremely valuable in introducing clients to BusinessLink, as were those of his three partners. Dr. Molchanov explained why they entered consulting:

> All of us were professors at the University, and this was the most interesting business for us. We saw Russia opening for business, and we had lots of Western friends. We continued to get recommendations, and more and more clients came to us.

As the business grew, a number of key managers were hired, including Viktor Konyaschenkov, who became the company's advertising specialist and headed the growing advertising department. He was a graduate of the robot technology program at St. Petersburg Technical University, spoke fluent

English, and had work experience that made him well suited to BusinessLink. He also attended a seven-week executive development program at Manchester Business School in England, and an additional short course at Rank-Xerox. At BusinessLink, his assignments included working closely with Procter & Gamble's marketing staff. He developed a strong background that soon allowed him to start up and head a full-service advertising function for BusinessLink's clients.

GROWTH CONTINUES IN 1993 AND 1994 DESPITE TRAGEDY

Tragedy struck the company in early 1994 when two of the partners were killed in an automobile accident. Despite the terrible loss, the company remained on a positive course. Dr. Molchanov elaborated:

> We have grown fast enough, and have sought to achieve a balance between growth and reputation, while developing the right type of management. We wanted to build a good reputation, be professional and manage well, and wanted to create stability. In our first years, we thought the risk might be too much for us and that we might not get the needed contracts and new clients, and we were not so confident.

The company had never sought bank loans, and financed growth from its profits. Sales in 1993 reached $1 million, with $2 million projected for 1994, and company executives were confident of obtaining bank loans if they wished to do so.

The company was still structured as a partnership with a central management overseeing BusinessLink's four business units. The partners, Dr. Molchanov said, were not yet taking any remuneration, but were "investing in the company's future." In 1994, discussing future plans, he stated: "Next year we will officially become a holding company with four separate companies under one umbrella. Actually, that's the way we are operating right now." BusinessLink's corporate governance included a board of directors, which met each week for two hours to discuss the issues, problems, and opportunities of the company's four businesses. The managers and key professionals in each business also held meetings to share information and discuss their own situations. Dr. Molchanov spent three eight-hour days each week in his office, and also visited clients. These reponsibilities, coupled with his duties at the University, required that he work 14-hour days on a regular basis.

Dr. Molchanov believed that the economic environment was improving: "Economic factors are mostly stabilized, both in St. Petersburg and Moscow." Privatization was going well and inflation was down, amounting to only four percent for the month of August 1994. He added, however, that defense conversion to commercial production was a problem, though one tank factory in St. Petersburg was beginning to produce municipal buses. Dr. Molchanov noted that BusinessLink kept current with economic information for itself and its clients, with middle-level managers scanning major newspapers and other sources.

By mid-1994, the company was in its third phase of office expansion, growing from a 20-square-meter space to 1,000 square meters in a refurbished office building in an upscale area of St. Petersburg. Dr. Molchanov believed that attractive and professional office space was important for creating the right impression with clients, as well as providing a professional environment for employees.

Employees and Organizational Culture

BusinessLink had grown to 40 full-time employees and utilized another 100 part-time workers on a project-by-project basis. Dr. Molchanov explained that his people were overloaded, and that there was a shortage of professionals to fill the company's needs. He said:

> The only limit to the development of our firm is the shortage of the best people, which is our key resource, much more important than money. We can find specialists, and also people who speak English, but it is very difficult to find people with both skills.

Dr. Molchanov found this situation ironic since BusinessLink itself operated a search firm as one of its four businesses. The company's full-time staff members were generally 30 to 40 years old, and had experience in other companies. Some of the part-time people were younger, such as those who worked on marketing research assignments.

Dr. Molchanov noted: "Our company is almost all Russian, with occasional use of Westerners, such as students from American business schools like the University of California at Berkeley." The company wanted to hire Western professionals, but had difficulty because, as Dr. Molchanov claimed, "they expect high salaries, and it is often psychologically difficult for them to work in the Russian environment because they see it as too chaotic."

Recognizing the problem of attracting people, BusinessLink's senior managers tried to create conditions that would retain the best people. They provided an attractive and comfortable work environment in prime office space, and treated employees with respect. Dr. Molchanov stated: "We have a good team and a friendly atmosphere, and try to promote a family feeling. We celebrate everyone's birthday, have social events, and encourage cultural activities." For instance, paintings and other artwork that decorated the offices had been created by BusinessLink employees. The company offered flexible work hours for the professional staff, with no fixed starting or ending time. Dr. Molchanov said:

> Initially, we paid salaries that were too low, but now we have increased them to be much higher than the average Russian competitor. However, Western companies pay a little more than we do, even though we have a good level of salaries now. Maybe we'll have a new motivation package within six months.

Explaining the trial period for new employees, Dr. Molchanov emphasized BusinessLink's positive culture:

> We have a test period of one to three months for new members of the family. Staff members evaluate new employees during this period, and emphasize the importance of values to ensure the newcomers fit into the company's culture. Not all of them fit, and some do not stay, but we are not afraid of strong individuals, and good competition is welcomed.

Clients

BusinessLink initially offered services only in the St. Petersburg area, but by 1994 advertised in their promotional literature that "we also offer services for those clients that are expanding throughout Russia and the CIS through BusinessLink Moscow and representatives in other major cities." Virtually all of the company's clients since its inception were Western companies, primarily multinationals doing business in Russia. They numbered more than 50 American, British, French, Scandinavian, German, Dutch, and Japanese companies, including British Petroleum, British Telecommunications, DHL, Gillette, Procter & Gamble, RJR Reynolds, and Coca-Cola. Dr. Molchanov explained: "We developed a good reputation and understand the expectations of Western companies, the way they expect to be served."

Dr. Molchanov felt that, in addition to the many Western contacts of the founding partners, early entry as a first mover into its main services was a key to the company's success. In addition to referrals and recommendations, BusinessLink utilized several other methods to locate and attract clients. Employing direct marketing techniques, they contacted target companies, trade missions, and industry organizations, particularly in Scandinavia. These organizations were sent information about BusinessLink's services and the clients they served. The company also organized seminars in countries such as Finland on how to do business in Russia, which usually were attended by 30 to 40 top managers.

Dr. Molchanov believed that Russian companies were becoming more able to appreciate BusinessLink's services, and stated that the company was working to develop domestic clients, even if the business was not initially profitable. He explained:

We will take Russian clients from the cradle and teach them advertising, for instance, and will even do it at a loss. They are coming more and more to us, because even the larger Western companies have Russian subsidiaries with Russian personnel and managers who seek us out.

Four Business Areas

BusinessLink's client services, which began with consulting and expanded early into personnel searches, diversified in 1993 and 1994 into advertising and public relations, as well as real estate development. By the end of the two-year period, each of the four businesses accounted for approximately 25 percent of BusinessLink's revenues.

Consulting

Working exclusively for foreign multinationals, the company's consulting services staff specialized in three areas—market entry strategies, legal consultation, and market research. Market entry services included identification of business and acquisition opportunities, evaluation of potential business partners, feasibility studies of proposed projects, advice on the corporate structure appropriate for operations in Russia, and registration of a client's foreign company as a Russian legal entity. Consultations centered on corporate, industrial, tax, and foreign trade issues, as well as Russian legislation. Legal consultation was performed by leading St. Petersburg lawyers hired on a project basis. Market research included developing information on potential demand in the Russian market, identifying suppliers of local raw materials and components, and brand marketing for the Russian market, including presentations and promotions. Charges were based on either a flat fee or the time spent on projects, with top consultants being billed out at a $100 hourly rate.

Consultations were conducted by core teams and additional specialists as needed, all of whom were selected by the senior consultant in charge of a project. Four senior consultants had complete responsibility for two to four projects simultaneously. Activities involved assembling the team, defining the project, budgeting, pricing, and assessing the quality of performance, as well as ensuring that the project operated within budget. While senior consultants approved the project and presented it to clients, four middle-level consultants were responsible for conducting most of the research and preparing drafts of the report. Training of middle-level consultants was a priority; some had been sent abroad for six-week periods to obtain international experience, and one employee was scheduled to go abroad for one year to obtain an MBA. The permanent staff also included six students who collected information and conducted preliminary research as junior consultants. After 18 months, they were expected to prepare short reports for their teams.

The senior consultants and managers were eligible for bonuses. A new bonus system was being developed for all employees in 1994 that focused on team performance, but with each member evaluated and rewarded individually. A company profit-sharing plan was also under consideration. Senior managers and consultants did not receive additional income for developing new business as in many Western consulting firms. Dr. Molchanov considered this to be a basic responsibility of all senior people: "This is a basic part of their job, and we don't provide bonuses for doing just part of a job, since employees should be interested in doing all functions well."

Personnel search

A natural outgrowth of the company's consulting activities was identifying and selecting Russian personnel for Western clients. BusinessLink's array of search services grew to include developing reports on hiring practices, salaries, and management structures, conducting executive searches to identify senior- and middle-management candidates, developing and placing newspaper advertisements for lower-level managers and staff, building a database of candidates for these lower-level positions in fields of interest to clients, and screening and testing applicants' aptitude and suitability for positions. BusinessLink gained experience in many of these areas by engaging in joint projects with Western international HR firms. Newspaper advertising was utilized for lower-level candidates, while executive searches were conducted through personal contacts in the business and academic communities. To conduct personnel testing, several psychologists worked on a contract basis. The company, upon request, also conducted quarterly salary surveys within the St. Petersburg area, and planned to do so on a regular basis when sufficient staff became available.

Competition in HR services came from a number of international firms, such as the then-Big Six accounting firms and Hill International. Dr. Molchanov believed that early entry into this sector had given BusinessLink an advantage, and there was not yet any serious competition from the dozen Russian firms that entered the market later. BusinessLink's pricing strategy was similar to its approach in other businesses, pricing somewhat below major Western competitors, but higher than Russian firms.

Advertising and public relations

BusinessLink's entry into advertising services was in response to the widening needs of its Western clients. Services included planning advertising campaigns, producing commercials and other advertisements, and selecting media outlets such as newspapers and television. Activities grew rapidly and soon absorbed all the time of Viktor Konyaschenkov who assumed responsibility for building the business. Russian companies were slow to develop as clients for advertising services because they had no experience with, or appreciation for, such activities. Viktor summarized: "Russian companies are not ready for advertising services yet." Advertising in Western terms was virtually unknown to most Russians, but was fast becoming an important element of entry strategies for Western firms. Viktor explained further:

> Our challenge in addressing Russian consumers is to deliver the message in a consistent way so that the advertiser's intended meaning is clear to them. We want to bring Western products to the Russian mind by conveying the same philosophy, but just a literal translation is not enough. At first, people used to watch TV commercials almost like a movie, but that is not true any longer. The average Russian family lives in a small apartment with one TV set. Everybody might be watching the commercials, so you can access many consumers at the same time, but it's hard to target specific market segments. Yet, we do know, for instance, that soap operas are watched mostly by retirees and young people.

Just as they adapted the advertising of Western products in ways that would be meaningful to Russian consumers, BusinessLink also helped clients adapt their products to the Russian market. Viktor stated: "It's up to us to find out what the client really wants, and we try to help them by finding out how the Russian people react to these ideas using techniques such as interviews and focus groups." He explained that BusinessLink usually started with such marketing research techniques and followed through with a complete list of marketing services comparable to those offered by Western advertising agencies. He added: "Even though the basic ideas of Westerners are very good, the marketing and advertising of Western goods must be developed and adapted to Russian consumers." Similar to their pricing strategy for consulting, BusinessLink priced advertising to Western clients lower than Western competitors to gain a foothold in that market. But their prices were higher than most of their 200 Russian competitors so as to differentiate the quality of their services. The company tried to follow Western standards in not asking for advance payments, except for placing advertising in various media.

A relatively new but expanding service for BusinessLink was offering clients assistance in public relations. Initially a function of the advertising group, by 1994 it had become important enough to be managed as a separate activity, but was also headed by Viktor Konyaschenkov. Services included government relations, public opinion research, media monitoring, event planning and promotion, and editorial services. These services, consisting mostly of special projects, began as a response to requests from Western clients who utilized BusinessLink's other services. The company was also beginning a marketing campaign to promote a new service that involved advising how to deal with new Russian holding companies that had emerged as a result of recent legislation. Lobbying government and business officials was a particularly important function in which BusinessLink provided guidance. Viktor described the process as follows:

It involves taking our clients by the hand and leading them through the government and business bureaucracy. Our philosophy is to make it happen for the client. This is especially important because frequent changes in city and other levels of government make lobbying difficult even for us.

Real estate development, construction, and investment

Although the company's real estate activities were initially limited to a consulting role for large multinationals such as Coca-Cola and Procter & Gamble, by 1994 it had expanded as a real estate developer and construction company. New activities consisted of real estate development projects, acquisition and leasing of industrial facilities, and assistance in finding office space and expatriate housing. BusinessLink had a ten-percent share in the private stock company that owned the building it occupied, and paid rent to the stock company. BusinessLink's managers planned to open a business center, develop and invest in office buildings, and rent space to clients. Their present building housed Procter & Gamble as well as Gustav Paulig, a major Finnish coffee and tea distributor. Dr. Molchanov explained: "We would like to own buildings as good investments, and it's not too expensive right now to do so. Maybe we will have a joint venture with Western partners." BusinessLink's managers had initially approached this new business cautiously because it provided a slower return on capital, but were now getting more involved.

A related new business, which did not have the large capital requirements of real estate development and construction, was a foray into managing construction projects for clients. BusinessLink's role was to handle all aspects of such projects from start to finish. The company's analysts would identify specific sites, analyze technical conditions for construction and infrastructure availability, ensure that plans conformed to local design and architectural requirements, work with city officials to expedite agreements and licenses, identify local contractors, architects, and specialists to assist in the planning and construction phases, and even expedite the procurement of construction materials. The company brochures stated: "We simplify each step of the often long and complicated process of making things happen in Russia."

All Business Areas Booming After Five Years

Dr. Molchanov summed up the company's situation late in 1994:

> Now we are sure of success in the near future, more or less sure about tomorrow, anyway. The economic situation is becoming better and better. We are keeping our clients and have attractive facilities, good computers, and nice furniture. We are looking ahead now. All segments of our company are booming at the moment. We consider all of them growth areas, and have lots of clients in all of them. We are also looking into other businesses such as a travel agency.

He attributed much of the company's success to employees' understanding of Western business philosophy in all service areas, and their ability to overcome cross-cultural barriers. They also wanted to continue learning from Western clients, and often asked them for suggestions to improve their services.

CONTINUATION OF PROSPEROUS GROWTH IN 1995

In September 1995, Dr. Molchanov stated that the past year had been highly successful in all business areas. Projected revenue for 1995 was $3.5 to $4 million, a very substantial increase over 1994's results of slightly less than $2 million. The number of clients had increased to over 100 foreign firms across the four businesses, including numerous American companies, 20 Finnish firms, and other European and Asian clients. Dr. Molchanov added: "Compared to a year ago, we also have more and more Russian clients, since the situation here in Russia is much better, and I am optimistic." The company's pricing policy remained unchanged, positioned between major Western and Russian competitors, and BusinessLink's competitive advantage continued to be quality and reputation.

Growth had continued in all four major business areas, with real estate development and advertising each contributing 40 percent of revenues in late 1995. Consulting and personnel search, the two original businesses, each contributed only ten percent by year's end, but remained important. Dr. Molchanov clarified:

> Consulting is very important because it is usually the first stage of involvement with a client. The company's full-service strategy requires all four of these businesses. Procter & Gamble is a good example. From their first step here in Russia, we have worked with them over time, and they now utilize all four of our businesses. We did the same thing with Coca-Cola, and are even very active in all stages of the planning and construction of their factory.

The growing number of projects necessitated that staff be increased to 50 full-time and nearly 200 part-time employees, twice the number of temporary staff members of a year earlier. Dr. Molchanov himself had left his full-time university appointment in June, but remained as an advisor to the rector. BusinessLink's management was still in the process of formally converting from a partnership to a holding company. It had been operating in that mode for some time, with its individual segments being treated as relatively independent business units.

Russia's improving environment was one reason for BusinessLink's rapid growth. Dr. Molchanov emphasized the importance of having reasonable economic and political stability if businesses were to continue to grow:

The economic situation is a lot better. The market is coming faster and so is evidence of economic stability. Competition, however, is coming as the market opens more and more, and it is getting harder to make money. Many companies and their managers won't be able to operate successfully within the changing market conditions. The political situation seems stable for the rest of the year and into next year, but it is still very uncertain. Most of our major problems are with federal government regulations, whereas the city is much better. Mayor Sobchak has developed a young, professional, skilled team of deputies, so good people are writing the laws. Privatization rules, for instance, are the best here in St. Petersburg. The economic environment here is also attractive, with banks paying eight percent lower taxes than in Moscow.

Marketing Activities for Clients Still Central

Although all business segments experienced growth, the consulting area with its marketing focus, combined with the advertising area, accounted for half of BusinessLink's revenues. The advertising business had tripled its staff to 18, and also tripled revenues over the past year. It now ranked among the 20 largest agencies in Russia, including international firms, and was one of the top Russian-owned agencies. In response to rapid growth in marketing-oriented consulting and advertising, the company started a subsidiary, BusinessLink Media. Its mission was to buy advertising time or space in various media, primarily print media and billboards. For instance, BusinessLink had entered into an 18-month contract with *Cosmopolitan* magazine to advertise personal care products for a British client. BusinessLink Media was also the first Russian agency to buy audience research data from Gallup Russia Media Monitor. Company literature described this service as "giving us the possibility of providing to customers media audience research, planning and monitoring of campaigns, and conducting media evaluation of competitors' activities."

Advertising programs were developed by an in-house team that competed with several external freelance teams to see which team's program would be selected. In producing programs for clients, BusinessLink did not use in-house facilities, but claimed to employ the best studios, printing houses, and professional expertise available. Company literature noted: "Our creative philosophy is developing brand personality, not an agency advertising style." The company's growing list of advertising clients included Procter & Gamble, DHL Worldwide, Coca-Cola, RJR, Tambrands, Tchibo International Gmbh, Twinings, Reckitt & Coleman, and Paulig. A recent assignment for RJR, for instance, was to introduce a new brand of cigarettes called Peter the Great. BusinessLink also worked on programs for the Russian Property Fund, as well as for the Russian National Olympic Committee which was seeking to bring the 2004 summer games to Russia.

Finnish Subsidiary and Scottish Joint Venture in 1995

One of the company's major new directions in 1995 was the opening of BusinessLink Nordic in Helsinki, Finland. Although the company had started efforts there in late 1994, operations began in earnest during 1995. The major objective was to attract Finnish firms to the services of BusinessLink companies. The subsidiary also sought to service Russian companies wanting to develop business in Finland. BusinessLink Nordic was officially a Finnish company and was temporarily 100-percent owned by the Finnish managing partner. Yet it was clearly a BusinessLink company with Dr. Molchanov in charge. He explained:

> She is the owner at the moment, but we plan to register the shares in our name later. We are following Finnish laws, and it's easier and faster to be a Finnish company first. I am the chairman of the board, and we have agreed that I would develop a strategy for the company. It's difficult for me to be an official partner because of Russian legislation.

The Finnish managing partner was fluent in Russian, and had business relationships with BusinessLink managers for several years. She had been employed at a small Finnish consulting company, but was dissatisfied with the firm's activities. She welcomed the opportunity to manage BusinessLink's new Helsinki office which also employed a secretary. Dr. Molchanov explained:

> We wanted to be closer to our clients. We're expecting some of them will become more interested in developing their business in St. Petersburg. And psychologically it's much easier to attract them if you have a Finnish manager in Finland, because the Finnish language is quite difficult and their mentality is a bit different from ours.

Through her marketing efforts and contacts, the Finnish managing director had succeeded in attracting 11 of the 50 largest Finnish companies as clients for BusinessLink. Although virtually all of the work for clients was done in St. Petersburg, plans included creating a full-service office in Helsinki as client needs developed. The company had also attracted its first Russian client seeking to develop business in Finland. Given BusinessLink Nordic's successful start-up, Dr. Molchanov expected the company to be financially self-sufficient by the end of the year. He added that, following BusinessLink's customary policy, all profits would be reinvested in the growth of the business, and that no dividends would be paid for the foreseeable future.

Another new direction was undertaken in July, when BusinessLink entered a joint venture with Reiden, a leading Scottish real estate company. The firm was well-known in Europe, and had offices in Canada and South Africa. The JV's main activity was to evaluate real estate and businesses in Russia. The general director was from Scotland, and the JV employed two Russian nationals. Other initiatives included plans to establish a professional financial consulting business by the end of the year. Its primary activity would be to provide auditing services to Russian firms, and a woman from St. Petersburg University had been hired to help start the business. BusinessLink's rationale for entering the field was that the service was badly needed by companies, and that Russian auditing firms were not providing good quality service. To illustrate his point, Dr. Molchanov noted that his organization had fired the firm that had done BusinessLink's audit. BusinessLink had also started a small legal services operation, as well as a new construction subsidiary within the real estate development group.

Key Role of Human Resources

As a people-intensive service organization, BusinessLink could operate and grow only by attracting, developing, and retaining excellent people. Dr. Molchanov emphasized: "Our biggest problem is to find good people, and we are always looking." BusinessLink had very little turnover, losing only two key people in four years, both from the personnel search area. One took a position as personnel manager of Wrigley's Moscow office, tripling her salary. Dr. Molchanov hoped to attract her back within a year, emphasizing the scarcity of such talented professionals. Most BusinessLink employees were under age 30, with only ten employees over 40, and one person over 50. Through his contacts at the university, Dr. Molchanov was able to find talented people, including his nephew who worked part-time at BusinessLink while attending business school.

When asked what his secret of success was, he answered:

> It's the employees. We created a crazy team of workaholics, and we work ten-hour days. Also, from the start, we have looked for the best people, and our key ten to 15 people are very good, and all speak English.

Dr. Molchanov spent a lot of time selecting team members and encouraging their professional development. For instance, one employee was sent on a three-week training program to France, and a lawyer was sent to the UK for a six-week course. Dr. Molchanov was in the process of hiring a new personnel director, and was arranging for her to take courses in St. Petersburg and abroad. In another initiative, he arranged for a woman working in advertising to pursue her MBA in Europe at BusinessLink's expense. Dr. Molchanov noted that his marketing-oriented company had not yet found its own marketing manager, adding wryly: "The shoemaker has no shoes."

Dr. Molchanov discussed his own role:

> My job is to create the right climate in the company, such as giving people
> pride and status in their own business segments. For instance, new business
> cards have been prepared for the lead person in consulting with the title,
> Director of BusinessLink Management Consultancy. A year ago it was
> Manager of the Consultancy Department. Right now, we are trying to give the
> impression to employees in each of our businesses that it is their own company,
> and the main person is the director. In Russia, psychologically there is a
> difference between manager and director, and a director is considered to be
> much more important.

Similar decisions had been made in the personnel search business, which
continued to grow, but now constituted only ten percent of company revenues.
As an example of the segment's growth, BusinessLink had requests from
clients to fill 40 jobs in a recent one-month period.

Emphasizing the team atmosphere in the company, Dr. Molchanov noted
that he viewed Viktor, the advertising director, as a partner rather than an
employee. The secretary-receptionist, Tatiana, also explained that the team
atmosphere was a major reason for her working at BusinessLink. She
considered this company attribute rare in Russia, and stated that her former
employment in a large, diversified Russian firm had been good, but lacked a
team orientation. She attributed BusinessLink's team spirit to the weekly team
meetings that she attended, as well as the lack of emphasis on hierarchy or
authoritarian management. Team spirit also was evident in the company's
social activities. For instance, outings were frequently arranged, such as a
three-day ship excursion for 60 people that was subsidized by the company.

In spite of the many positive aspects of the company's climate, Dr.
Molchanov was disappointed in his own failure to develop an effective
financial reward system. He explained:

> We did implement the reward system developed last year, but I don't like at all
> what we have, and it was my mistake. It was too simple, with the main
> principle being that each department received dividends based on their unit's
> profit, which was distributed among the employees. But to my mind, this
> system is too primitive, and we want to introduce a different way of giving
> bonuses that will create the right climate for the entire company. The danger is
> that the company could split into independent businesses, and we want to avoid
> that.

Dr. Molchanov believed it was crucial that employees as well as clients
view BusinessLink as one company. He felt that, although the businesses were
given great autonomy, maintaining the one-company climate was the crux of
his job, and that BusinessLink's full-service competitive strategy was based
upon this premise.

Strategy Evolves to Include Financial Investments

Dr. Molchanov explained how the company's strategy had evolved to include major financial investments:

> If you compare the situation to a year ago, I can say that we are no longer only a consultancy and service company. We do a lot of projects for ourselves, especially in the real estate development area where we are investing our own money. You know, privatization is here, and to my mind it is foolish not to use the chance to buy real estate very cheap, or to buy industrial facilities or shares of companies which are also very cheap. That's why we will invest as much as we can. The real value is if you have management control of a joint stock company.

Dr. Molchanov's financial strategy was to reinvest all profits in the businesses, as well as in real estate investments. As in prior years, the firm financed itself from operations during 1995, and had not resorted to borrowing. Financial demands were growing, however, with the firm's increasing emphasis on investing in real estate projects for itself, rather than for clients. The company had, for instance, increased its ownership of the building it occupied to 20 percent, from ten percent a year earlier. Management was contemplating purchasing the entire building, presently owned by a joint stock company in which BusinessLink had a 20-percent stake. Dr. Molchanov explained that BusinessLink would likely form a new joint stock company to own the building if they went ahead with their plans to purchase the remaining shares.

Such major investment projects were occupying an increasing amount of Dr. Molchanov's time. Whereas marketing had been his primary focus in earlier years, over the past few months two major real estate projects occupied 70 percent of his time. One involved the purchase of the company's office building which required top-level government negotiations in Moscow, and the second was a large real estate development project. A major advertising account was his third main area of activity. He emphasized: "All of these projects are key to the company's future." The rest of his time was spent on overseeing daily operations, and continuing the development of BusinessLink's team with the objective of holding the various businesses together as one company. He also realized that he would likely have to scrutinize some businesses more carefully, given the company's increasing need for capital to finance new investments. He stated that he would make a decision before the year's end on whether to continue the fledgling travel agency that employed several people. The unit had not been performing well, which Dr. Molchanov attributed in part to "the manager not being aggressive enough." He realized that all of these decisions ultimately fell on his shoulders, since by 1995, he was the only one of the four original partners still active in running the business. As noted earlier, two others had died in an accident, and the third, Dr. Yeremeev, had decided to remain relatively passive while directing the Russian Language and Cultural Center at St. Petersburg University.

DRAMATIC GROWTH AND ORGANIZATIONAL EVOLUTION IN 1996

Following its successes in 1995, BusinessLink was well on its way by the next fall to meeting its 1996 annual revenue target of $8 million, with a seven to ten percent profit margin. Achieving this goal would nearly double the company's 1995 revenue of $4.2 million. Full-time employees had increased only 30 percent, from 50 in 1995 to 65 in 1996. Managers continued their policy of utilizing part-time employees as necessary to fulfill client contracts, thus limiting the risk and fixed costs associated with large increases in full-time employees. Productivity also continued to increase as a result of the performance-based reward system.

As planned, BusinessLink formalized its holding company structure during 1996. Individual businesses were now structured as completely autonomous units, coordinated strategically and financially by BusinessLink's board of directors. Despite the organizational change, the company remained entirely owned by the two remaining partners. Dr. Molchanov devoted all his time to the business, and the board attempted to ensure an overall corporate orientation in the company's activities and financing. The ten-person board was entirely internal and included the two partners, the directors of the four major units, and four other senior managers. They met weekly to coordinate strategy and to discuss major corporate issues as well as those of the business units. Individual units also held weekly meetings to coordinate their own operations, as well as monthly strategic meetings.

Company managers explained that the holding company structure had been prompted by market considerations. One senior manager noted:

> It's a very different company now, and the market is asking for different services and faster response. Initially we intended to provide full services for clients, but now clients decide for themselves which services they want. Although some clients work with all of our businesses, many now work with only some of our businesses, or only one.

The new structure was expected to facilitate quick and direct response to clients by the appropriate business unit or units, and overall coordination was provided by the board of directors. A senior advertising manager offered an additional reason for this structure:

Clients were becoming confused by our many businesses under the one corporate structure. This could be negative for us in advertising, such as when The Gillette Company said they would do no advertising with us because of earlier problems with BusinessLink's personnel services. Now, presentations to new potential clients start with the new structure of the business to avoid confusion.

BL Advertising Becomes the Largest Agency in St. Petersburg

Olga Lozgacheva, one of the firm's account managers, provided an update of BusinessLink's advertising activities in 1996. Following the philosophy of the new organizational structure implemented in that year, the advertising business unit was renamed BL Advertising, and a distinctive new logo was being developed to differentiate it from the BusinessLink holding company. This change also reflected the importance of the advertising sector given its growth and relatively large size. In fall 1996, 25 of BusinessLink's 65 employees worked in BL Advertising, up from 15 the previous year.

Ms. Lozgacheva stated that BL Advertising was now the largest advertising agency in St. Petersburg, and the only wholly Russian-owned firm in the city positioned to compete with major international advertising agencies. The strategy of BL Advertising was to compete with these agencies for the business of major international companies operating in Russia. In 1996, for instance, the American multinational RJR was BL Advertising's largest client. Company management expected BL Advertising to be more profitable in 1996 because they were adding new clients, and had increased their commission on ads to 15 percent, which was the standard for major advertising companies. This decision was a departure from the earlier pricing strategy, which placed BL Advertising's rates below those of major international competitors.

BL management was committed to staying in St. Petersburg for the present, but realized that most international companies started up operations in Moscow or soon moved their head offices there. Yet, one manager stated: "We compete well from St. Petersburg for international company advertising business, but we will get more aggressive as needed to keep and gain market share." The implication seemed to be that BusinessLink was willing to open a Moscow office as business opportunities developed.

The firm was attempting during 1996 to make deeper inroads with major Russian companies. The few Russian clients already working with BL Advertising were primarily consumer goods companies. Others had become interested after witnessing the dramatic positive effects of advertising on President Yeltsin's successful re-election campaign. One BL advertising manager noted: "After the election, two large Russian companies approached us and asked, 'Did Yeltsin win just because of advertising?'"

A number of Russian firms had begun to advertise and to use agencies, but BL Advertising management saw that some were unhappy with the international advertising agencies. BL Advertising managers believed this dissatisfaction presented an opportunity for their firm, and they were committed to the strategy of increasing dramatically the proportion of Russian firms among BL clients. One manager explained: "BL Advertising is getting to know potential Russian clients so they'll sign with us in a couple of years. We're working for the future, and it takes a lot of time. These firms are very picky."

Many Russian firms still had misconceptions about advertising and were reluctant to use it. Some firms were still quite secretive and reticent about disclosing information to companies like BL Advertising. One client, for example, would not discuss its distribution system even though it would have been very helpful in developing a marketing and advertising program. Few Russian firms had marketing or advertising departments, and BL Advertising often had to work with sales representatives. With experience in advertising lacking among clients, communications were often difficult and lengthy. Such problems made it difficult to develop business with Russian clients, and a relatively long time horizon was necessary.

Human Resource Policies and Issues

The shortage of qualified candidates for positions within BL Advertising led management to consider slowing the unit's rate of growth. This situation was representative of virtually all units within BusinessLink, but was most severe within the fast-growing advertising business. A major problem was the lack of time to train new employees. Another particularly acute problem was finding people to fill managerial positions who could think strategically from the start. The best candidates were those who had managerial experience in universities or internationally. Filling such positions internally was difficult in this young company. The average age in the advertising group was 24 and ranged from 18 to 34, which was somewhat younger than the company's average age of 30.

Olga Lozgacheva, the advertising manager explained that "the group had always spent a great deal of time screening candidates to match a person to a position, and also to assess the suitability of the individual for BusinessLink's team-oriented culture." She added, however, that not as much time was being spent currently in this very important activity. One result was that the advertising managers had fired several people in the past year who didn't fit into the culture. She acknowledged:

> It's hard now starting out here with little supervision or formal training. It's up to the person to ask questions of everybody and take initiative, and we start them out right away working as part of a project. It's really hard for those who don't have the right attitude, and we have also fired people who could not accomplish their individual work.

Decisions were made about new personnel after a three-month probationary period when an oral interview was held to assess their progress. In discussing BL Advertising's performance appraisal system, Ms. Lozgacheva noted that there was as yet no formal career planning or progression. The company did groom people, and she noted that "last week we took an individual along to a client to learn the ropes, and we will monitor progress to see if the person is promotable." Important elements in appraisals were how well employees tied personal goals to those of the company, and how successful they were in accomplishing their goals.

BusinessLink's compensation philosophy was to pay for performance. Olga explained:

> At the end of last year, Viktor did an employee survey and asked everyone how much they wanted to earn for the coming year. We are rewarded on individual performance, and management is careful to make sure that everybody knows their company goals and personal goals. Since we see each other every day, it's easy to see who produces. Management takes into account your performance as well as how much money you make for the agency.

She added that salaries were kept confidential. New employees in 1996 started at $250 per month for the first three months, and then new salaries were negotiated. Olga had started four years ago at $80 per month, but inflation accounted for much of the difference between starting salaries over time. The shortage of qualified personnel put pressure on starting salaries, resulting in salary compression which some managers felt had not yet been addressed. Nevertheless, salaries were considered relatively good, with computer operators earning $400 per month, for instance. Olga felt that employees were quite satisfied and were not generally looking for new opportunities. They would receive some salary increases depending upon company profits. Olga herself preferred a stable salary, and was pleased when the company temporarily discontinued its bonus system.

When Olga Lozgacheva started at BusinessLink four years earlier as one of the first 15 employees, she began working in marketing and was promoted to marketing manager. She was one of the five senior managers reporting to Viktor Konyaschenkov, the director of BL Advertising. As one of the two account managers, Olga recommended the hiring of candidates for her group, with the final decision being made by Viktor. Her biggest problems, she explained, were allocating assignments among her staff members, as well as organizing paperwork. In fall 1996 she was devising a computerized system to help her staff document their work with clients.

Personnel Services and Real Estate

Although the advertising unit had become the largest and fastest-growing business within BusinessLink's portfolio, most of its other units also continued growing, except for the travel agency that was disbanded. The mission of the personnel services unit was changing because clients did not want to train new hires. BusinessLink thus focused on sourcing very scarce higher level, experienced executives. The unit also became more involved in training potential candidates, and saw this service as a promising extension of its business. For instance, they had trained a number of secretaries and were able to place all of them.

The company's real estate business was reported to be profitable, and was still conducted through its joint venture with a Scottish partner. The partnership continued to develop properties which it owned, as well as to manage construction and development projects for others. For example, a major project in late 1996 was developing a building for Tambrands on Kirovsky Prospekt. These activities were extensions of BusinessLink's consulting experience in surveying properties, as well as subcontracting construction and development projects to others.

Coordination and Planning

The planning process in BL Advertising is illustrative of the planning activities conducted in all units of the company. The director, Viktor Konyaschenkov, held weekly meetings with the two account managers and the managers of the art, media, creative, and production departments. Recent weekly meetings included discussions about the previous week's business, operational and client issues, status reports of important projects, and future business. One manager noted that this meeting was the only time during the week that all managers got together. She added that strategic and long-term issues would be discussed at other meetings, usually every month.

Like other units, the advertising group also did an annual planning exercise in which they set objectives for the number of clients to target, the number of people to hire, equipment to buy, and revenues needed to cover salaries and other costs to produce the targeted profit. BusinessLink's board of directors approved and consolidated the plans, and finalized corporate strategy and financial plans.

DOUBLED REVENUES AND REAL ESTATE GROUP DOMINANCE IN 1997 AND PRE-CRISIS 1998

For the second straight year, the BusinessLink companies nearly doubled their revenues in 1997 to $14 million. In 1996, they achieved revenues of approximately $7 million, somewhat less than their goal of $8 million. Profits in both years ranged from seven to ten percent. Real estate development became the fastest-growing business segment, while advertising continued its robust expansion. By mid-1998, BusinessLink employed 200 full-time professionals, up from 110 in 1997. Part-time employees were also hired as needed.

The umbrella or holding company concept developed by the board of directors became operational during 1997. The structure was applied first to the advertising group of companies called BL Advertising, which had its own logo to differentiate it from other BusinessLink units.

The real estate development arm, which originated in 1992, had become a separate full-service enterprise by 1997 and contained independent entities within it. The real estate company umbrella included two Russian construction companies that BusinessLink had started.

Also in 1997, the personnel search activity was reconstituted under new leadership with the objective of providing a full-service human resource function for client companies. Business consulting continued to be a mainstay, and was organized as another separate unit.

Dr. Molchanov explained that the reason for the company's success was that its competitive strategy was still based upon attracting the best people to serve its clients: "That's why we're sure we'll survive, because we have the best people." In implementing BusinessLink's strategy, Dr. Molchanov believed that the most effective approach was to keep each company separate, and to require each to be self-financing. The company's board of directors was constituted entirely by insiders in mid-1998, but Dr. Molchanov had "recently begun thinking about inviting outsiders to board membership in order to take advantage of particular areas of expertise they might have."

Motivating employees was one of Dr. Molchanov's key roles, as it was for the directors and board chairmen of the operating companies. Dr. Molchanov favored keeping salaries tied to the dollar rather than rubles, believing that the resulting stability was a strong motivator for his people. Consistent with his objective of delegating authority, Dr. Molchanov required all top managers to recruit and hire their own people. As in the past, the company had organized excursions for employees and their families to Finland and Novgorod. The company subsidized 30 to 50 percent of expenses for such trips which had become more frequent during 1997 and 1998.

Real Estate Development Group

During 1997 and 1998, the Real Estate Development group had become in many respects the most important unit under the BusinessLink umbrella. Dr. Molchanov spent much of his time arranging financing for its projects. The group was headed by general director, Vladimir Bogratchev, who had been with BusinessLink since 1992, primarily leading real estate activities. Mr. Bogratchev, age 39 in 1998, was a civil engineer with an extensive background in engineering and project management. His experience had been in both the military and government sectors where he had been in charge of building and renovating major facilities, including office buildings and industrial plants.

The group consisted of 25 full-time project managers, engineers, cost estimators, financial planners, and support staff. It was a leader in the St. Petersburg real estate development market, having entered the field fairly early during the growth years of the 1990s. Activities included investing in commercial and multi-unit residential real estate projects, participating in real estate development projects, managing construction projects, and constructing and renovating buildings. Mr. Bogratchev explained that the primary business was to develop property projects: "We acquire buildings, land, and rights, build or renovate real estate, and then manage or sell them." The company undertook multiple projects, at times participating in 15 or 20 simultaneously, with four or five being large undertakings.

Developments were usually done in partnership with Russian or international organizations that sometimes were only financial partners, but in other cases were full operating partners. Mr. Bogratchev explained how projects were financed: "When we develop residential buildings we receive advances from future owners, and when we develop office buildings we use bank financing which we repay with money coming from the leases." These buildings were often built or renovated for the development group to lease out as apartments and offices to tenants. In other cases, building and renovation were accomplished for clients who occupied the premises, as was the case with PepsiCo, or who leased space to other tenants. BusinessLink also built and renovated factories, and most such projects were carried out by the group's construction unit. Dr. Molchanov stated: "We have been successful in our development efforts because we know where the good locations are and we know how to complete projects."

BL Advertising Group

BL Advertising Group was the largest revenue producer of the BusinessLink companies in mid-1998, and second in profitability after the real estate development group. Dr. Molchanov explained that BL Advertising was one of the largest advertising firms in St. Petersburg and was considered a leader, being the only St. Petersburg firm in the business with a Moscow office. He stated that, by 1998, BL Advertising was a smaller umbrella company in its own right within the BusinessLink holding company, and included five separate legal entities in which BusinessLink held the majority of the shares. Three of the entities were established in partnership with other Russian companies. Four of the advertising companies were located in St. Petersburg. The fifth was started in Moscow in the summer of 1998.

BL Advertising, still headed by Viktor Konyaschenkov, offered services that were typical of a sizable advertising agency—creative, marketing, corporate communications, corporate marketing communications, and general marketing. These units worked directly with managers who handled projects for international and Russian clients. The departments were located on various floors within the Business Link offices. This diversification had started by early 1997 when BL Advertising began to divide its business functions into profit centers. Viktor implemented this diversified structure with the thought that these departments might compete among themselves, especially in creative activities. By mid-1998, the advertising group had 80 employees.

Viktor estimated that the advertising market in Russia for 1997 was $1.8 billion and was forecasted to grow to $2.3 billion in 1998. BL Advertising's revenues were $13 million in 1997 and were projected to be $17 million for 1998. Seventy percent of revenues came from international clients who constituted half the company's client base. Russian companies made up the other half of clients, and accounted for 30 percent of BL Advertising's revenues. A major source of revenue during 1997 and 1998 came from establishing Russian trademarks and brands for international clients.

Helping clients position their products in the Russian market was another advanced service that went beyond simply introducing products to the market. These activities supported BL Advertising's objective of creating the perception that these international clients are Russian companies. It also fostered the corollary objective of helping Russian-owned businesses, which often had little marketing experience, extend the range of their marketing activities. Many of BL Advertising's new activities were initiated by its strategic planning unit, established in 1997 to work with clients toward achieving these objectives within five years.

Seventy percent of the company's clients were located in St. Petersburg, but the biggest accounts were located in Moscow. Significant Moscow accounts included RJR Tobacco and a well-known British manufacturer of feminine and baby care products. Staffing the new Moscow office during 1998 involved transferring key personnel from St. Petersburg. Viktor explained, however, that skilled personnel were generally more available in Moscow, especially creative and account specialists. Competition, on the other hand, was more intense for BL Advertising in Moscow than in St. Petersburg, where the company had built a strong reputation over the years. Viktor described clients in Moscow as being "more sophisticated and harder to please." Nonetheless, the company had achieved many successes, and continued to receive requests from new clients to participate in competitions for their business. This activity was called a Peach competition in Russia, and Viktor was proud that, in a short time, BL Advertising had won two such competitions, one for an international company, and a second for a large Russian client.

Each individual department or company under the advertising umbrella was headed by a general director reporting to Viktor who was the chairman of the board of BL Advertising. Viktor held weekly meetings with his St. Petersburg managers to discuss the status of projects and client relations. These were called closing meetings, and were held every Friday. Viktor was also very involved with the new Moscow office, and spent every Wednesday and Thursday there working with his staff. Monthly meetings held in St. Petersburg included senior people from the Moscow office, and were devoted to longer-range issues, problems, and opportunities for BL Advertising and its member companies.

Viktor described his major managerial problem as delegating authority to people who were not accustomed to accepting responsibility. He told them that he "wanted them to run things themselves on a daily basis." He had developed a way of instilling this responsibility in his staff: "As a general rule, when somebody comes to me to discuss a question, they must have at least one answer before I offer my comments." Viktor noted that he rewarded employees commensurate with their performance. Individual bonuses were paid quarterly and annually based upon client billings or client acceptance of ideas, as well as programs developed by the creative department.

BL Advertising had not experienced the chronic problem of collecting receivables that plagued many Russian companies. Viktor explained: "These have been our long-term clients and they pay us since they understand the difficult situation that nonpayment would put us in." With their newer or shorter-term clients, however, the company did encounter many delays, as well as excuses which these clients hoped would justify late payment of their bills. Viktor also explained that the company tried to get clients to commit to specific amounts of business for extended periods to allow BL Advertising to plan projects and cash flow.

Personnel Services

Although considerably smaller than the company's other businesses, the Personnel Services group had doubled its revenues during the 12 months ending in July 1998. The revitalization of the business unit was due to the leadership of a newly appointed general director, Dr.Valery Katkalo. He was appointed in October 1997, and still retained his position as dean of the management school at St. Petersburg State University where he had been an associate of Dr. Molchanov. Dr. Katkalo's new strategy for the group was to move it from being primarily a search and placement firm to providing full-service human resource functions for clients. Another strategic initiative he introduced was to more actively seek business with Russian clients. Foreign companies, which had been the company's mainstay since its early days, constituted the majority of the unit's 40 clients.

Search and placement, the initial activities of the unit, were still important. Dr. Katkalo noted that the company was successful in finding people at all levels for clients, "starting with secretaries and going up to general manager positions." The wider range of services required by the new strategy necessitated additional staff, and the group had grown from five to 15 people during the last year. Like other BusinessLink units, the Personnel Services group had expanded beyond St. Petersburg, opening a new branch in nearby Novgorod. Two full-time employees there were supplemented as needed by professionals from St. Petersburg.

New activities included training and organizational development for clients, and BusinessLink Personnel opened its own training center. Dr. Katkalo explained that his group was expanding its client offerings in human resource development, organizational development consulting, recruiting, and training. Some clients were utilizing the full menu of services, while others made use of one or two offerings. Much of the group's work was still with international clients including Gillette, PepsiCo, British American Tobacco, KPMG, and Stimorol, a large European chewing gum company. All of these companies had factories or other operations in St. Petersburg, and were attracted to the personnel service offerings of this BusinessLink company. But Dr. Katkalo noted: "Russian companies are not used to paying for HR services."

Dr. Katkalo was particularly pleased that some clients the company had lost had returned to BusinessLink in recent months. This success occurred in spite of the increasing level of competition from major international search and placement firms including Ward Howell, Amerol, Kelly Services, and Manpower. Competition from Russian companies also was increasing, with about a dozen mostly smaller newcomers opening their doors during the past year or two. In Dr. Katkalo's view, these companies competed primarily on price, with little emphasis on quality of service, and worked primarily for Russian clients. In this increasingly competitive environment, Dr. Katkalo had maintained the pricing policy of charging the same rates to international and Russian clients, and setting prices between those of international and Russian competitors.

To accommodate the company's growth in 1997 and 1998, the group increased its office space within BusinessLink's facility. The 15 employees included marketing managers, recruiters, and assistant recruiters, as well as one administrator. As had always been the case for BusinessLink companies, finding qualified personnel was a problem for the Personnel Services group. Just as Dr. Molchanov had looked to St. Petersburg State University to recruit Dr. Katkalo, the latter recruited faculty members to serve as consultants within his business unit. He had hired two recent graduates to become full-time employees, and had hired personnel away from competitors.

In addition to changing the company's strategy, Dr. Katkalo wanted to instill a new performance-oriented culture. His objective was to initiate performance-based rewards and develop a marketing orientation. All personnel were expected to develop business with current and new clients. During 1998, he changed the organization's compensation schedule to a bonus system in which employees earned monthly commissions on successful client transactions. Although he was pleased with the group's progress, Dr. Katkalo stated in September 1998 that "Personnel Services contributes only a minor amount to BusinessLink at present."

Successful Financing of Growth

Dr. Molchanov described his own activities during 1997 and 1998:

> Much of my time has been spent restructuring the company, especially during 1997, and obtaining capital for the real estate development activities in St. Petersburg. Attracting financial resources to the firm had not been difficult for BusinessLink during these years because of its profitable operations and strong reputation.

Banks had been happy to do business with his company, he noted, and financing growth had not been a problem. Normally, he worked with several medium-sized or large Russian banks, and BusinessLink had also obtained loans from several international banks. In summary, Dr. Molchanov felt that 1997 and 1998 had been very positive for BusinessLink, at least until late August 1998.

CUTBACKS AFTER THE CRISIS OF AUGUST 17, 1998

Although the country's financial crisis that began in August 1998 inflicted many difficulties on BusinessLink, Dr. Molchanov felt that the company was healthy and fairly well positioned to survive and retain a substantial amount of its business. He emphasized in mid-September, however, that the company was attempting to assure a positive outcome by cutting expenses and emphasizing marketing and sales activities to retain clients and attract others. He described the situation as "very difficult, and we feel it very sharply right now." He noted that many clients had lost a great deal of money during the first month of the crisis, and that purchasing power had declined by a factor of three due to the devaluation of the ruble.

Dr. Molchanov explained that the advertising business, for instance, was "going down rapidly right now since international clients have drastically decreased advertising while waiting to see what develops with the government." Viktor estimated that the total Russian advertising market for 1998 would be $1.2 billion rather than the $2.3 billion projected a year earlier, and that BL Advertising would fall far short of its goal of $17 million. The number of advertising employees totaled only 40 by mid-September, half the number of a month earlier. Viktor explained:

> We understand that we are a service business, and that such layoffs are necessary when business decreases severely. We feel sorry, but that's life. We are thinking about the future and kept those who fit best. We kept the people who would work hardest and take on more jobs, the most productive and prolific. We will stay close to others so that we can bring them back when the situation improves. It is better to take the best people and give them a good salary rather than to keep everyone and pay them less.

Viktor continued with a discussion of strategy:

> Our strategy now is to survive. We have the benefit of time now and our strategy takes strict shareholder financial considerations out of management. This makes it easier to survive because we can think in terms of the business rather than only ownership and profits. Now we take on some jobs to keep people busy, jobs that we would not have taken in the past. We try to get commitments from our clients to help us keep our people working, even on a freelance basis, so we can stay close to them and rehire them in the future.

The real estate development group in September 1998 was involved in over 15 projects, a third of which were considered very large. Most clients were international and primarily European. These included Finland's Nokia, Stimal of Denmark, Rehal, a large German construction company, and Procter & Gamble's Tambrands subsidiary. Mr. Bogratchev emphasized that the market had been very active over the years, producing high yields to developers that were comparable to those in the US and Europe. By mid-September, however, he emphasized that it was very difficult to begin new development projects because financing was extremely scarce. He added:

> Our business is continuing: we don't stop our life. I am trying to keep an objective, realistic course. I don't want to be overly optimistic, but I don't think that the market is going to collapse. I understand that people are not buying apartments as they used to, but there are other segments of the market, and hopefully these will stay more favorable. So our goal now is to continue the projects that we have, and follow the time frame that we have planned. But I would say it looks like new projects are going to be delayed.

He explained that the large international clients to whom BusinessLink leased space were paying their bills in a timely way since they were less affected by Russia's financial crisis. Dr. Molchanov added that "new sales in the real estate area have stopped and we need to cut expenses, but we have ongoing projects which are quite profitable."

BusinessLink Personnel, like the other business units, was experiencing a downturn in its business. Plans to expand office space were put on hold and staff reductions had been made. Nonetheless, Dr. Katkalo stated: "I will not characterize the situation as completely dramatic." His organization had about 40 clients at the time, some of whom had frozen their contracts and were not planning to increase their activity. He added: "We still have enough clients which would not permit us to live in luxury, but would allow us to continue with our business."

His approach during the slowdown was to downsize cautiously, since he recognized that "this business is relying fully on human capital. That is why we are now adapting to the situation by adding more marketing activities." His organization consisted of a newly hired marketing manager, as well as recruiters and assistant recruiters who were engaged in marketing in addition to their other responsibilities. The unit had not yet reduced prices to retain and secure business, but Dr. Katkalo realized that this could become necessary.

With regard to his own activities during the crisis, Dr. Katkalo was spending a great deal more time working with important customers: "These days, working with new clients and potential clients is most important for me. I would say business development is now most important for all of us."

Other decisions in September 1998 included which banks to continue working with to finance real estate development, and which personnel to keep or to lay off. Regarding the family of organizations under the BusinessLink umbrella, Dr. Molchanov noted that his strategy was for each company to be self-financing, with some qualifications:

> If in the future we come to the worst situation, we stand ready to share resources among the companies, if necessary, to ensure their survival. We are not now in deep enough problems to do so, but we may sometime have to step back to our 1992 strategy and structure of being one company. It is too early now to think of goals even for next year. Our strategy now is to try to overcome these difficulties.

10.　Aquarius Systems Inform

STARTING OUT WITH FOREIGN PARTNERS

Aquarius Systems Inform is a computer company involved in assembling and distributing personal computers and related products. The enterprise evolved from a joint venture with foreign partners to an independent stock company. For a short time, it became an affiliate of a holding company called Aquarius Systems Interface, and eventually reverted to the status of an independent stock company.

The firm began operations as Aquarius Systems Integral in April 1989 as a joint venture between five Russian founding organizations and the West German trading company, Teb Impex. The JV was created to develop a computer business, including construction of an assembly plant in Russia. The Russian and German parent companies had previously been affiliated with Aquarius, a Taiwanese firm founded in 1983. That company sold its ASI computers in many countries, and had become the largest supplier of computers in the CIS. The new JV soon developed a strong reputation for quality products at reasonable prices, with management stating that their quality met German standards. Additionally, it provided customers with two-year maintenance warranties. The agreement was the first Russian-Taiwanese joint venture signed after the USSR joint venture law was passed in 1988, and the firm was very successful during the early years of perestroika.

In August 1990, the joint venture began assembling computers for the Russian market, with its major customers being high-level government agencies. Shortly after production began, however, a number of organizational changes occurred. Because the JV's German general director wanted the firm to sell imported computers rather than assembling them in Russia, he left the company, along with six other people. Two months later, all of them returned, but the problems had not been fully resolved. The West German partner had initially agreed that the JV should purchase production equipment from Taiwan, and JV representatives spent a month there to learn production operations at Aquarius' main facilities. However, the German partner later decided it did not want to invest in plant and equipment. The Russian partners found the necessary investment funds elsewhere, and built the plant.

For the first two years of operations, the JV bought computer components through Teb Impex, the German partner. Later, the Russian managers realized they could purchase the components themselves on the world market at a cheaper price, without incurring Teb Impex's markup. A number of differences of opinion arose, including the Russian partners' claim that Teb Impex had failed to live up to its obligations as a JV partner. As an example of this negligence, the Russian partner pointed to Teb Impex's failure to obtain office space in Moscow for the JV. As a result of such disagreements, the Russian partners bought the Germans' JV share in late 1992, and became an independent company. In October of that year, the new firm was registered as an open stock company called Aquarius Systems Interface. Contacts with Aquarius in Taiwan became very infrequent, mainly because it had been bought by another large Taiwanese company that brought in new management. As a result, the Russian firm's reliance on Taiwanese components declined sharply as its own plant increased production of parts.

THE COMPUTER INDUSTRY IN THE EARLY 1990S

In the early 1990s, the computer business was not profitable for private firms in Russia due to a number of factors. A major obstacle was larger state-owned enterprises monopolizing the market by selling computers at lower prices to gain market share. Also, the government imposed a 200-percent import tax on computer components, making domestic assembly prohibitively expensive. As a result, firms that had been highly successful, including Dialog and Interquadra, stopped production. According to Aquarius CEO Igor Galkin, the State Committee for Computer Technology and other ministries, such as the one for the Radio Electronics Industry, invited only Aquarius to submit bids for business.

By 1993, industry conditions began to improve with a reduction of the import tax on components from 200 percent to ten percent. A new wave of Russian computer firms appeared on the scene but most focused on sales and service. No major competitors emerged for Aquarius in production and assembly operations. To demonstrate the superiority of its products, the company organized a number of public relations activities. For instance, in mid-1993 they hosted a trade show in their plant where representatives of 30 competitor firms displayed their products. Potential customers at the event were invited to evaluate and rank the computers of all the exhibiting manufacturers.

NEW STRATEGIES AND SYSTEMS IN 1993 AFTER HEAVY LOSSES

Product and Pricing Strategy

Aquarius' objective during the early 1990s was to produce and sell high quality computers. Although Mr. Galkin recognized that price was an important factor in customer decisions, he noted that it had become less crucial by early 1992. Competitors' products imported from Asia could be purchased for 20 to 30 percent less than Aquarius' models, but were of lower quality. Western models with quality comparable to Aquarius' products were priced lower. A large portion of Aquarius' costs came from heavy plant operating expenses, including relatively good wages to the 120 plant workers. Management contrasted their situation with that of Russian competitors who assembled computers "on the desk." Without heavy plant expenses, they could afford to sell at a lower price. In the face of such competition, coupled with burdensome government policies, Aquarius encountered serious financial problems. The firm lost 20 million rubles in 1992 after government price liberalization caused runaway inflation. Mr. Galkin noted that "on the darkest day" in the summer of 1992, the dollar-ruble exchange rate jumped 50 percent. In response, Aquarius was one of the first in the industry to initiate a dollar pricing system, and other firms followed their lead.

Regarding their relations with the government, Mr. Galkin explained: "The government made a lot of promises but, while it did not provide any support for us, it did not interfere either." He acknowledged that "former enemies from ministries such as the Radio Technical Ministry are now friends," and some ministry officials who had formed technical consulting firms actively sought Aquarius' expertise to help them with technical issues.

In early 1993 Aquarius changed its sales strategy and began creating a dealership network throughout the country. The first phase of this expansion included supplying computers to a government organization. Management, however, soon decided to stop relying on the government ministry market, especially since many ministries were being disbanded following the break-up of the Soviet Union in 1991. Aquarius management also realized that few large enterprises were in a position to buy computers in large quantities. On the positive side, the new dealership system was effective in reaching new commercial customers, and Mr. Galkin believed that Aquarius had the best domestic dealer network in the industry.

A major reason for the company's success was that it sold products on consignment, in contrast to competitors who required immediate payment from customers. Although selling on consignment was risky, Aquarius had sold several hundred computers throughout Russia on this basis, charging a slightly higher price for that payment option. Customers were typically smaller enterprises, including banks. While government agencies were interested in buying equipment, their budgets were often not adequate. And although state orders had declined markedly, Aquarius had begun reviving its old contacts with the government network. The company, for instance, was negotiating with the State Statistical Agency for an order, and had retained the State Committee for Computer Technology as a consultant. The vast majority of Aquarius' products were sold in the Russian market, with 10 to 15 percent exported to other CIS countries such as Ukraine and Uzbekistan.

Aquarius managers said that they were not afraid of selling on credit, and since long-term credit was not available to them, they took short-term credit and "moved it around" like a revolving credit system. Their highly entrepreneurial approach was evident in activities such as providing newly renovated office space in their building to the bank that financed the renovations.

Opportunistic Business Strategy and a New Organization

Although a number of Aquarius executives considered computers to be their main business, this activity generated only a percentage of the company's $50 million annual revenues. This was the result of Aquarius having diversified into numerous other businesses that appeared to have good profit potential. Mr. Galkin described the opportunistic approach to growth as a "mushroom strategy," which many saw as being similar to that of the Korean chaebols. Most such opportunities arose as Aquarius gained experience in its growing computer business, created new management systems, and acquired physical facilities to operate in the emerging market economy. These new business activities also helped Aquarius survive cash-flow problems arising from late receivables collections in its computer business. Although most customers paid for computers within a few weeks, others took as long as a year.

In mid-1993, Aquarius began organizing as a joint stock company that would be involved in eight highly diverse businesses. The first was the original computer production and sales activity already in operation. The second undertaking, a financial services business, provided cash-flow management services to assist enterprises in their efforts to obtain bank financing. This business was started in early 1993 when Aquarius helped the giant enterprise AZLK, producer of the Moskvich car, obtain two billion rubles from banks within three weeks. A loan agreement of this sort normally took one year. Plans for the financial services business included creating a bank inside the company. Management recognized the potential benefits of Aquarius having its own internal bank since the company held shares in several other banks, and managers were aware of the various ways that banking services could help Aquarius' financial position.

Legal services, a third new business, had developed from the expertise that Aquarius' lawyers had acquired in solving the company's various legal issues which arose as a result of the new transitional economy. Five lawyers who were working on privatization issues to support Aquarius' operations had begun to sell such services to other firms as well. Typical assignments involved preparing legal documents for customs, real estate, and share auctions, as well as guiding clients through bureaucratic channels. This new business, however, had limited prospects for expansion due to the scarcity of specialists in various legal issues.

A fourth business involved providing information systems to customers involved with import-export operations. The company, for instance, had signed an agreement with the Kalmyk autonomous republic to create an information system to support trade with other regions. A fifth business, production of window frames for buildings, was an offshoot of the company's experience with a Hungarian firm that supplied frames for Aquarius' own office renovations. Aquarius planned to open a new factory in summer 1993 using French equipment and Austrian technology. Customers for the products included the City of Moscow and various foreign firms. Plans were also underway to open another plant in summer 1993 to manufacture heaters for homes, which involved a new technology and components supplied by the AZLK auto manufacturer. Mr. Galkin stated that this sixth business activity already had orders for 10,000 heaters.

Computer monitor assembly, a seventh business, was to be started with a South Korean supplier of components and a Kalmyk firm as partners. Also targeted for a summer 1993 launching, this new business involved assembling computer monitors in a vacant factory in the Kalmyk region, and selling them along with Aquarius' computers. For tax purposes, Aquarius was designated as the customer for the monitors since this arrangement avoided the VAT (value added tax) that would be imposed if Aquarius were to receive parts and materials rather than assembled monitors. The Kalmyk firm was to benefit from the relationship by having the monitors sold through Aquarius' distribution network.

Aquarius' management foresaw large-scale real estate development and construction management projects as a potential eighth business. This idea originated when Aquarius had buildings constructed for their own use. Their construction crews had worked alongside Finnish workers, and learned valuable construction methods that were in demand throughout Moscow. Aquarius envisioned building a 40-story luxury office building on Moscow's prestigious Kutuzovsky Prospekt that would be leased to various clients. They were negotiating with an American firm that would manage the property once it was built. There was also the possibility that the Americans might become joint owners if they decided to invest in the project. Aquarius was also seeking partners for an international customs service center on the Minsk highway that would include a hotel and gas station complex. Partners were also being sought for a project to build 50 cottages and resort facilities located on ten hectares on the outskirts of Moscow.

Aquarius was expected to become a stock company in July 1993. Executives realized that the importance of the computer business to the overall organization had been overlooked during the company's diversification into other businesses. They decided that computer services would be thoroughly integrated into the new organization. To gain tax advantages, a central accounting system was to be created to consolidate all the businesses in one set of financial statements. Each business would be allocated its budget from the central administration based on performance, and each would function as a profit center. Mr. Galkin noted that transfer prices across businesses would be an important factor in determining each unit's profits. However, business units could sell to customers outside the company at higher prices to generate additional profits, and distribute the excess to employees as they deemed appropriate.

Top Management Team

Top management consisted of a diverse group of talented and experienced people who enjoyed working together as a team. Mr. Gassian, the former CEO who left the company for a period of time to enter politics, was a lawyer by training and had experience in three joint ventures. A highly intuitive individual, he generated many of the initial ideas for the company. Mr. Galkin, the head of the computer business, had a more conservative nature, and thus the managers were good complements to one another. Other members of the original team were the head of sales, and the deputy of commercial operations for the non-computer businesses. The controller was well qualified, with a degree from the economics department of the Oil Institute, and possessed excellent experience in finance with a large semi-privatized firm. She developed many creative ways of financing the company's growth, and her effective personal communication style and wide range of contacts were valuable assets. She had been in the position for two years, having replaced the previous controller whose style was considered too rigid by Aquarius executives. The top management team reviewed company operations and established continuous communication through weekly meetings attended by the heads of all the company's divisions.

Progressive Human Resources Policies and Reward Systems

Recognizing the importance of a talented and committed work force to the company's success, Aquarius' top management developed a number of progressive human resources policies to attract, motivate, and reward employees. Management viewed the company as a family, and held frequent company meetings and social events to promote an atmosphere of participation and inclusion. They also invested in employee development, and sent a number of key people abroad for training, including the chief accountant who studied in Germany, and computer specialists who trained in the Netherlands. Benefits paid by the company included daily lunches, health care services at one of the best hospitals and clinics in Moscow, vacations at company-sponsored facilities, tuition at nursery schools and private high schools, trips abroad, and gifts of consumer goods. The company had once owned an import store, but later sold it. It also had a fleet of 30 cars that were used as a taxi service. Senior managers had access to the vehicles for official business as well as for personal use on weekends. Employees were eligible for benefits upon being hired, without a waiting period.

In another gesture demonstrating sensitivity to employees' needs, management remedied the erosion of salaries created by hyperinflation. During the first six months of 1993, salaries were recorded in dollars in the company's accounting system, and converted to rubles at the rate prevailing for the previous month. This procedure provided employees with reasonably stable salaries during a period when monthly inflation reached exorbitant levels.

A new compensation plan was being discussed in 1993 to give management greater flexibility in rewarding performance. Initially, executives considered making employees' salaries entirely variable, with pay awarded according to performance, but they quickly realized that this arrangement would create problems. Because Aquarius was a high tech company, it needed people to pull together, which would be unrealistic if employees were paid under a totally individually-based reward system. Instead, only sales personnel were compensated entirely by commission, while all others received a salary. However, the system being considered in mid-1993 for non-sales employees called for 80 percent of compensation to be fixed at the beginning of each monthly pay period, with the remaining potential 20 percent being dependent upon performance. Department managers would determine the variable payments for their staff members by evaluating their performance. While department managers would have full responsibility and accountability for their unit's activities, top management would keep close control over the compensation system for the entire company. Monthly sales volume was the main criterion for determining the bonus pool.

Mr. Galkin emphasized that competent people were crucial to the company's growth, and that new businesses were created only if qualified people could be found to run them. "It's hard to find good leaders," he noted. Turnover, on the other hand, was not a major problem: "We try to keep people working here, and not going elsewhere." Most employees worked exclusively for Aquarius, although some also worked in other companies, a common practice at the time. Some of them, Mr. Galkin acknowledged, were hoping to start their own businesses after gaining valuable experience and contacts at Aquarius.

Successful in 1993, But Seeking Greater Profits

Igor Galkin summed up the company's situation in mid-1993: "We consider ourselves successful, but are not satisfied with our profit levels." He referred to the successful diversifications in the company's business, as well as their success in holding on to valuable technical personnel. The company's products were well regarded, and sales were increasing, especially for Aquarius computers. With regard to the business environment, Mr. Galkin cited a number of major obstacles that interfered with the company's growth objectives. One was the unstable laws that made it difficult to plan for changing business conditions. Frequently changing customs regulations made it difficult to project costs, while a lack of laws to support entrepreneurs afforded few advantages to private firms. Finally, frequent and often drastic fluctuations in the ruble-dollar exchange rate created serious financial and banking problems.

RESTRUCTURED HOLDING COMPANY AND PORTFOLIO STRATEGY IN 1994

By early 1994, Aquarius Systems Integral had been restructured to a holding company and renamed Aquarius Systems Interface. The computer unit was renamed Aquarius Systems Inform. The new organization oversaw the activities of ten daughter firms including the original computer business. The objective of the restructuring was to allocate finances among the businesses, some of which were already profitable, while others in earlier stages showed potential. With the businesses in the portfolio having a range of short- and long-term payoff periods, each unit operated as a self-sustaining legal entity, and company executives recognized that each business needed its own distinct management style. All fixed assets remained under the control of the mother company or holding company. Although none of the daughter companies was to receive funds from the holding company after the restructuring, the holding company assisted them in obtaining bank credit, arranged financing for all ten companies, and paid taxes as one corporation.

Some of the businesses had grown during the year, while others had diminished. For instance, the construction company had created joint ventures with two American companies, McHugh, and McCann Construction, to sell construction materials. Additionally, a new firm had been organized to plan a five-year project to build a facility for the Moscow Stock Exchange. The same business unit also constructed a new hotel as the first phase of a customs facilities project. Other changes had occurred in the legal services and transport businesses, with both having been absorbed into the corporate administration of the holding company. Aquarius management had abandoned plans to create their own bank, realizing that it would be an extremely long and complicated process. Instead, they relied on two independent banks that they had helped other companies to organize. Aquarius was not a founder and had no financial interest in these banks. Yet, the advice and personnel they provided gave Aquarius considerable influence in the banks' activities. A possibility was that branches might be created inside the Aquarius organization.

Computer Business Under the New Holding Company Structure

Igor Galkin became the head of the restructured Aquarius Systems Inform, the computer production business that was 51-percent owned by the holding company. He was responsible for all aspects of the business including sourcing, production, sales, and financing. He pointed to the company's success in reducing inventory by 50 percent, from three months to six weeks, which produced a significant improvement in working capital management. Mr. Galkin emphasized that the main goal of Aquarius Systems Inform was to increase sales. He complained, however, that a major obstacle to achieving this objective was that "the holding company takes too much money from us as corporate taxes." The computer company was still an important business after the restructuring, and employed 100 of the holding company's 300 employees.

Building Government Relations

Aquarius and other computer companies had become actively engaged in lobbying the government to support the industry. Aquarius was the top firm in computer production, while Stipler, which was mainly a distributor, was the leader in sales. The ten largest domestic computer producers had formed an association to build relationships with the government, primarily through the State Committee for Information Technology. Aquarius had signed an agreement with a competitor, EVK, located in the high tech center, Zelenogorod, outside Moscow, to sell computers to government agencies. The companies viewed this alliance as a defensive measure, since both faced stiff competition from imports such as Dell and Compaq. These computers were often preferred by government officials for their prestigious image. Aquarius management claimed that their computers were of the same quality, but were lower-priced.

Pricing for Inflation and Setting a Customer Credit Policy

A major problem in late 1994 was the rampant inflation that continued to erode the value of the ruble and seriously threaten profits for companies like Aquarius. Because of a new government ruling that prohibited product price lists quoted in dollars, Aquarius had to abandon that practice. Instead, the company set ruble prices at the dollar equivalent, with a two-percent surcharge to cover currency conversion costs. Top management also developed a three-step credit policy to protect itself from the devastating effects of inflation-ridden accounts receivable. First-time customers were required to pay on delivery, second-time customers were required to pay a deposit, and only those who had passed these stages were permitted to buy fully on account. Credit limits were established for customers, and terms varied by the quantity of computers ordered. Although fines were imposed for late payments, numerous customers paid the penalties, and then ordered more products. Mr. Galkin noted that they had developed this credit policy themselves, and that other firms were adopting it as well. Although Aquarius had lost some money with this approach, he concluded that it was very effective overall.

Cash Registers and Home Computers as Potential New Products

Aquarius' management was considering adding new products that would use many of the same components contained in its existing line of computers. Management planned to begin assembly of cash registers in late summer 1994, and was also negotiating with foreign firms to assemble other computer-related products in their plant outside Moscow. Another niche that Aquarius was hoping to develop was home computers. Company leaders recognized that price was an important factor in that segment, but if the product could be offered at a relatively low price, a great potential market existed. Currently, this segment was undeveloped. To help stimulate the market, Aquarius executives had been holding discussions with government officials in hopes that a government-supported program would be created to help consumers purchase home computers on credit, payable over a three-year period. In 1994, a home computer cost about $500. Aquarius management proposed that consumers be allowed to obtain low-interest bank loans, with Aquarius receiving payment directly from participating banks. The company also needed to raise funds to set up production facilities for home computers, and hoped to create a consortium of computer manufacturers to develop and produce the products.

Igor Galkin's Management Style

During 1994, Igor Galkin, who had headed the entire firm during the former CEO's absence, again became head of the computer company when the former CEO returned to the new holding company. He had left Aquarius to serve as deputy prime minister of Kamatia in the Caucasus. Mr. Galkin, however, still remained very involved in the holding company because of his experience and good relations. He also believed he was able to "make tougher decisions and manage more strongly than others." In his new position, Mr. Galkin found he had even less free time than before, frequently working 14-hour days, and often seven days a week. Despite a grueling work schedule and heavy decision-making pressures, Mr. Galkin was very optimistic about the future of Aquarius.

AN INDEPENDENT COMPUTER COMPANY IN 1995

Top Management Changes in the Holding Company

Substantial management changes took place in 1995. The holding company's CEO and chairman of the board, who had returned in 1994, was replaced by a younger executive from the company's financial area. Seeking short-term profits, the new CEO sold the computer plant and moved the corporate offices to less expensive quarters in the Oktiabrskii region in the northern part of Moscow. The holding company continued its involvement in construction projects, window production, and most of its other activities. At the same time, the computer firm was experiencing difficulties. It had begun producing cash registers, but found few customers for them in the early stages. Also, Aquarius no longer produced computers since its factory had been sold. It had become a dealer for Hewlett-Packard, selling and servicing HP computers. The consortium that had been established to develop home computers was not successful, largely because the companies did not develop an appropriate strategy, and the market segment was undeveloped.

Buying the Computer Business

When the holding company was formed, the computer operation was registered as one of the daughter companies. Mr. Galkin explained that the holding company did not pay enough attention to the computer business, except to utilize the funds it generated. In response, he and some associates decided to buy out the business. Unable to obtain bank loans, they acquired funding from personal contacts who stipulated that the money be used to reactivate the computer business. By mid-1995, the debts were paid off, and

Aquarius Systems Inform became a solvent, independent company. Soon afterwards, the company began to finance its operations by attracting capital from several banks, as well as from an American investment fund.

In September 1995, the computer company signed an agreement to purchase 100 percent of the shares of the Shuya computer factory, and by the fall of 1996, had paid off the debt incurred in this transaction. The purchase was made possible by the company's success in diversifying into cash register production. Mr. Galkin explained: "This new type of product gave us the opportunity to survive and keep the factory going. Although we put cash registers in second place after computers, today they bring in more profit than computers, and they helped us pay off our debts."

Aquarius' decision to become an independent company was timely, since shortly afterwards the holding company went bankrupt and all its businesses were sold. Like the computer company, the unit producing windows also got out at a good time, and continued operations as an independent firm. Mr. Galkin believed that the holding company had failed as a result of its over-diversification, a mismanagement of its "mushroom strategy." He elaborated: "Also, the principle of one-person centralized management was maintained, and it is difficult for a single individual to manage a diverse business. It's not possible to be a professional in all spheres of activity." He explained that this over-diversification, as well as the financial policies of the holding company, had a very negative effect on the computer business:

> To start businesses in diverse sectors requires monetary investments. But at the time, only the computer business was making money. Consequently, the top management simply took money from us. But it was not possible to develop the computer business without money. That is one of the reasons we wanted to become independent. In no case should money be taken from an operation that is alive.

FORGING AHEAD IN 1996: COMPUTERS, CASH REGISTERS, AND SOFTWARE SYSTEMS

With the repurchase of its computer plant, Aquarius resumed assembly of computers, and expanded its product line by 1996 to serve the needs of several market segments. The company produced two lines of computers, Aquarius Standard and Aquarius Professional, to sell in different market niches. Aquarius Standard was considered to be equivalent to the company's earlier model, while Aquarius Professional was viewed as a high-level Pentium-equivalent model that was sold to government organizations. Competitive products for Aquarius Standard were Russian-assembled computers including those produced in Zelenogorod. In explaining the company's positioning of this product, Mr. Galkin noted: "Price has major significance, and we give a two-year maintenance guarantee. But by technical characteristics, this isn't a great computer, it's standard." In contrast, he explained, the Aquarius Professional line was positioned to compete with Western products. This model contained components sourced from the US, Germany, and Taiwan, and was certified for use in educational settings that had stricter radiation emission and eyestrain standards. Aquarius wanted to produce its own computer components, but realized it was not price-competitive to do so because of taxes on production.

In deciding what types of activities to pursue as a newly independent company, Mr. Galkin stated:

> We had a lot of discussions about what was missing in Aquarius. We didn't have a marketing service. We had a pretty good idea what it was but, as we say, we know everything but we don't do it. That, unfortunately, is our weakness.

Nonetheless, Aquarius soon became involved in producing cash registers when the government mandated that such equipment be installed in all retail establishments. The technology was similar to the computers Aquarius had been producing, and with a Bulgarian partner supplying components, Aquarius launched itself into the cash register business alongside the computer operation. The company had also begun exploring the possibility of producing some cash register components, which were taxed less heavily than computer parts.

Another business venture was launched when Aquarius management realized the potential for designing and selling complex systems that linked cash registers with computers utilizing customized software. They believed the company had strong potential to become a leader in the emerging systems integration market niche for retail establishments where no serious competition yet existed. Company leaders saw product strategy as encompassing three lines of business: computers, cash registers, and software systems. Mr. Galkin outlined the company's strategic direction: "Certain priorities will be made so that, in the near future, sales of new systems will move from third to second place, and some time after that, to first place."

Management planned to focus on relatively inexpensive integrated systems for small retail establishments. Unlike the sophisticated point-of-sale computerized cash registers used by many large stores that cost as much as $7,000 each, Aquarius offered a far cheaper solution. For $2,000, they provided a system in which up to eight far less expensive cash registers could be used as terminals, and be connected to one computer that performed information processing functions, including reading product bar codes. Thus, Aquarius' $2,000 price for the software system allowed retailers to install a much more affordable configuration than eight stand-alone computerized cash registers costing approximately $50,000.

Aquarius executives envisioned many applications for their integrated system. Mr. Galkin noted that it offered numerous advantages to customers. Because the system recorded and monitored transactions instantly, owners could easily detect pilferage by comparing electronically recorded sales with those reported by store employees. After using the new system for one week, the owner of a chain of stores fired all the store managers, realizing that they had been cheating him. In another application, Aquarius had received an order from a chain of gas stations to automate gas pumps as recently mandated by the government. The contract involved modernizing mechanical pumps and connecting them to cash registers and computer systems, as well as installing the system on new electronic gas pumps. Mr. Galkin noted: "With the help of our system, we can solve the problem of optimizing inventory, be it fuel or goods in a store's warehouse."

Another promising contract for the integrated computer and cash register system was the fast food industry. Management was discussing the possibility of a contract with McDonald's to service the Western-made computerized cash registers in their restaurants. Mr. Galkin hoped that McDonald's would accept Aquarius parts for their repairs. The company was also negotiating with one of McDonald's new domestic competitors, Russkii Bistro, to install its system in the 800 cafes expected to open in Moscow by the end of 1997. Russkii Bistro managers preferred the system used by McDonald's, but could not afford the nearly $8,000 per unit cost. The Moscow city government, which owned the controlling shares in Russkii Bistro, would not fund that amount from its budget. Mr. Galkin explained:

> Officials from the city have looked at our system, and seen that it is a lot cheaper, yet does the same thing. And since this will all be done on the city government's budget, the Moscow government wants to collaborate with us. But the storeowners and managers want everything to be like McDonald's, so signatures on the agreement are being held up.

Surviving as an Independent Company

In late 1996, Mr. Galkin explained that Aquarius was evolving from the survival stage to the profit stage of development, and noted that management had to improvise several ways to stabilize the company. For instance, when Aquarius had become independent, it had no money to pay rent at the expensive corporate offices. Instead, executives decided to renovate the cafeteria of one of their other buildings, and the entire corporate staff occupied the cramped 150-square-meter space for a year. In late 1996, when business improved, they moved to an 800-square-meter office in northern Moscow. Mr. Galkin mused:

> That means that the business is developing and we are able to do some things, but this is nothing like the beautiful offices we had on prestigious Kutuzovsky Prospekt. Maybe in a year we'll be able to do better.

Another step that the company took to stay in business, following the lead of many other companies, was to develop expertise in transactions involving government securities or promissory notes called "veksels." The financial director was sent for training on how the securities market operated. Management saw an opportunity to increase sales to government agencies if Aquarius would accept government securities rather than cash as payment. Mr. Galkin added:

> But we will have to do something with these government securities rather quickly to transform them into money, and most importantly, without any losses. This is a completely new type of work for us, and it is not related to the computer business. But the circumstances are forcing us to get involved in it.

Aquarius also took a creative approach to advertising and finding potential customers by using public relations opportunities and becoming involved in industry associations. Mr. Galkin noted:

> When we became independent, we didn't have any money and couldn't advertise, so we took a different route and started to use public relations, which cost considerably less than advertising. We had articles written about us, appeared on TV, and held press conferences. In publications we pursued one goal—to establish a good name in the computer market. But at the same time we were publicizing our new cash register business.

Seeing a need to establish links with government agencies for new business, Mr. Galkin disclosed that company managers "revived old personal contacts there and started to create new ones." Aquarius executives were among the founders of the Russian Computer Association and the Moscow Information Technology Club, and they also became members of the International Congress of Industrialists and Entrepreneurs. Such associations had already provided promising business opportunities, with the Russkii Bistro negotiations being the direct result of Aquarius' membership in the Moscow Information Technology Club. The club's president, in fact, was also the director of information management in the Moscow city government, and as Mr. Galkin explained: "With the help of this club and directly with the help of the president, we have a potential customer."

191

Human Resources, Culture, and Management Style – "A Union of Aquarius Veterans"

As an independent company at the end of 1996, Aquarius employed approximately 30 people in its Moscow offices and 50 in the computer factory. Plans called for hiring more staff to develop the systems product for the retail sector. CEO Galkin credited a small core of loyal staff members for helping him through the difficult transition of moving the firm from its holding company status to independent operations:

> Essentially, the skeleton of the firm remained and was transferred into the independent business. Times were very tough at the beginning, but people believed in me. If I alone were to have counted on turning this idea into a reality, it wouldn't have turned out because I had only a general idea of what to do with the company.

Mr. Galkin added that several valuable employees who had left during the early 1990s returned to the newly independent Aquarius. The former manager of the programming department in the original company returned as executive director of Aquarius, after working at Lotus and IBM in the West. Mr. Galkin valued such expertise, and was having discussions with several other former employees who were also considering returning:

> I in no way judge those people who at one point left us and are now coming back. And there is a trend for them to come back to Aquarius. We try to support talented specialists. The executive director is a good example of this. Having received a larger salary at IBM than what he gets here, he nevertheless returned because the spirit of Aquarius has important meaning for him.

Mr. Galkin noted that the same good relationships existed with a number of other former employees who had left to work in large computer firms. He spoke fondly of them:

> We consider them our people there, and a number of commercial projects that we have in those companies are with our former colleagues. All of them have maintained good relations with Aquarius. We even want to create a "Union of Aquarius veterans."

As 1996 was ending, Galkin had high praise for his staff, but he wanted to encourage more initiative, creativity, and responsibility among some employees:

> We are trying to introduce delegation of authority. People must have their rights, but they must accept their responsibility as well. There is a category of employees who are good implementers but who wait for assignments. We would like all managers in all divisions to come up with their own ideas, even

stupid ones, because even in stupid ideas you can often find something worthwhile.

DISTRIBUTION, QUALITY, AND SERVICE IN 1997 AND 1998

Distribution Agreements and ISO 9002 Certification

In 1997, Aquarius continued to enhance its products and services, seeking primarily to improve distribution. The company established a relationship with one of the country's strongest distributors, OCS, which distributed Western-made computers as well as its own. Aquarius also became listed as an official supplier for many government ministries of the Russian Federation including the office of the President, the ministry of defense, the ministry of internal affairs, the federal customs service, the federal security service, the state tax inspection service, the Central Bank, and the Federal Social Insurance Fund. Its products were also used in large commercial organizations and banks including Inkombank and the United Industrial Bank. Its high-end PC was sold with a three-year warranty and promoted as being of top quality and compatible with government environmental and ergonomic standards. By the end of 1997, the company provided service through more than 100 technical service centers in 50 regions of the Russian Federation.

With more than 50,000 machines in use, the computerized cash register system, Aquarius KKM, gained increasing popularity as the company developed new models during this period. The products could be used as stand-alone units or integrated into a system which recorded and transmitted to a central processing facility the transactions of all units in a retail business. Parts and subsystems produced by Aquarius were certified under the Russian Federation's certification system. An increasing number of these parts were provided by other Russian factories, although most were produced at the company's Shuya plant which had an annual capacity of 120,000 electronic components.

In 1998, Aquarius became the first Russian computer company to be certified as being in compliance with ISO 9002, the highest international quality standard. The company was also testing its PCs and cash register systems for compatibility with Windows 95, OS/2, Warp 4.0, and Novell systems. Up to this time, Aquarius had distributed its products primarily in the commercial market. In 1998, it established a strategic alliance which made its products available to small businesses and consumers. An agreement was reached with Multimedia Delo and its subsidiary, Landata, which had a successful retail network through which Aquarius computers would be distributed. Aquarius President, Igor Galkin, spoke enthusiastically of the alliance:

> The strategic partnership with Landata is moving to a new stage. We are now not only in project businesses together, but also in retail trade. The union of two strong partners expands opportunities for both of them in the Russian computer market.

Another milestone reached early in the year was the signing of a much broader contract with the Russian distributor, OCS. It was the first such distribution agreement entered into by OCS for computers assembled in Russia. That company had traditionally assembled its own computers from Russian-made parts, and distributed Western-made computers. Aquarius offered special terms and favorable pricing to the OCS network in recognition of the large volume of orders. Some dealers sold computers with their own trademarks, and Aquarius saw this as an opportunity to sell or license its technology to these companies for use in their own branded computers.

Major Networking Project for a Government Agency

Aquarius' reputation continued to develop during this period. In early 1998, with support from Landata, Aquarius acted as general contractor in establishing a computer network for the central administration of the Social Insurance Fund of the Russian Federation. The network utilized equipment of the Canadian company, Newbridge Networks Corporation, and the project involved coordination by Aquarius of more than 80 computer companies throughout most regions of Russia. At its conclusion, the project would utilize 3,000 Aquarius computers. Initial work took place at the fund's 30 branches in the Moscow region for which Aquarius developed the solution that was later implemented nationwide. OCS was also involved as the distributor of peripherals and networking equipment, and worked in various regions with many of its own partners who performed the actual implementation. This complex project brought Aquarius to a new level of competence and recognition. Management explained that it was the first time in Russia that a centralized computer technology project had been completed for a federal government ministry. The project's success brought a great deal of attention to Aquarius, and aroused interest among a number of other government organizations with a similar regional structure.

Divisional Structure Created

With the increasing complexity of its business, Aquarius Systems Inform, ASI, developed a divisional structure in which ASI was the managing firm for three operating daughter companies – Aquarius Data, Aquarius Register, and Aquarius Shuya Factory. ASI was responsible for marketing, finance, R&D, quality systems, and production planning, as well as setting the strategic direction for the operating units. Corporate management was also responsible for formulating the overall strategy of the Aquarius group, as well as ensuring implementation. Aquarius Data was responsible for computer network projects such as the one involving the Russian Social Insurance Fund, as well as development and enhancement of PC products. It also was responsible for the overall management of production, distribution, and servicing of PCs. Aquarius Register was a separate production and distribution company which developed, sold, installed, and serviced cash registers and systems linking point-of-sale devices to central processing units. The Aquarius Shuya Factory produced parts and assembled the company's line of cash registers and computers.

BUSINESS OPPORTUNITIES IN POST-CRISIS 1998

Although the country's financial crisis put additional pressure on Aquarius, it also provided opportunities. Western firms became less involved in Russia's computer business, and domestic companies were increasingly careful with spending. As a result, Russian suppliers began to receive increasing attention. Aquarius, with its well-priced, high quality line of computers and cash registers, was able to meet the needs of these commercial customers as well as those in government. The financial crisis was also instrumental in the development of the company's relationship with the distributor, OCS. Previously that company had sourced parts and components from many locations, but it proved to be uneconomical to coordinate this dispersed supplier network after the crisis. Thus, they turned to Aquarius as a cost-effective source of assembled computers. The firm appeared to be weathering the crisis better than most other production companies, and Mr. Galkin was guardedly optimistic about the company's future.

11. Platinum Russia

FOUNDED BY A WESTERN-EDUCATED RUSSIAN WOMAN

Platinum Russia Ltd. was founded in 1994 as the exclusive distributor of accounting and manufacturing software products in the countries of the former USSR for the American company, Platinum Software Corporation. The firm was started in Moscow by Olga Peterson, a young Russian woman who had returned to her native country in 1989 after studying and working for 10 years in the United States. Before founding her company, Dr. Peterson worked for several years in Moscow in software systems development and consulting at Deloitte & Touche, as well as at Ernst & Young where she had been director of an information technology group. Her objective for her own company was to participate in Russia's growing accounting software and systems field. She and her American husband, David, were the sole owners of Platinum Russia, which quickly became a successful operation. The firm, in fact, contributed five percent of Platinum Software Corporation's total sales revenues within its first year. The company developed, customized, and sold Platinum software to Western and Russian companies including Mercedes-Benz, Polaroid Corporation, and Soyuzcontract.

At age 18, speaking little English, Olga Peterson left Russia for the United States with her parents. It took her little time to learn the language, and she acquired an industrial engineering degree at Northwestern University. This accomplishment was followed by an MBA at the University of Chicago and a Ph.D. at Moscow State University several years later. She gained valuable work experience in industrial engineering and strategic marketing while employed for five years at Motorola Corporation. These experiences were followed by a position as a management consultant at one of the Big Eight US accounting firms. Dr. Peterson's description of her experience upon leaving Motorola provides some insight into her drive and ambition. The international division's vice-president reportedly asked her: "We paid for your degree, and we're trying to promote minorities. So why are you leaving?" In response, she quoted one of her University of Chicago professors: "The University of

Chicago gives grads smarts, not loyalty." In describing herself, Dr. Peterson stated:

> I'm very goal-oriented, to the point of obsession. My father says that I am more like a train because I don't see anything outside, just my goal.

All of Olga's employees were Russian, except for her American husband and partner, David. She claimed to have the brightest people as employees, with many having Russian Ph.Ds. At the time of the company's founding, management's average age was 30, and in their prior careers some had been high-ranking communist party members, physicists, theoreticians, or linguists. Her deputy, Viktor, age 50, had been a doctoral student under the Nobel laureate physicist, Andrei Sakharov. Dr. Peterson felt that such people could fully utilize their intellectual capacities in well-paying jobs at Platinum:

> There is no money to be made working in universities, and everybody here makes a lot of money. We find great ways to play with the high technologies and make money with them.

The technologies Dr. Peterson referred to were software development, English-Russian translation of software, systems analysis, and various computers and network systems. As a licensee and distributor, the company offered a product line similar to that of Platinum Software Corporation. The centerpiece of their offerings was a general ledger package which, like other products, could be used alone or integrated with other Platinum products to provide a complete financial information system. Platinum, like the major Western accounting firms, often had to train clients, especially Russian companies, in internationally accepted accounting methods and systems. The company was thus soon drawn into consulting on systems development as a prelude to installing its software packages.

PARTNERSHIP WITH PLATINUM SOFTWARE USA CORPORATION IN 1994

Olga Peterson signed her contract with Platinum Software Corporation in April 1994. That company was experiencing serious problems which had been ongoing since negotiations began in late 1993. Platinum USA's capitalization had plummeted dramatically from its high of $330 million, and its staff had declined from 150 to 30 as a result of a drastic reorganization. Dr. Peterson explained: "There was this crazy turmoil around the time the contract was signed, when Platinum USA went through a major upheaval." A former Platinum USA executive explained that a serious problem had been discovered in the way orders were recorded:

Senior managers, including the founder, were forced out and the staff was slashed drastically. Platinum was being sued and went through a year and a half of hell. Anyone else would have run as fast as they could in the opposite direction, but Olga said she just had to get a contract because she already had begun client work and claimed she had invested over $100,000 in her business.

Dr. Peterson's contract was signed by the newly appointed CEO, whom she said at first regretted the terms, and tried for almost a year to renegotiate. In a complete turnabout, the original five-year contract was later extended to ten in recognition of her company's excellent performance. The former Platinum USA executive later explained: "Company management saw Olga as being very successful, and critical to their goal of having a strong international organization."

Platinum Software Corporation was founded in California in 1984. It was a publicly-traded firm which developed and marketed integrated financial and information management software systems to thousands of customers worldwide, including AT&T, Barclay's Bank, General Electric, Goldman Sachs, Occidental Petroleum, and Voest Alphine. Platinum utilized a direct sales force as well as over 1,000 authorized dealers, distributors, systems integrators, and software consultants. Strategic partnerships had been formed with major hardware and software vendors such as IBM, Digital Equipment, Hewlett-Packard, Sun Microsystems, and Microsoft, as well as with large consulting firms including Arthur Andersen and PricewaterhouseCoopers.

Platinum USA executives and Dr. Peterson realized that together they could take advantage of opportunities in Russia's rapidly developing business sector by combining the American company's sophisticated product line with Olga's extensive knowledge of customers and market conditions. The company's product family consisted of over 20 modules that could be utilized independently as single-user systems or integrated with other modules on a local area network (LAN). The company concentrated on extending its product line from single users to LAN-based products targeted at small businesses, as well as to intelligent client/server company-wide software systems for international organizations.

RAPID SUCCESS IN 1995

Sales Topped $3 Million in First Year

During 1995, Platinum Russia's sales topped $3 million, comprising around five percent of Platinum Software Corporation's total sales revenues. By that time, Dr. Peterson's company had offices in Moscow and St. Petersburg, employed 66 people, and had more than 60 client firms. Among customers were the American firms Procter & Gamble, McDonald's, Motorola, Colgate-

Palmolive and Caterpillar, and a major Russian investment bank, Renaissance Capital. Virtually all of these accomplishments occurred during the company's first year of operation. In recognition of her organization's growing importance to Platinum Software Corporation, the US company's CEO visited Moscow in mid-1995. Dr. Peterson was proud of her company's achievements, but added that there were easier ways to make money:

> My deputy, Viktor, jokes that if we really want to make money, we should throw away all consultants, put some cases of vodka in here, and turn the offices into a vodka warehouse.

Localization and Translation of Software

Speaking in rapid, fluent English, Dr. Peterson described some strengths of her company: "We are similar to the major international accounting firms, but in many ways we are a lot better. We provide better value." A senior manager at Arthur Andersen stated in a published interview that Platinum's manufacturing resource planning system (MRP) was the best software system for manufacturers because it could be integrated with a company's financial system. This endorsement was seen as evidence of the value added by Platinum Russia in its high quality localization and translation of Platinum USA's software. Speaking of competitors, Dr. Peterson noted: "We don't anticipate a lot of Western competition in this market because it is expensive to support." The company, in fact, listed several major international accounting firms among its clients, and although they could be potential competitors, Olga had created cooperative alliances with some of them.

Platinum Russia's primary function was to translate and localize for the Russian market a dozen of the US company's 20 products. The main offering was a general ledger package which, like other products, could also be linked in a more complete financial system. Modules in addition to the general ledger included accounts receivable, foreign currency, payroll, and MRP systems. Dr. Peterson likened the company to an anthill of busy, hardworking employees:

> Twelve man-years of localization went into this product to modify it for the Russian market. Ten programmers support development work and localization of modules including fixed assets, payroll, and materials requirements programs, while 20 people work in language translation. Other people support program maintenance, while a consulting department looks at the product from an accountant's perspective. What task anyone is working on at a given time is hard to say. Everyone has his or her own project. Everything is tested in-house, and there are no beta sites.

The programmers did not have the casual appearance that is common to programmers in the US. At Platinum Russia, Dr. Peterson required employees to dress in a business-like fashion to set a professional tone for clients visiting the company's offices. "The office is quiet. Some people work at home, which is encouraged in an effort to reduce office overhead," she added. The company occupied 300 square meters in Moscow and another 160 in central St. Petersburg in modest but very expensive office space.

Multitalented Executive Team

Dr. Peterson provided Platinum Russia with its business direction and vision, and shared many managerial activities with her deputy, Viktor, who held the title of technical director. With a Ph.D. in astrophysics, he had been a student under the Nobel laureate Andrei Sakharov. Before joining Platinum, Viktor had spent over 20 years with an institute that developed digital signal processing hardware and software for space missions. Dr. Peterson said: "I was lucky to find Viktor. He and my husband David, who are cofounders with me, are the smartest." A former Platinum USA executive described Viktor as "the most impressive person I have ever met on an intellectual level."

Viktor, like Olga, saw the two of them as having complementary skills and roles. He described Olga as a strong personality, an extrovert, and very aggressive in a positive sense. "She likes to talk to people, and often talks to several people at the same time." A former Platinum USA executive said of Olga:

> She's so emotional, so overly emotional, that she needed some steady voices just to calm her down. That's where Viktor and David come in. Olga was constantly in tears, and said this was very Russian. She's got one foot in the American style and one foot in the Russian style.

Of her personality, Olga noted:

> I'm very aggressive. Therefore, it's sometimes better to have somebody else tell a customer he screwed up—somebody softer. That's why I have a team of people, and I become more of a background person. I do marketing, but really what I am best at is strategy. There is no question about it—strategy, general management, and organization are my strengths.

As for strategic planning, Dr. Peterson stated simply: "When I have time, I work on strategy." After a brief pause, she added: "I make time when I need it."

Viktor saw himself as more introverted, preferring to focus on one project, problem, or person at a time. His initial assignment at Platinum was to organize all the in-house jobs and to assign appropriate personnel after deciding whether the job required translators, programmers, or consultants. He described himself as having "general responsibility for all technical aspects, for the development of the company's technical strategy in Russia, and the development of methodologies for integrated accounting software."

Explaining her husband David's role, as well as those of other company employees, Dr. Peterson added:

> David is a tinkerer by disposition, not by training. He has psychological insight, which is needed to market our sophisticated products. He speaks well, and with his tinkering he has investigated technical aspects, so we ask him to explain the program to the customer. He handles customers really well. He will not go into a lot of technical detail, and gives them an overview. For more detailed information he sends them to Viktor who will take them deep. Then the customer gets an office tour, and during that time, my management style is not to speak, but let others speak. It's like a theater. Different people have different roles. The impression that we're trying to make is that it's not a one-man company; the customer gets a whole organization of very talented individuals. There are different roles for different people. A woman customer from Volgograd wants older salespeople. Victor can help such customers. Ivan, the marketing manager, is younger and looks very Western. He was a professional translator, so he handles Westerners. I greet them from a high level perspective. I just come and say hello, ask how are you, and give my level of energy and leave.

Russian clients, on the other hand, "don't expect a woman to be in charge," Dr. Peterson noted. Once, a client who met with her and Viktor shook Viktor's hand and said of Dr. Peterson, "what a pretty girl," not realizing that she was the CEO. So when new Russian clients came to Platinum, she avoided being introduced to them. If necessary, she was introduced simply as "an expert from Chicago." She preferred not to let such clients know that she was in charge, feeling that "then Platinum can't make the sale, or it takes too long." She believed that outside the US, being a woman in business was definitely a disadvantage, even though it was only one of the parameters. Still, Olga maintained that being a woman could sometimes be an advantage.

Recruiting and Managing People

Dr. Peterson initially recruited staff from universities as well as through friends and word of mouth. She also took some people with her from the Russian office of the Big Six firm when she left. As the business grew, she added more formal recruiting methods including advertisements, a relatively new approach in Russia. She explained her hiring philosophy:

> I hire people myself and really try very hard to find a spot for them. I'm looking for smart people. I'm not talking about skill, but about attitude. Like some Big Six firms, we hire talented people, train them, and let them develop skills. There are definite skills demanded, such as programming and accounting.

A former Platinum USA executive stated: "I was overwhelmed with the technical ability and quality of every single person I met. They could talk about many things, were so well educated and well rounded."

Dr. Peterson also explained how individuals at the company complemented one another:

> There is always a spot here for smart people, and when they get bored, they can move to another department. But there is also a spot for people who are not so smart. In a lot of ways I'm one of those. I'm more of an executor. When discussing which way to go with a high-end product and the technical people are talking bits and bytes, my response to them is, 'Don't confuse me. I'm getting a headache! Just decide. See which choice we as a company should take, and then tell me, because I will help you push it through.' I compensate them for that, not just in money but also in good words.

A former Platinum USA executive noted: "She didn't make it easy on her staff. She would work them to the bone, but then she'd turn around and be extraordinarily generous. She gives credit where credit is due."

Dr. Peterson said she hired some Americans whom she later had to fire. She insisted that she hated firing people, and tried never to do so, but the Americans just didn't fit in with the company. She explained the difference in cultural backgrounds:

> Americans are different because they were raised as part of a system that works for the consumer. You go to the store in the States and everything is there for you. It's too easy. The people are so much a product of their beautifully developed system that when they come to Russia, they are absolutely lost. The system is much more complex here, and because of that, this country has not advanced as much as America. There, you are a little piece of a big machine that is very beautiful. Here, you have to do so much in order to achieve the same thing. Here in Russia, just learning to survive, that's the challenge, the ultimate challenge.

Dr. Peterson said she also solved problems, but claimed to become bored with very complex problems. She said she was much better at a lot of very simple things, which were the type of problems she solved every day. For example, she came up with an idea of calling customers to ask when they were planning to pay. She explained: "Administration is a very important thing because a business is a system. If you don't collect from a customer, you have a bad system, so you'd better work on your collectibles." She no longer made such calls herself and had trained others to perform this task.

Dr. Peterson delegated significant amounts of responsibility to people whom she felt were capable of doing the job. Platinum's office in St. Petersburg, for instance, was managed by a woman in her late twenties. Dr. Peterson said of her: "Irina is incredible. She is the sharpest person, a very good manager." The dozen staff members Irina hired worked together very well and had gone to the Moscow office for training. Peterson believed that Irina probably wouldn't be as effective if she worked directly for her because Olga would overprotect her. Instead, Olga gave her autonomy, traveling often to St. Petersburg on weekends for discussions with Irina, whom she valued as a good friend as well as a business colleague. Irina explained: "Olga and I do everything together. She helps a lot in evaluating the current situation and deciding long-term goals, while I handle short-term goals. She understands the market very well and can see fluctuations from the very first moment."

To Dr. Peterson, the business was like a family:

> I think that because I'm a woman, I look at it like a mother. I just like to take care of it. To a man it might be more like sports or a competition. I think it's good to be a woman in this business because I have a different perspective.

Six percent of Platinum Russia employees were women, virtually all holding professional positions. Olga noted:

> There are more young women attending college in Russia every year. Women can't do heavy physical work with their bodies, but their minds are just as good as men's. However, they are different and they bring a different perspective.

Plans to Dominate the Mid-Range Market

Olga was responsible for the financial performance and condition of the company. She outlined a near-term goal for Platinum as well as a three-year outlook, including the possibility of giving up some ownership of the company:

> Our near-term goal is to move from $50,000 to $150,000 in implementation service revenue per customer. In terms of moving geographically, we are discussing it and we would like to see 150 sites throughout Russia. Also, we would like our products to be sold through distributors that are Russian companies. Our company is all Russian, with the exception of my husband, who also loves Russia and speaks the language fluently now. Our product is expensive, as it is sold at American prices. People here will pay such prices for it because it has more features than competitors, and is recognizable to Western financial institutions that lend at much lower rates than Russian banks.

Dr. Peterson also outlined a three-year outlook for Platinum Russia. According to her forecasts, a good scenario would see Platinum as a dominant force in mid-range accounting software in the $20,000 to $60,000 price range, with distributors throughout the former USSR. In three years, she projected it would be the number one company with sales of at least $5 million. This outcome could happen, according to Dr. Peterson, because Platinum Russia employees worked hard and had a good service orientation. There was also some discussion regarding the possibility of expanding into Eastern Europe, but Peterson said she didn't like to travel. She felt she could conceivably go to Warsaw for short stints, but her home was really in Russia.

As sole owners of the company, Olga and her husband intended to retain majority ownership. Nonetheless, they had begun looking for other investors. Peterson felt it would be prudent to give up some ownership and increase capital, but the business was hers and would stay that way, at least for the foreseeable future. As to how others would obtain part ownership, Dr. Peterson said that she and her husband were discussing the issue, and that it had to be done right. She wanted to ensure that the people instrumental in building the business would have early access to part ownership through stock options, or shares which would likely be sold first within the company. Up to that point they had been working on operational issues, but recently she and David had begun talking to investment bankers.

Dr. Peterson's Values and Management Style

Dr. Peterson expressed other feelings she had about business:

> I love business. It is what I've done all my life and I'm very good at it. I like being among my friends doing business together. I like being around people a lot smarter than me. I get a kick out of it. That my deputy was Sakharov's student makes me feel great.

When asked about her personal values, Olga remarked that she loved her work so much that she took most things in stride:

> I work here because I like it. I don't need to work, I have enough money to retire, but what am I going to do with all this energy?

She recalled that when she was fired from her second job at a Big Six firm in Moscow, she went back to school for a Ph.D. in management at Moscow State University. She tried teaching for a while, but discovered that university life was not for her: "It's very complex and you have to concentrate. I like to teach, but not in a class. What I like is feedback, so I need to ask questions because that aids my professional growth."

She described the situation at Platinum as being almost perfect for her:

> I like my job, and I like being a manager. I don't necessarily like being an owner in a lot of ways, because in Russia right now that is like running around the streets with a big diamond ring. I really don't like having things, and I actually live quite poorly. I like making money, but I don't like spending it, almost to the extent of it being a sickness. But a person should be centered on good values rather than being attached to their car. My three-room apartment is okay for Russia, but by American standards, you would be shocked.

Olga explained the personal connection she had with the company:

It is just a project which I'd like to tie up and package like a present so that it's all done, like my Ph.D. So the company should not be an end in itself. When I think about my life, it's just another successful aspect of it. Sometimes I think how I'd like to sell the company and become financially independent—but I already am. If I did sell, I would stay as a manager if other owners came on board. I'd still like to have a job with this company. I'd like it to be a lot bigger than me and to go public one day. I'd like it to be another Microsoft.

Olga applied her approach to business to her personal life as well. She explained: "My whole life is projects. Even my baby is a lifelong project who has to be well managed." Olga stated she wanted her child to get an exceptional education, learn several languages, go to music school, and visit places like the Hermitage Museum in St. Petersburg. "In other words, I want her to have everything I had as a child and more," she concluded.

Speaking of herself, Olga emphasized that she loved Russia and speaking Russian, and often traveled to St. Petersburg where she kept an apartment overlooking the Palace Square and the Admiralty. When asked how she could enjoy living in such an unstructured country while her life was highly structured, she quickly clarified:

You are talking about life and I am talking about me. I am projects, I am structure. I am the leader. I take the unstructured environment and make it into structure. This is why I add value. There was nothing here before, and now Platinum Russia is the number one distributor.

A former Platinum USA executive also observed: "Platinum Russia is intertwined with Olga and her unique personality." When asked if she truly considered herself a leader, Olga responded without hesitation:

Absolutely. The company is like a child: it grows up with your values, and the values of the environment. You'll always see yourself in it. This company is me. I'm a general manager. I'm a good manager. When the company needs other personalities to manage it, I walk away. I hire people who are smarter than me. The company, like a baby, needs a life of its own. In many ways I'm like Steve Jobs was to Apple—a charismatic leader. People remember me because of the way I talk, and that's an asset. That's why I could not be a consultant, because a consultant has to listen, and I don't just listen. I have ideas of my own.

According to Dr. Peterson, Platinum's success was not based solely on the fact that they might have better products. "It's the quality in whatever we do." She believed in what she had learned in university, and drew ideas from a few favorite texts, especially those in psychology. One of them, *Psychology of Flow*, was written by a University of Chicago professor. "He talks about quality. He says: 'Do whatever you do with quality, because quality improves our lives. Always finish projects. If you start, you finish. If you promise, you deliver.' It's my bible," Olga explained. She then applied this approach to her own company:

> So what's the niche for us? What's our strategic advantage? It's the quality: the quality of people. We pay people a lot more money; we pay people more than the Big Six. It's the quality of relationships, the relationships that are formed and the respect that people have for each other, because this is more like a university. This is not me naturally; this is something that I learned. It's the quality of treating the customer with dignity. This is what you really should do. What these books say is that everyone around you should benefit. That's really my goal. Everyone around me should see a positive impact. I am very lucky that I can make other people's lives better—customers, colleagues, employees, and family. And I think that the people around me are very lucky.

Explaining more about her style, she added:

> I'm a manager. I just like to give advice. I even go home and give orders. But people like me because I give clear instructions and they can get things done in the right way.

Dr. Peterson emphasized her admiration for high quality people. She noted that those at the Big Six firms were hard working, very bright, quality people who got things done. She herself worked at Platinum much the same way as she had in other companies. The projects were similar and she was still involved in organization and administration, not technical issues:

> I administer things and people, that's what I do. My life is very interesting and the decisions that I make are very interesting. Business to me is not all just rational; it's the expression of my talent. I am a manager. There is no question about it, because I don't want to know the programs, and I don't know technology. So I would say that I'm a professional general manager. That's what I do. Whenever I want to do something, I hire people. Even the business plans are prepared for me. I don't work by myself, and can't even work on Saturday by myself. But I coordinate, and I manage the process, and this is why our company has been so successful. I am just a coordinator.

CONSULTING GROUP CREATED IN 1996

In 1996, Dr. Peterson described her company as very profitable and well regarded. A major development was the completion of a conversion from a DOS to Windows operating system. Although this was a costly process, Olga believed it was essential in order to stay competitive. Another important step was the addition of consulting as a necessary service to customers, enabling them to implement new software systems. By late 1996, more than 60 of the company's 150 employees worked as consultants for clients. At that time, the company had five offices and 120 clients.

Olga and Viktor noted the changes in the company's organization as customer needs resulted in the creation of a consulting group. The additional complexity required a more pronounced sharing of responsibilities between Olga and Viktor. Viktor focused on technical direction and management of technical personnel, while Olga set overall business directions, formulated expansion plans, established internal policies, dealt with Western customers, and participated in hiring decisions.

The consulting business developed primarily because many customers did not know what they needed in terms of accounting systems. Feasibility studies were necessary, and proposals had to be developed, both of which required consultation as well as an examination of the client's current systems. Technical designs related to Platinum's systems were developed and client training was implemented. Systems had to be tested and run before final approval by customers. In short, Platinum's business had expanded beyond selling software packages to providing complete information systems consulting and implementation services.

When asked whether they competed or cooperated with the Big Six, Dr. Peterson answered: "One Big Six firm we cooperate with loves Platinum, while another hates us because we have entered their consulting niche." She claimed that Platinum had to provide consulting services in order to move its product in the developing market. But she added: "Now I think there is an equilibrium where we all know our place. We all work together."

ONE OF RUSSIA'S TOP WOMEN EXECUTIVES IN 1997

Summing up her view of Olga, a former Platinum USA executive stated:

> She's a businesswoman, a sharp businesswoman. She's gutsy. It's why she's successful. She's predicting that this year's revenues will be double what she did last year, at a good profit. She's very savvy and she'll survive no matter what. I can't think of another person who could have pulled off what she has pulled off.

An April 1998 cover story in *Russia Business Review* portrayed Dr. Peterson as one of Russia's best women executives in its coverage of 14 leading women. The article made it clear that Olga and her company were doing extremely well in the Russian software and systems consulting market. She reported her 1997 revenues as $6 to $10 million, and employees numbered 120 in the Moscow and St. Petersburg locations. The article described the qualities that made Olga a successful businesswoman: "Her disposition brings leadership and strategy to the company and is combined with a solid business background, most of which she acquired in her ten years in the United States."

Olga openly expressed her admiration for the US:

American business is really magnificent, the way they created the structure of companies, and the work ethic. It's something for other nations to learn, something for me to learn for sure. I have a lot of respect for America, but it's not mine.

Feeling a great need to come back to Russia several years earlier, she explained the circumstances leading to the decision: "My last job at Motorola was in international and I tried to convince them that they needed to open an office in Russia. But Motorola is too conservative—they didn't want to do it at that time." She explained that this was a major reason she left Motorola to join Deloitte Touche in Moscow in the early 1990s.

It was clear from the article that Dr. Peterson still retained the enthusiasm, confidence, energy, and vision that she had demonstrated from the start. Explaining her role as Platinum's leader, she was quoted as saying:

I got into this role of general manager ... and it just clicks all of a sudden. I'm in charge and I have this voice inside of me telling me what to do. It doesn't mean I don't make mistakes, but my judgment gets better and better, and I love it.... I am a general manager at heart.

The article concluded about Olga:

Now she is calling the shots. She is calling for Platinum to be a leader in this very huge and undeveloped market ... and provided the firm continues in a successful vein, Peterson sees a 10-fold increase in Platinum's business over the next three to four years.

ONE OF TOP THREE ACCOUNTING SOFTWARE FIRMS IN 1998

Heading for a Record Year

The first half of 1998 saw continued success in Platinum's business, with growth in revenues, employees, and customers. The company appeared to be on the way to a record year. The fundamental mission and competitive strategy remained consistent with earlier years, and the variety of customers and software applications had expanded. However, the shortage of qualified personnel limited growth, and remained a problem which the company tried to address. It also tried to retain employees by offering bonuses for increasing sales and for keeping themselves fully billed to clients.

Still, the company was able to achieve impressive results, and emerged during 1998 as one of the top three accounting software and consulting firms in Russia, according to Dr. Peterson. In 1996, the company had set an objective for 1998 to increase average revenue per customer from $50,000 to a level of $150,000 to $200,000. This objective was achieved in 1998 while continuing to sell directly to clients rather than utilizing distributors as they had considered doing in their 1996 planning exercise. The number of customers also expanded dramatically during 1998 to 300 firms, including major multinationals such as PepsiCo, Coca-Cola, and Caterpillar Inc. Olga Peterson continued to guide the company through its dramatic growth, setting the strategy and guiding the organization's development, while seeking new opportunities for Platinum such as finding new investors.

Still Healthy in the Post-Crisis Environment

In fall 1998, Olga Peterson reported that the company's situation was still healthy, but like most firms, it had suffered setbacks as a result of the country's economic crisis. She expected that Platinum's revenues for 1998 would be $6 million, which was less than planned but still impressive given the difficult circumstances. She noted that the company had been profitable during every year of operation, and remained so even during the crisis. Her major concern was that foreign customers would continue to leave Russia because of the difficulties, and that Russian companies would not be able to afford the types of services offered by Platinum. Another consequence of the crisis was that some potential investors withdrew from discussions that had been very positive before the crisis.

Olga stated: "Business is going well, but it is scary to think about where my country is going with the incapable and corrupt government." In response to the country's deteriorating situation, the company had downsized in an effort to cut costs. By the fall, Platinum employed 100 people, including 30 consultants, down from the 1996 level of 150, of whom 60 were consultants. Aggravating the company's human resource situation, two of Platinum's key managers had left earlier in the year. Olga's deputy, Viktor, left Platinum to start a printing firm, while the senior marketing executive started a competitor software firm. Management of day-to-day activities became the responsibility of a manager who was promoted to that position. Olga's husband, David, assumed more responsibilities in marketing and sales, in addition to those of managing the overall company as a partner with Olga.

Dr. Peterson saw the crisis as having a possible positive outcome for Platinum in that competitors were rapidly exiting the industry. The reasons, she said, were the country's highly unstable political situation, as well as the technological difficulty of maintaining products that complied with both Western and Russian accounting principles. Yet, the times posed a formidable managerial challenge to Olga and Platinum. She explained:

> Not very many companies are going to remain in business, and this is the challenge for me. There is trouble in this country, and it will be another test for

me as a manager and as a leader to see if I can guide my company through this crisis.

PLANS FOR THE FUTURE

Facing the very difficult situation in the country, Olga remained realistic but positive about the future. She and David still owned Platinum but planned to offer shares to employees in the coming years. She planned also for the development of additional software products as well as new related services. If conditions improved dramatically, she saw the potential for Platinum to achieve annual revenues of $50 million within five to seven years.

Her near-term objective was "to become one of the few survivors in the industry thanks to the quality of Platinum's products, services, people, and reputation." In addition to benefiting from decreased competition, Olga saw potential business from selling accounting solutions to new customers who had become more oriented to cost controls as a result of the crisis. Additionally, she planned to capitalize on the opportunity to hire excellent managers who had left competitors or customers due to layoffs. She would still continue to reduce expenses in all areas such as salaries and rent, which she saw as a realistic approach, given the decreased demand in the country for people and facilities. Olga summarized her views:

> It is my obligation to myself, my employees, and our customers to do my best to get through this crisis.

12. Vybor

TRADING COMPANY FOUNDED DURING PERESTROIKA

Vybor, the Russian word for "choice," was formed in 1986 as a consumer goods trading and publishing cooperative, shortly after new government legislation allowed non-state-owned businesses to be created. The founders were two brothers in their thirties, Aleksandr Mikhailovich and Valentin Mikhailovich Buianovskii, who each had 50-percent ownership of the company. Both had been highly talented and accomplished in their academic pursuits, with Valentin winning the Lenin scholarship as the top music student of his year, and Aleksandr taking top honors as the best mathematics student. Aleksandr, who was fluent in English, subsequently worked as a computer programmer. In managing Vybor, the look-alike Buianovskii brothers worked very closely together, shared an office, and split everything equally. Each time they created a new business, they set it up as a profit center in which each brother had a 50-percent share, and they rotated the roles of president and general manager in each business.

The Buianovskiis had looked into many different business opportunities and concluded that a trading company would be the most profitable. Aleksandr's plan was to stay in the business as long as it remained profitable:

> I've put a lot of effort into it, and I'll stay until it's not so profitable. Then, I'll make a change.

ONE OF TOP FIFTY TRADING FIRMS BY 1993

Three Customer Groups

Vybor got its start as a trading company importing consumer goods from China, Malaysia, Turkey, and other countries. Initially the company sold goods only to large customers, but as competition increased, it dealt with three customer groups: large enterprises that purchased over 10 million rubles of goods annually, medium-sized stores purchasing from 1 to 10 million rubles, and small customers such as kiosk vendors who bought under 1 million rubles.

Vybor had a small showroom in central Moscow where customers selected and picked up goods including leather goods, shoes, television sets and VCRs, tape recorders, confectionery products, perfumes, and soaps. Virtually all products were imported. In 1993, an expediting service was added to transport goods from Vybor's warehouse to customers. Vybor also held shares in daughter companies at 40 locations in other parts of Russia. Aleksandr reported that by 1993 Vybor was one of the top 50 import-export firms in Russia and had become highly reputable, with banks giving them credit based solely on their name.

Difficult Business Environment, But Inflation an Advantage

A major challenge for Vybor was the uncertain business environment. For example, shipping goods to Russia was very difficult, and the banking system was undeveloped. Additionally, the firm was unable to contract out services such as cleaning and shipping to other firms. Another brother who had emigrated to the US was able to do so in a similar business there, thus allowing him to operate with only ten core employees. Uncertainty about the laws was another concern, as Aleksandr explained: "It's hard to know what the laws will be. But I can cope if I know what they are."

Two economic realities, corruption and inflation, that caused problems for most firms, were not particularly troublesome for Vybor. While corruption was a serious problem for many retail businesses, Aleksandr did not consider it a major problem: "Corruption doesn't really hurt us because the mafia realize that our business must stay viable." Even inflation had a positive side for Vybor:

> Inflation actually helps us because people want to get rid of their inflated rubles and buy our goods.

Overall, Aleksandr favored a market economy in Russia, but felt "it should have been introduced with less tragedy and less use of uncivilized methods." Although he believed that the country was moving too fast to a market economy, he viewed the future with guarded optimism.

Management of Employees, Organizational Structure, and Decision Making

In addition to the difficult business environment, management of employees was another major challenge. In summarizing human resources issues, Aleksandr stated:

> The main problem is the psychology of people. It's hard to organize them to work hard and give 100-percent effort after 70 years of socialism.

212

Vybor employed over 500 people in its Moscow operations, as well as five to ten people in each of the 40 daughter companies outside Moscow. The average age of the Moscow work force, including managers, was 27 to 30, with some employees as young as 18 in lower-level jobs. Women comprised 30 percent of the management team, and filled 50 percent of lower-level positions.

Finding experienced and reliable people was very difficult. The Buianovskiis looked for individuals whose personal characteristics included high intelligence, quick reaction to change, high energy level, and a highly motivated attitude. Since few people had relevant work experience, Vybor provided training for many of its employees.

The brothers encouraged managers to create small companies within Vybor to keep them from leaving to start their own businesses, which some had already done. Corporate and unit profits were calculated, and managers were permitted to decide how to spend their units' profits. In addition, several businesses were allowed to retain three percent of their sales revenues for managers to reinvest at their discretion. Every morning the brothers held a meeting with Vybor's 40 managers to make decisions and share information. The Buianovskiis made the top management decisions together, but gave managers of the various businesses autonomy to make most internal decisions that did not require additional funding. Each business, such as Vybor Shoes, had its own legal status, accounting unit, and directors, and no board of directors existed for Vybor as a whole.

To motivate managers of the various businesses, the Buianovskii brothers developed an incentive system that allowed managers to become owners. Each year, top-performing managers became eligible to own ten percent of their own businesses, up to a maximum of 50 percent over five years. This system would involve a transfer of ownership from the brothers who currently owned 100 percent of each business. July 1993 marked the first year that the ownership plan would take effect, and the eligibility of four managers was being considered at that time.

Senior managers were also eligible for profit sharing, and Aleksandr stated that there was "no limit to the amount that they can earn." Such was not the case for managers at other levels, however, and they were a harder group to motivate as a result, Aleksandr admitted. The Buianovskiis tried to link pay with performance but found performance hard to measure in many jobs. For the past two years they had adjusted salaries for managers and clerks to take total sales volume into account. However, the system did not work very well, and Aleksandr explained that some employees engaged in "the Pavlik Morozov Syndrome" of complaining about each other's performance. This syndrome referred to a famous incident during the Stalinist period that had become common parlance. Management offered other incentives to employees as well. For instance, all 500 employees in the Moscow operations were invited to a restaurant for a Christmas season celebration in 1992.

A Strategy Like Roulette

"My strategy is like roulette," Aleksandr stated. Before 1993, little competition existed, but he considered the Russian market to be 70-percent saturated by 1993. Aleksandr explained: "Others use our price list and compete against us, so we must take action based on our experience and authority."

When the government freed prices in 1992, there was little impact on Vybor because, "as before, we had room to set prices," Aleksandr clarified. Each time they started a business, competitors followed them, as was the case in their book publishing and brokerage ventures. These businesses were very profitable at first, but as competitors entered, Vybor's profits declined to a more moderate level. Initially, according to Mr. Buianovskii, profits were 100 percent, but they reduced prices under competitive pressure and profits declined to around 30 percent.

Mr. Buianovskii explained that he was constantly looking for other business opportunities in case he needed new ways of generating profits. For instance, he had established an investment fund by buying vouchers or shares of various enterprises, but planned to wait until conditions became more favorable before taking action. He was also interested in buying small businesses and would do so when the time was right. "Raising capital is not a problem for us," he asserted, adding that their Irish partner in the import-export joint venture, Virgin East, was only one source of funding. Each partner had a 50-percent stake in the JV.

Largest Customers in Siberia and the Far East

Sales from Vybor's four retail stores generated less than two percent of sales. The largest customers were independent firms located in Siberia and the Far East. Long-term contracts were negotiated with them, typically one-year agreements with options for renewal. Inventory turnover was four times a year for imported goods, and ten times for domestic products. Vybor's specialization in consumer goods was a departure from its initial business as a broker selling unfinished goods to enterprises. That business became unattractive, Aleksandr stated, when the government increased taxes, freed prices, and stopped paying its debts to enterprises. This soon resulted in enterprises not being able to pay for goods ordered. An additional obstacle was the negative attitudes that enterprise managers often harbored toward middlemen and other brokers. "The mentality is that if you don't produce goods in an enterprise, you're a crook," Aleksandr explained. Nonetheless,

Vybor still maintained a small brokerage department that operated at a modest profit.

Television Advertising and Direct Sales

Vybor marketed its products in several ways. The company found it profitable to advertise on television, targeting retailers rather than consumers as is typically the case in more developed market economies. It also engaged in direct sales campaigns to potential customers, and sent product information to current customers. Another effective technique involved going to large enterprises on paydays and selling goods directly to employees on site, often selling out their stock in one or two days.

MAJOR STAFF CUTS TO STAY PROFITABLE IN 1994

Downsizing and Employee Issues

Vybor continued to be profitable throughout 1994. This success was made possible as a result of a major downsizing in which half of the employees were let go. This decision was made when profits began declining despite no significant downturn in business volume. Aleksandr Buianovskii attributed the need for this action to the country's unstable economic and legislative conditions, especially high inflation and taxes, and unpaid wages. The main problem for Vybor was that customers lacked money to pay for goods because of huge government and interfirm debt. Barter and diversification were Vybor's primary ways of coping with the cash crisis. Barter agreements included paying for imported goods with Russian-made knitwear, as well as paying the employees' salaries of Russian suppliers in exchange for manufactured goods.

Exorbitant tax rates and frequently changing tax legislation were large problems, but Aleksandr did not consider them insurmountable. He took a pragmatic approach to managing Vybor's tax exposure, noting the valuable information contained in books such as *25 Ways to Avoid Taxes.*

Implementation of the massive downsizing decision was delegated to managers who followed general corporate guidelines. Aleksandr pointed out that downsizing was in managers' personal interests because staff reductions improved profits, and managers were eligible for corporate profit sharing. The downsizing activity had other positive aspects in addition to contributing to corporate profitability. Aleksandr noted: "Now we have more experienced personnel and fewer problems with them." He added that the main motivational tools included money, the company's reputation, and tight administrative and disciplinary policies:

> The problem of mistrusting some employees is still very serious, and we need to monitor them as they don't always perform as we expect.

Vybor's compensation level was considered to be slightly higher than competitors', with sales managers' monthly salaries being around $300. The incentive program in which managers had the potential for 50-percent ownership of their business units was still available, and was considered effective by the Buianovskii brothers. In contrast, their decision to give company shares to lower-level employees was not as well received. When they distributed small dividends to all shareholders—largely as a symbolic gesture of profit sharing—some employees resented that dividends were paid to other shareholders as well as to themselves.

Continuing Wholesaler Strategy and Diversification into Financial Markets

Company executives used a six-month sliding planning horizon in developing strategy. Vybor's various companies were still involved in the same businesses of shoes, clothing, electronic goods, and the like, but were now structured as different legal entities. The company's strategy was to remain as a wholesaler and distributor. Aleksandr emphasized that they had no intention of opening more retail stores, since they viewed retailing as a completely different type of business that was very complex and not cost effective. He noted that some competitors had opened retail outlets but closed them after some time.

The joint venture with their Irish partner was flourishing, the relationship had become even stronger, and many of Vybor's goods were purchased through the joint venture. Vybor's main suppliers remained the same as in 1993, with most being from abroad. The three criteria used to evaluate suppliers were quality, price, and reliability.

Aleksandr was also exploring the possibility of selling to other firms a computerized pricing system that had recently been developed by one of Vybor's programmers. The software package allowed a large number of variables affecting pricing policies to be analyzed, and the inflation factor it contained was especially useful in light of the rampant inflation the country was experiencing.

The major strategic change in 1994 was Vybor's diversification into financial markets. Management saw this development as a long-term strategy to subsidize their main business, and built upon experience they had gained by being involved in bond and pension investment funds for the past two years. Aleksandr held shares in 30 enterprises, often obtaining them in exchange for goods to shareholders at reduced prices. This barter technique effectively circumvented the country's pervasive cash-crunch while also increasing Vybor's sales volume.

Foreign Competition Intensifies

Throughout the year, competition had increased to several dozen firms, primarily foreign companies including some from Belarus. Vybor responded by advertising its products on television and in newspapers. The company also offered lower prices on some items when management decided not to adjust prices in lockstep with inflation. Vybor did not hold special sales, Aleksandr explained, "because people don't believe the word, 'sale,' and often think it is untrue."

Although Aleksandr admitted that Vybor was not much different from its competitors in its product offerings, he believed the company had four primary sources of competitive advantage: experience as an established firm, a good reputation, an effective distribution channel, and a central location, with Moscow accounting for 50 percent of its market. Rich oil-producing cities were another profitable market, but Vybor avoided the St. Petersburg market due to strong competition there.

Community Involvement and Charitable Work

The company was involved in a number of charitable activities, and frequently responded to requests for help by social organizations. For instance, they sponsored a children's soccer team, and provided funding for a bakery that employed disabled people.

Top Management Devotes More Time to Strategic Issues

As the company evolved, Aleksandr Buianovskii began to change the focus of his activities. Until 1994, he had worked primarily on organizational-level issues. Now that the business had become more established and employees had become more experienced, he increased his delegation of operational decisions to trusted staff members. He devoted more time to strategic issues, especially in prospecting for and organizing new businesses. Although his work hours were still long, he reduced his schedule from 12 to 10 hours a day, and from 6 to 5 days a week. In addition, he made time for exercising at a health club, but declined offers to join expensive business clubs which he felt provided little value for him.

Optimistic, But Wanting Government Stability

Aleksandr's wish for the future was for the government to create greater stability for doing business. He hoped that the government would stop passing retroactive laws and abruptly raising prices, and that it would make taxes more predictable. He acknowledged the importance of a solid tax base, but added:

I'm not asking for reduced taxes. What is needed is a set of clear rules of the game. People need to be educated about the rules, and the rules need to be enforced. The government also needs to provide some guarantee for business people to prosper, rather than pulling the rug out from under them. Even so, I'm optimistic about the future of Vybor.

RESTRUCTURING AND SPECIALIZATION IN 1995

Sales Slump in Tough Economic Environment

Hyperinflation and huge interfirm debt plagued the economy in 1995, and their combined effects took a toll on Vybor. With economic conditions much worse than before, trading division sales were slashed in half, with revenues in one of Vybor's outlets, for example, plummeting by $100,000 to a mere $5,000. Aleksandr attributed much of the decline to "a sea of competition," inflation eroding their prices, and enterprises not paying wages on time. He explained that the latter caused a chain reaction in the economy that affected Vybor in several ways. Most importantly, consumers lacked cash to purchase goods, thereby reducing Vybor's revenues. Additionally, firms that went bankrupt or had other financial problems often negatively affected banks' loan funds, which in turn made it more difficult for Vybor to obtain bank credits.

Taxation continued to be a serious issue for Vybor, with laws that took effect retroactively being particularly frustrating. Aleksandr stated that taxes had a heavy impact on profit margins, and believed that, "in the US a ten-percent profit might be fine, but it must be at least 50-percent in Russia in order to stay in business."

Shedding Businesses to Stay Profitable

Despite these serious obstacles, profits for Vybor's businesses, including the investment fund, were unchanged from the prior year, thanks to significant cost cutting and product specialization measures taken by top management. Aleksandr's major strategic decisions in 1995 were to shed unprofitable businesses, specialize in shoes, and explore new business ventures. He also decided to sell only goods that would yield at least a satisfactory profit margin, and was in the process of selling off stock of imported clothing which had become less profitable due to high customs duties. Faced with strong competition, he decided to discontinue the consumer electronics line as well. Aleksandr claimed that other "more privileged" firms apparently did not pay the customs duties that he was required to pay. Since duties on imported shoes, however, had not increased, Aleksandr decided to specialize in sport shoes and women's shoes imported from several countries.

In the process of shedding several businesses, the work force was again reduced drastically, from 120 to 25 people. Nonetheless, the incentive system of salaries and commissions was still in place. Employees who had earned $300 a month in 1994 averaged $450 in 1995, in step with inflation, and some individuals earned up to $2,000 a month. Aleksandr's brother and business partner, Valentin, was no longer active in managing Vybor, having left to start a consulting business in auditing.

Focus on the Shoe Business

Vybor purchased leather and synthetic sports and women's shoes from several countries including Hong Kong, China, India, and Portugal. Vybor's main supplier was Sprandi, which was owned by an Indian family living in Hong Kong, whose factory was located in China. Aleksandr claimed that Vybor obtained shoes at the lowest price of all of Sprandi's customers. Vybor paid Sprandi every 10 days, and cash flow was not a problem because customers now paid upon delivery or by a bank transfer within a few days.

Shoes were purchased in container lots that were then sold in smaller quantities to distributors. Vybor had about 250 customers for its shoes and clothing. Marketing representatives prospected for new customers, and ads targeted at wholesale distributors were still placed in newspapers. However, television advertising was dropped because it was very expensive.

Retail prices for the footwear product line ranged from $7 to $70, and prices were sometimes reduced to stimulate sales or in response to competitors' prices. Consumers could purchase as little as one pair of shoes, and discounts were given for large quantities. Signs in the Moscow showroom noted that sales were made "only by prepayment."

Purchase of a Sewing Factory

In September 1995, Aleksandr was completing negotiations to buy the well-regarded local sewing factory, Moroz. This decision was motivated by Vybor's strategy to buy a factory related to their business expertise. Having experience in imported clothing, they expected that their knowledge would be transferable to a domestic operation. They had set up the plant to produce work clothes from high-quality but relatively low-cost fabric imported from China and Korea. No problems were foreseen with financing since Vybor's investment fund owned 80 percent of the business, and the 200 Moroz factory workers owned the remaining 20 percent. Factory operations were to be run by Vybor personnel since Aleksandr believed no one else was qualified to run the new plant. In September 1995, he appointed a plant manager with whom he discussed such issues as which workers to keep from the Moroz operation, and whether to reduce the plant's total work force.

Declining Activity with Irish Joint Venture Partner

Vybor's joint venture with its Irish partner was in decline. A serious warehouse fire resulted in a major loss of inventory, and a drop in sales ensued. Another result of the fire was that the Irish partner felt Russia had become a dangerous place to do business, and was looking for opportunities elsewhere.

BANKRUPT IN 1996

In early 1996, Vybor went bankrupt. Aleksandr Buianovskii elaborated:

> The firm now exists only on paper. It owes a huge $2 million debt to Inkombank, and everyone is absolutely certain that it will never be repaid. We returned the remaining goods to suppliers, distributed vacation pay to most of the employees, transferred a few employees and the building we occupied to another firm, and closed our doors. We gave Inkombank some warehouses as partial forgiveness of debt, and from time to time I have to provide the bank various documents to show we cannot pay them.

Aleksandr himself wasted no time in starting two new businesses. His main job, which he began in mid-1996, was as the director of a plastic pipe manufacturing plant in the Ochakovo region of Moscow. Additionally, he organized a new company to distribute Sprandi shoes throughout Russia.

New Job as Director of a Plastic Pipe Plant

Aleksandr explained that the job of managing the plastic pipe factory came about through a friend who had bought the company, but apparently did not have time to manage the facility. His friend bought the factory in order to make use of electricity and other resources he had access to in another factory. Aleksandr explained his friend's decision: "Before he owned the pipe factory, he encountered some difficulties. To solve them, he bought the factory." His friend owned 51 percent of the company, Aleksandr owned 30 percent, and other top managers owned the remaining 19 percent.

The company was a former state-owned enterprise that had been producing plastic pipe since 1988. In 1994, the plant began producing pipes for the domestic gas industry in collaboration with Gas France. The official agreement to finalize the joint venture, Gaztrubplast, was signed in mid-1996 shortly after the new owners took charge of the plastic factory. The French partner was responsible for quality control of the ten percent of the factory's pipe output accounted for by the venture. The remaining 90 percent of pipes were produced and inspected in the Russian section of the factory.

Aleksandr described the two types of pipes:

The 10 percent produced for the joint venture is sold with a different brand name and by special order. It is a different color, comes with a guarantee, and is sold at different prices. But basically the two types of pipe are absolutely the same. Moscow customers use Gaztrubplast pipe, and customers in other regions of Russia use our other pipe.

Part Owner of Sprandi Shoe Distributor Firm

At about the same time as he became involved in the plastic pipe factory, Aleksandr also began a new venture with the international shoe company, Sprandi, which had been one of Vybor's key suppliers. He chose Sprandi to help develop a new business since its sales in Russia had doubled in each of the three years that Vybor had been its distributor. The Indian owners of the international firm held 75 percent of the new Russian company, also called Sprandi. Aleksandr owned the remaining 25 percent, and received a salary that was deducted from his share of the profits. He described his role as that of a consultant, and worked most evenings for Sprandi in Vybor's former office space after finishing his workday at the plastic pipe factory. In fall 1996, he estimated that 10 to 20 percent of his total work time was spent on Sprandi business.

The company became the distributor of Sprandi footwear in Russia, Ukraine, Belarus, and Kazakstan. It employed 15 people in Russia, including five Sprandi family members from Hong Kong who relocated to Moscow, and 10 Russians, some of whom had previously worked at Vybor. The parent company's strategy was to compete internationally in the second tier of athletic shoes against such brands as LA Gear and Hi Tech, but the company also produced some top tier shoes for Nike. Aleksandr explained that Sprandi management had begun a television and magazine advertising campaign in Russia on which they had spent $350,000 in the past year.

Still Optimistic About the Future

In fall 1996, Aleksandr was cautiously optimistic about the future of his businesses, in spite of many unfavorable economic conditions. He summarized his views:

> The government takes all the money from the market. Everything is dormant now. But I am hopeful for a better future. We have some political stability, now that the war in Chechnya is being resolved. But the government has to create positive conditions to encourage investment. If these are implemented, then business activities will increase, and banks will find it more attractive to invest their funds. I hope that this will happen soon. Our enterprise is also taking part in expanding the market, and we believe we can increase our sales by 50 percent annually. The business environment is somewhat better than before. For instance, it is easier to find people with experience in the market, as I found recently when I hired an experienced marketing manager. Also, many people

now realize that they have to work hard and that they need to understand how to do business properly. A few years ago, a lot of people practically wanted to steal what they could from their companies and then leave. Now they want to work for what they get. So I'm optimistic. To live without optimism is impossible.

PART FIVE

Analysis and Conclusions

13. Enterprise Progress During the Capitalist Decade

APPLYING A STRATEGIC MANAGEMENT FRAMEWORK

Earlier chapters have described the changing environment for Russian business during the 1990s, as well as the progress of ten enterprises during that time. The business environment was analyzed in four different stages which we identified as the Commercialization, Privatization, Nomenklatura, and Statization stages. The ten enterprises were grouped into three types: state-owned enterprises, hybrid organizations, and entrepreneurships. We emphasized the latter category since this was a new form of enterprise which developed during the decade. The focus of each chapter was an individual enterprise, and our goal was to present a detailed description of each one's strategy as it evolved during the decade.

Our objective in this chapter is to summarize the progress made by the three types of Russian enterprises during the 1990s. Such an approach can assist business managers, researchers, and students seeking an overall understanding of how different types of Russian businesses fared during the country's attempted transition to a market economy.

The conceptual perspective for this concluding chapter will be strategic management, which encompasses the business environment as well as the decisions and activities of organizations in the context of the environment. Because of the central importance of organizational goals as a starting point in that framework, the chapter begins by covering strategic objectives for the three types of enterprises—state-owned, hybrid, and entrepreneurships. The remainder of the chapter will discuss specific characteristics which further reflect strategic decisions for each enterprise type. These characteristics will be analyzed during four stages of the decade's economic and political evolution.

STRATEGIC OBJECTIVES

A strategic analysis of an organization requires identifying strategic objectives which subsequently guide decisions and organizational direction. In reviewing the reports of the executives who headed the ten organizations we studied, we identified a number of strategic objectives and assessed the importance of each. Objectives which have been traditionally emphasized in many Russian organizations include creating employment, and promoting social or environmental causes, or national defense. Others typically associated with Western market-oriented companies include growth, profit, and a market-driven orientation. Objectives common in both settings include ensuring organizational survival and developing intellectual capital.

We assigned a rating of high to objectives which could be considered drivers of strategy, medium to those that were fairly important but did not actually drive strategy, and low to those which were relatively unimportant in a firm's strategic direction. Our intention was to see how these organizations dealt with the change from the centrally-planned economy, and to assess the extent to which they adopted objectives more commonly found in a market-oriented economy.

State-Owned Enterprises

The two state-owned enterprises, the Central R&D Institute of Robotics and Technical Cybernetics and Toriy Research and Production Association, adhered quite closely to traditional Russian enterprise objectives of creating employment and supporting the nation's defense sector. Given their status as technologically-oriented firms, they also valued the development of intellectual capital as key to their futures. Each was also concerned with survival, increasingly so as the decade progressed. The Robotics Institute seemed more concerned with its survival than did Toriy. This was partly due to Institute employees' high level of patriotism and pride in Russia's technical prowess. Additionally, management saw the Institute as fulfilling a vital role as part of a threatened technological infrastructure and educational system.

When it came to the objectives of growth, profit, and market-driven orientation more commonly found in the West, both organizations showed moderate emphasis. The R&D Institute, however, seemed more aware than Toriy of the need to develop a market orientation, even at a fairly early stage. This profile of strategic objectives changed during the decade, with both state-owned enterprises putting more emphasis in later years on survival, profit, and market orientation, and less on creating or maintaining employment as a social obligation. This transition seems consistent with the country's continuing move toward a more market-oriented economy, coupled with less government support for state-owned enterprises.

Hybrid Enterprises

The three hybrid or semi-privatized enterprises, Mikromashina, Ekip, and Tonar, were generally high on social objectives, particularly Ekip and Tonar which embraced environmental issues as fundamental to their strategies. Mikromashina, because of its financial problems, was somewhat less concerned with them, but still placed a high value on succeeding as a Russian enterprise rather than becoming foreign-owned. All three were concerned with retaining or creating employment, with Tonar seeing this as a major objective, while the other two saw it as a relatively important goal. The importance placed on developing intellectual capital was highest in Ekip, which was primarily an R&D organization, but was still relatively high in Tonar and Mikromashina since both organizations dealt with an extensive number of technical and business issues.

Of the three hybrid enterprises, only Mikromashina was particularly concerned with survival before the later years of the decade. Nonetheless, Tonar's management seemed to place some importance on that goal, possibly because, as a new organization, it had quickly become involved in the relatively risky activity of operating plants and providing employment. When the three more Western-type goals of growth, profit, and market orientation were considered, these three organizations looked very much like the state-owned enterprises. The three saw these goals as being of moderate significance, although Ekip in its production-oriented projects did demonstrate an appreciation for meeting the needs of commercial markets. Tonar's management, too, saw the need to grow as the size of its projects increased.

Entrepreneurships

The five entrepreneurships generally showed little interest in strategic objectives grounded in Russia's past, such as maintaining employment, and displayed little orientation toward environmental or patriotic causes as business objectives. Most saw survival of their organizations as a primary objective. A notable exception was Vybor, whose owners showed little concern for the survival of the original enterprise, since making profits in any opportunistic business activity drove their strategy. The entrepreneurships placed different emphasis on the objective of developing intellectual capital, with the technology-oriented Platinum ranking it high, BusinessLink, Premier Bank, and Aquarius viewing it as quite important, and the trading company, Vybor, seeing little importance in it.

As for Western-oriented strategic objectives, the entrepreneurships as a group saw them as important goals. All five entrepreneurships had some business experience with Western firms, including partnerships in joint ventures, licensing agreements, and distribution arrangements. All these organizations seemed to appreciate the importance of learning to be market driven, and almost uniformly gave that goal a very high priority. Platinum, BusinessLink, and Vybor saw profit as a very important goal, while Premier Bank and Aquarius saw it as quite important. Growth, however, was not as uniformly embraced as an objective. BusinessLink, Aquarius, and Platinum had it as a primary goal, probably because of the high growth potential of the markets they served. The others, with less market potential, saw growth as being of moderate importance.

Evolution of Strategic Objectives

During the country's Commercialization stage, the state-owned organizations continued to operate much as they had in the past. And although their organizations were not heavily affected by privatization, they became somewhat market-oriented. As the decade progressed to the Nomenklatura and Statization stages, financial pressures caused them to become more concerned with survival. They tried to engage in more profit-oriented activities, while retaining more traditional goals as well.

The strategic objectives of the hybrid or semi-privatized firms looked very similar to the state-owned enterprises. Even though two of the hybrid organizations were started in the late 1980s, some values of the founders had been formed during their years of working in the Soviet system. They concentrated on long-term objectives and engaged in projects to reach their goals. Commercialization did not really affect their goals, which were more aligned to those of earlier times. Their objectives remained relatively consistent and did not change much during the Statization and Nomenklatura periods. These hybrid organizations exhibited some orientation toward both past and future.

From the beginning, the entrepreneurships showed a consistent inclination to adopt Western goals as their strategic objectives. Unaffected by the Privatization stage, they were quite consistent in this orientation during all four stages of the decade's economic transition. They generally had a strong market orientation, and saw profit, growth, and survival as important objectives. In fact, a profile of their strategic objectives looked very much like those of typical US companies. Being in different businesses, however, they varied in their views about the importance of developing intellectual capital. Generally, they did not place a high priority on the more Soviet-era objectives of creating employment and supporting environmental or patriotic causes.

Regardless of the objectives pursued during most of the 1990s, the country's financial crisis of August 1998 caused survival to emerge as the paramount strategic objective for the ten organizations, as it did for virtually all Russian enterprises. Although some continued to operate moderately successful businesses after that time, the possibility of business failure became foremost in the minds of leaders of these and most other enterprises.

STRATEGIC CHARACTERISTICS, DECISIONS, AND RESULTS

Our analysis of strategic characteristics, decision making, and results within the three types of enterprises focuses on those which supported competitive strategies. The critical decision areas involve products, markets, technologies, and operations. Strategies are considered within the context of the changing competitive, political, economic, and social environments. Financial and human resources policies and practices are also evaluated, including staffing, culture, structure, and systems. The ways in which enterprises implemented their strategies is also assessed.

State-Owned Organizations in the Commercialization Stage

The primary activity of the two state-owned enterprises was conducting basic and applied research in scientific and defense-related sectors. The Russian government considered the work of such enterprises in electronics, robotics, and cybernetics to be crucial to national security and sustainable industrial development. Yet, the disintegration of the country's central planning system had a negative effect on state-owned enterprises like Toriy and the Robotics and Cybernetics Institute. The primary problem occurred in the total disruption of the state-managed supply system, which resulted in shortages of materials needed for operations. The economic environment also began to deteriorate. Severe inflation resulted in partial payment or nonpayment of debts to these enterprises for deliveries to customers. The primary competitors were other state-owned enterprises which had duplicate capabilities. There was little foreign competition for the products manufactured by these enterprises, which had been part of the government's defense infrastructure.

The competitive strategy of these state-owned organizations changed very little from the earlier central planning period. They continued to rely on the government as their primary, and often only customer, depending on the product. They maintained their traditional areas of technological expertise, and attempted to develop new products based on these technologies. Although they experienced shortages of materials, they continued operating much as they had in the past. Since the cash-starved government was the main outlet for their production, these organizations were unable to develop customer interest in new products. And because they had virtually no experience working with foreign customers, there was no demand for their products from that source. Revenues from business operations suffered, and the enterprises were forced to cut expenses in virtually all areas. Government subsidies were also reduced, with the Robotics Institute, for instance, receiving only 70 percent of its previous allocation. Still, these organizations were able to carry on operations at a reduced level.

Retaining human resources was especially important to these technologically sophisticated organizations. It was clear that they would have little possibility of attracting new and younger talent who sought more promising opportunities in the entrepreneurial sector. Thus, they focused on their more experienced and talented scientists, and were forced to be creative in developing ways to retain and motivate these key human resources. Both enterprises were fortunate that their organizational structures included affiliations with major scientific and technical universities. The director of the Robotics and Cybernetics Institute worked diligently to maintain a culture based on scientific and technological values to retain his scientists. He also provided students from the affiliated Technological University to work as research assistants, to support senior scientists and to build a pipeline of younger professionals for the Institute. Toriy allowed its scientists to establish individual businesses as joint ventures with the enterprise itself.

Although Toriy and the Robotics Institute experienced major reductions in their work forces, they reported success at retaining their experienced senior scientists. Toriy's director, for instance, noted that the company lost workers and technicians, but no scientists during the Commercialization stage. Aggravating the situation in these enterprises, however, was a slowdown in orders and nonpayments by customers, as well as a recurring inability at Toriy to pay wages on time. Toriy employees occasionally received subsidies for food and medical care in lieu of wages.

Fundamental to the survival of the state-owned organizations were the dedication and influence of the two powerful CEOs. They displayed flexibility and ingenuity at this stage, much as the best enterprise directors had done during the Soviet period. Additionally, they utilized their networks of influence within governmental, scientific, and industrial organizations to benefit their enterprises. They shrewdly leveraged their positions as heads of elite organizations in the defense sector which traditionally had access to resources and influence with key decision makers. They presided as strong leaders with centralized power over hierarchically-structured organizations, and they were personally committed to the transformation of their organizations. This strong, authoritative leadership style was an essential asset to these enterprises as they experienced the transition from central planning to the Commercialization stage.

State-Owned Organizations in the Privatization Stage

Although the state-owned enterprises were not greatly affected by privatization, the CEOs' views on the subject differed. Dr. Lopota believed that it was crucial for the Robotics and Cybernetics Institute to remain state-owned to take advantage of the benefits it offered. Dr. Artiukh of Toriy, on the other hand, favored becoming a privatized stock company, since he believed private ownership offered more opportunities to the enterprise and its employees. The firm, in fact, did become partially privatized, with 49 percent of its stock sold during the country's Privatization stage to managers, employees, and others.

The environment continued to change dramatically from the days of central planning, producing uncertainty and requiring constant tactical redirection by enterprise leaders. The central government passed contradictory and seemingly nonsensical laws, particularly in the areas of taxation and foreign investment. The country began experiencing hyperinflation, which grossly complicated planning, pricing, and other strategic decisions. State-owned enterprises fared no better than newly privatized organizations during this stage, since all were buffeted by the same negative environmental forces. Toriy, for instance, had to pay extraordinarily high rates for energy, and the Robotics Institute reported constant threats that their energy sources would be disconnected if inflation-ridden bills were not paid on time. Demand continued for some products of both state-owned enterprises, though at a much reduced rate.

Toriy and the Robotics Institute began to face increasing competition from North American and Western European companies with advanced technologies and products that were well regarded on the world market. Both enterprises realized the importance of retaining technological expertise, and deploying it to meet new market needs. The competitive strategy for each firm was to reduce dependence upon the government as a customer, and to find new markets for products originally designed for the defense sector, which could be modified to meet commercial and consumer needs. In order to continue operations, the firms began seeking suppliers willing to work with them on the basis of countertrade or barter.

Financial problems increased, with the government's weakened financial position creating more pressure on the enterprises to become increasingly self-financing. The subsidy to the Robotics Institute was reduced to $10 million annually, significantly less than in the past. Its status as a state-owned enterprise, however, brought a favorable tax status which helped the Institute's cash flow considerably. Toriy, which was partially privatized, received even less in government subsidies. A fundamental requirement for both companies was to follow closely any opportunity which might produce profits, or even a contribution to cover fixed costs. Neither company, however, was able to develop all of the projects they had begun. Customers continued to delay payments, and Toriy even resorted to international arbitration to collect payment from one foreign customer.

The organizational structure of these state-owned organizations remained relatively unchanged during the Privatization stage. Toriy continued developing internal entrepreneurships, while the scientists in the Robotics Institute were given more responsibility for developing commercial business. Each enterprise downsized in response to declines in business, but Dr. Lopota insisted that he had not yet been forced to resort to layoffs. The leaders of both organizations focused upon retaining their key resource, talented scientists. Dr. Lopota believed that his major internal problem was "changing the psychology of people" away from expecting entitlements. Given the difficult economic environment including hyperinflation and the resulting low wages, he wanted employees to understand that they should expect to be paid commensurate with their performance. He instituted bonuses based upon results such as developing commercial business, and provided extra pay for involvement in special projects.

State-Owned Organizations in the Nomenklatura Stage

Because the Robotics Institute and Toriy remained either entirely or majority state-owned during the Nomenklatura stage, they did not experience as much change as enterprises more deeply involved in the privatized sector. It was in the privatized organizations that directors and other influential individuals began amassing for themselves ownership and control of the enterprises. These individuals, often acting in concert with government officials, bankers, and other members of the nomenklatura, hoped to become wealthy during the Nomenklatura stage which began in mid-1994.

The development of this new nomenklatura, including the infamous oligarchs, had a major influence on the economy as well as on privatized Russian enterprises. This group established its influence in the Yeltsin administration, as well as in virtually all other areas of government. Led by the oligarchs, they controlled the flow of funds to and from the government, and often had the power to divert payments to particular enterprises or away from others. On the surface it appeared to many observers that the political and economic environments were stabilizing. Inflation decreased dramatically, and GDP stabilized during 1996 and 1997. The country seemed to be making real progress in its transition to a market economy. The defense sector, however, was described by Dr. Artiukh as being in dire straits.

The competitive strategy of the Robotics Institute during this stage was to upgrade its technology and to exchange scientific information with the West. Managers had worked with an American company on a business plan, and decided upon telecommunications as a primary business focus. They attempted to develop formal and informal relationships with telecommunications specialists around the world. The Institute became a highly computerized organization, and developed advanced devices meeting the needs of the telecommunications market, space industry, environmental protection organizations, and the medical instrumentation field. The Institute used advertising for the first time, and many technical staff members were engaged in developing commercial opportunities. Toriy utilized its technological expertise to produce microwave and space communications equipment, television broadcasting products, and medical instruments, as well as acoustic speakers for the consumer market. Its products, such as electro-nitro simulators and high-technology scalpels, were very popular with some customers. The commercial segment increased from ten percent of Toriy's business to 70 percent during this period, with production quadrupling during 1996 compared to 1995.

Both enterprises succeeded in becoming more market-driven during the Nomenklatura stage. Despite a severe decline in government orders, each had begun developing relationships with commercial customers in Russia and abroad. The Robotics Institute, especially, increased its marketing efforts by involving its technical experts in domestic and international trade shows. Both enterprises continued their R&D efforts, although at a reduced level.

Financing enterprise operations remained the paramount activity for the leaders of both the Robotics Institute and Toriy. The nonpayment of debts between government and enterprises, as well as between enterprises, had become a virtual crisis, and the government owed Toriy 6 billion rubles in unpaid bills. Government subsidies decreased further, and cash flow was at a minimum in both organizations. More and more business was done on the basis of IOUs or barter.

Organizationally, both enterprises changed little from the Privatization stage. Toriy, however, continued to downsize dramatically and employed only 3,200 people in the mid-1990s, a sharp decrease from the 10,000 employees of the early Commercialization stage. Both leaders continued to utilize numerous techniques to retain their valuable scientists. These inducements included providing research assistants and entrepreneurial opportunities, and additional financial rewards for developing commercial business. Although the firms faced numerous hardships, they continued to focus on commercial opportunities to decrease dependence on the government.

State-Owned Organizations in the Statization Stage

The Statization stage was the unfortunate consequence of the Nomenklatura stage. The increasing role of government became inevitable, with more power concentrated in fewer interlocking hands. President Yeltsin began centralizing more and more power in the government, and continued changing cabinet ministers at an alarming rate. This action was partly in response to an outcry from international groups, as well as Russian citizens, against the excesses of the nomenklatura. The signs of economic progress such as stable inflation, improved production output, and slight increases in GDP were beginning to be seen as only superficial advances. Russian stock market prices had increased at a world-leading pace during 1997, but many analysts began to wonder whether there was a solid basis for the run up. The possibility became more and more likely that the country's economic bubble was about to burst.

By May 1998, such danger signals as decreasing GDP heralded a major disaster, which actually erupted during August 1998. The government defaulted on its foreign debt, and President Yeltsin continued replacing cabinet ministers, while he himself was under siege from many quarters. His relationship with notorious oligarchs like Berezovsky came under increasing criticism, and many in the country called for the president's resignation as well as punishment for the oligarchs. Under these circumstances, President Yeltsin drew more and more power back to the executive branch of the government. The communist-led Duma also favored bringing more power to their legislative branch, much of which had been lost to the president during the earlier years of the decade. By the fall, it was apparent that Yeltsin's power was waning, and as a result, he was forced to appoint Yevgeny Primakov as prime minister. Most observers saw the appointment of this conservative Soviet-era official as another force to promote an increasing state role in economic decisions.

Entering 1999, the country's economic situation continued to deteriorate as a seemingly passive government stood by in a posture of helplessness and inaction. Inflation rose to over 80 percent in early 1999, and the ruble tumbled 75 percent in value. Businesses, including state-owned enterprises, operated by issuing credits to one another rather than paying debts. Money transactions became less common as time went on, and the production of real goods declined dramatically. Those produced were often used to pay workers' wages or debts to other companies. The chaotic situation took its toll on many business leaders, and among the casualties was Toriy's Dr. Artiukh whose death was reported in early 1999.

Dr. Lopota of the Robotics Institute stated in late 1998 that he was operating much the same as in the previous four years, but that survival had become paramount. In spite of the difficulties during the Statization period, he continued to allocate 25 percent of the Institute's revenues to R&D projects. His primary strategy was to continue development in technological projects while diversifying markets to reach more commercial and foreign customers. There was still little change, however, in the Institute's customer base which included state enterprises, the Russian space agency, and large Russian and foreign governments and firms. Projects continued to focus on telecommunications technology, which Dr. Lopota believed had become the Institute's distinctive competence.

The Institute's increasing emphasis on survival during this stage was due to severe financial setbacks, with cash on hand having been reduced to a two-month level, down from an eight-month cushion during the previous several years. The primary reason for this financial deterioration was a decrease in government subsidies to only $500,000 per month, a small fraction of earlier support. Dr. Lopota noted that the chaos in the government, financial, and industrial sectors had created an increasingly hostile environment for his and other state-owned enterprises. He intensified the Institute's search for more contracts with commercial customers and expected all employees to participate. He explained that additional pressure had been applied on employees, especially older scientists, to produce or be replaced. His primary goal beyond survival was to maintain momentum for the Institute, even during the crisis. He emphasized that it was imperative that the Institute remain a state agency, following its present mission and strategy to the extent that resources permitted.

In summary, state agencies like the Robotics Institute and Toriy found themselves virtually cast adrift by the government. In spite of the government's increased centralization of power, its support for enterprises like these virtually disappeared. It seemed that President Yeltsin, Prime Minister Primakov, and his 1999 successors, Sergei Stepashin and Vladimir Putin, and even the communist Duma had declared a moratorium on decision making. All appeared to be waiting for the December 1999 Duma elections and the presidential election of 2000. In the meantime, the state agencies tried to survive, maintain their most valuable human resources, and continue some level of operations. The early years of the Statization stage proved to be a time to play a waiting game.

Hybrid Organizations in the Commercialization Stage

The three enterprises which we classified as hybrids were Mikromashina, Tonar, and Ekip. The term, hybrid, was chosen to identify several organizations which were neither entrepreneurships nor primarily state-owned during most of the 1990s. All, however, received some funding from central government agencies or municipal governments like the Moscow City Council. During the Commercialization stage, various government bodies were important shareholders of Tonar, and were minority shareholders of Ekip, and sole owners of Mikromashina. Historically, Tonar and Ekip, unlike Mikromashina, were never wholly-owned state enterprises. They started in the late 1980s, and thus government bodies acted more as investors in these two new firms. Tonar, in fact, was 48-percent state-owned, but it was understood that private investors were to retain majority ownership. Ekip had little state ownership and was primarily owned by its founder, Anatoly Savitsky. Additional minority positions were held by individual investors who entered into partnerships with Ekip by providing financing for individual projects. To raise funds needed in operating their firms, the executives of both companies drew heavily on contacts made during their earlier experience in large state-owned organizations.

The founders of both Ekip and Tonar were able to pursue projects that they had begun developing or had wanted to develop in their previous positions with state-owned organizations. Tonar's co-founders were scientists with international experience who for many years had held top positions in leading Soviet scientific institutes. Ekip's founder had also been a prominent scientist and executive. Mikromashina was led by its former chief engineer who had been with the company for over 30 years. He had also been involved during recent years with the company's Swiss and American partners in a successful joint venture which exported to Europe and the Middle East.

In spite of some successes, Mikromashina struggled as the country's central planning and supply system deteriorated. Management tried to depend on old contacts, such as suppliers and distributors, but found them to be unreliable. Imported products began to encroach on Mikromashina's markets since Russians were beginning to prefer the prestige of these newly available goods. Inflation and the ruble's devaluation put pressure on the company to lay off some workers and reduce hours for others. Ekip and Tonar saw the disintegration of the country's distribution, power supply, and transportation systems as business opportunities. Ekip's projects included some aimed at solving problems in air transportation and energy-conserving supply sources, as well as environmentally friendly commercial construction materials. Tonar began building a food warehousing and wholesale distribution network, as well as other large-scale environmentally beneficial projects.

Strategically, all three enterprises sought to produce products needed in the shortage-ridden Russian economy. Mikromashina had a history of successful operations, including a joint venture, and its products were noted for their quality. The company had a relatively new plant and reliable but inefficient production operations. In order to maintain employment, management allowed work to be performed manually rather than utilizing more efficient equipment. Management's strategy was to take the techniques and quality orientation developed in the joint venture and integrate them into its own product line. The company hoped that by doing so it could retain its markets in the face of increasing competition from imports.

The strategies of Ekip and Tonar were driven by ethical principles, as well as environmental and social objectives of improving both the natural environment in Russia and the lives of its citizens. The leaders of both companies hoped to do this by commercializing the abundant technology which had been developed during the Soviet era. Ekip's scientist-founder published an ecological encyclopedia that aimed to increase knowledge and awareness of environmental issues. The company also received a good deal of publicity for its prototype of a "flying saucer" aircraft capable of landing on both water and land. Ekip was also experimenting with a new fuel-efficient commercial aircraft, and had developed a fuel-saving device for fishing vessels. Tonar's projects were aimed at providing employment for and improving the lives of Russia's citizens. Its early projects centered on food distribution, and the production of polypropylene which was needed by many Russian companies. These activities attracted financing from various government sources.

The organizational structure of the three hybrid firms showed some similarities as well as marked differences. Mikromashina operated a single plant, with management on site operating both the company and its joint venture. Decisions for the most part were made in a hierarchical structure, except for the joint venture which had its own manager. Tonar functioned differently, having headquarters in Moscow and offices in five major Russian cities. The company operated on a project basis, and by utilizing only three management layers, decentralized decisions to project managers who were experienced operating executives. Ekip, with its 20-person headquarters, operated in a fashion similar to Tonar. Projects were headed by individual project managers, with Dr. Savitsky exercising varying amounts of involvement in each.

While Tonar and Ekip were adding employees to their growing organizations, Mikromashina's work force had decreased to 1,300 after a reduction of 400 employees during the Commercialization stage. The joint venture continued to employ 45 people. Mikromashina's management group worked to set a direction for the firm, while Tonar and Ekip sought to attract talented scientists to develop products and head projects. Dr. Savitsky felt that the interesting nature of the projects provided sufficient incentive to attract and retain technical leaders needed in Ekip, since most products were in the creative developmental stage. Tonar, in contrast, utilized three different remuneration plans for its higher level managers, one of which was very dependent upon company profit. Mikromashina had begun introducing team bonuses which were tied to productivity and quality.

In spite of the uncertainties and numerous problems in the political and economic environments, the Commercialization period was a relatively positive time for these enterprises. They received enough government funding to pursue their projects and objectives. Tonar reported profitable operations, as well as equity infusion from some foreign investors. Ekip had few problems with funding since the founder was able to attract funds from various sources who saw great potential in a number of his projects. Mikromashina was initially able to finance itself from cash flow and government subsidies, although the company's position had deteriorated by the time the Commercialization stage came to a close. Overall, it was basically a time of relative optimism for all three firms.

Hybrid Organizations in the Privatization Stage

As these hybrid firms entered the Privatization stage, the economy seemed to be developing in a more organized fashion, but numerous problems persisted. Tonar viewed itself as a successful firm that was on its way to becoming one of the leading companies in Russia. Management's major organizational objective during the period was to reduce governments' minority ownership in the company, a goal consistent with the new environment of privatization. Ekip, already a primarily private organization, was little affected by the privatization laws, and saw its major objective to be moving projects beyond the developmental stage at a faster pace.

Mikromashina was the hybrid firm most affected by the country's privatization legislation. The majority shares were now held by management and the workers, although there were some individual outside investors. Mikromashina was also a 60-percent owner of its international joint venture. The acting director's primary objective was to develop a successful organization which would provide employment to as many of the company's workers as possible. Other managers, however, being new shareholders, seemed to want a quicker return for themselves, and were anxious to hold the company's first shareholder meeting to set new goals.

Like the state enterprises, the three hybrid firms were negatively affected by the deteriorating business environment during the Privatization stage. The drastic decrease in purchasing power due to rampant inflation caused slowdowns in sales for both Tonar and Mikromashina. Nonpayment of debts by companies and the government hurt all three enterprises. The deteriorating supply chain put additional pressure on costs and drove up prices, thus making exports unfeasible, especially for Mikromashina. Ekip experienced increasing difficulty in financing its projects, especially for aircraft which required large investments. The same problem existed for environmental clean-up projects in which both Ekip and Tonar were involved, and they also felt the effects of the government's reduced support for high technology initiatives.

The competitive strategy of Mikromashina was to continue to produce every day, although at a relatively low level because customers were few. Even if they could be found, they usually delayed payments for deliveries for very long periods. Management searched for international partners for whom the company could do contract manufacturing, and possibly produce their own branded products as well. They rented out plant space, and found employment for some workers at the companies which rented space. The joint venture continued to operate profitably, but Mikromashina used its share of the profits to pay its own payroll. It also sold additional ownership in the JV, as well as a ten-percent stake in Mikromashina itself to its American partner. In spite of all its stopgap measures, however, the company's financial position weakened considerably and debts increased to $500,000 in 1994.

Both Tonar and Ekip continued pursuing the projects they had been involved in for several years. In addition to investigating other opportunities, Tonar's managers were engaged in three primary projects. They constructed and began operating a polypropylene plant, worked with a foreign partner to develop a food distribution network, and made plans to build a solid waste disposal and recycling plant near Moscow. These projects were aimed at developing raw materials for the revitalization of Russia's infrastructure, as well as improving the ecological environment. The company also accelerated activities in developing small scientist-run companies which were meant to take advantage of the country's scientific talent. This was consistent with Tonar's objective to act as a bridge between entrepreneurs and the government, primarily by securing government funding for these entrepreneurships.

Ekip continued developing its technologically advanced, environmentally friendly products. These included fuel-efficient aircraft, energy-saving devices such as a wave mover for fishing vessels, and highly efficient electro-gas generators. The company was also developing an environmentally friendly insulation material for the construction industry. In addition, it was involved in a new joint venture to reclaim oil from industrial and oil well sites. Besides overseeing the company's development projects, Dr. Savitsky's primary activity was raising funds from industrial partners, private investors, and the government. It was apparent by this time, however, that funding such a large number of projects was not feasible.

Organizationally, Mikromashina attempted to make its way as a newly privatized stock company. The chief engineer had been promoted to the position of acting director until an election could be held at a shareholders' meeting. It was clear that there was dissension within the management ranks regarding the company's direction. The acting director expressed fears that the company would be destroyed by some young managers whom he viewed as opportunists. They, on the other hand, seemed to view him as clinging to the old ways of Russian enterprise directors, emphasizing employment and stability rather than profitability. It was clear, too, that the acting director wanted to keep Mikromashina as an independent Russian company rather than become foreign owned.

Tonar was run by an eight-member board of directors and seven committees which oversaw the company's major functions. It operated three primary divisions, each of which was subdivided into two departments. Management continued to employ a team approach and group decision making, and emphasized decentralization. The company continued to retain a relatively small corporate office, and a relatively small number of its 2,000 employees were managers. The firm's business approach was impressive enough to attract key people, as well as foreign and Russian investment for major projects. Still, management expressed concern with the scarcity of market-oriented entrepreneurs, as well as the company's inability to retain the best of these who often found other opportunities in the expanding privatized sector. The company promoted people on the basis of performance, and was considering issuing company shares as an additional incentive.

Even though Ekip was a private stock company, it received major support from the government, particularly the Committee for Science and Technology. Dr. Savitsky, in fact, considered the government as a partner he could trust without fear of losing key scientific talent and knowledge. The company continued to use joint ventures for many of its projects, and Dr. Savitsky's involvement in each varied. His family, especially his brother and sister, also played important roles in overseeing projects from marketing and accounting perspectives.

Overall, the Privatization period was a time of adjustment for the three hybrid organizations. Mikromashina became a private stock company, with 20-percent ownership remaining with the government. It had a new management, increasing operational problems, and an uncertain direction for the future due to strong disagreements among managers. Tonar experienced successful growth, and its management grew more experienced in operating a highly decentralized, complex organization. Ekip remained closely-held and controlled, and operated primarily as a research and development organization engaged in a large number of technical projects.

Hybrid Organizations in the Nomenklatura Stage

Although the hybrid firms fared relatively well during the early years of Privatization, they faced increasing challenges during the Nomenklatura years. On the surface it appeared that the country's economic and political situations were stabilizing, but negative forces were at work due to the rising power of the oligarchs and other opportunists. Some of this influence appeared to have penetrated Mikromashina as some of the new owner-managers seemed to be trying to increase their power and potential wealth.

The senior executives of both Tonar and Ekip noted the increasing prevalence in the country of unethical practices on the part of both business managers and government officials, and Tonar's managers also noted the sharply increasing power of the mafia over Russian businesses.

Mikromashina's competitive strategy changed little during the early years of the Nomenklatura stage, but evolved as the stage progressed. The company's problems intensified. Competition from imported goods became fiercer, and company sales decreased by 60 percent during 1994. Its financial problems became more acute, layoffs continued, and the company resorted to bartering with customers and suppliers. Management continued attempts to establish ventures such as joint manufacturing with international companies. The firm hoped to develop exports, which seemed more feasible with the decrease in inflation and more stable prices. The company became more involved in trading, such as importing and distributing parts from China. The company's new general director also succeeded in putting together a creative opportunity which involved the Lada automobile company and the Moscow city government. Still, all managers were increasingly concerned with the firm's survival, and the value of its building was recognized as a key asset in this quest. In fact, Mikromashina's strategic focus changed from production to real estate as the company leased more and more of its space to small businesses.

Tonar's mission and basic objectives remained focused on developing projects with social benefits. The company's broad network of relationships with government organizations and other companies continued to bring opportunities and financing until late 1994. The diversification strategy demonstrated in its portfolio of projects had proven successful. The company had also started its own bank to provide project financing to the firm at discount rates. By the end of 1995, however, the company experienced more difficulty in attracting funds for large-scale long-term projects, and as a result, management began focusing on fewer activities. They continued work on their three major projects, and often found it necessary to utilize foreign contractors and equipment because Russian companies could not provide the requisite levels of technology. Management also sought strong international partners to provide financing and share risk. As time went on, management remained optimistic, but cautiously so because of the increasing uncertainties in the environment, which appeared to be improving, but only superficially.

Ekip initially seemed the least affected by developments during the Nomenklatura stage. The company had gained experience and achieved success in several projects. Management was able to demonstrate that some equipment the firm developed was less expensive, simpler in design, and more reliable than competitive products. The government in 1994, in fact, provided one billion rubles for an aircraft project, and foreign companies including Europe's Airbus and Boeing of the US showed interest in joint ventures with Ekip. But in 1995, the company, like Tonar, experienced increasing difficulty in attracting financing. Some projects were cancelled and others delayed. Projects were categorized into three types: those producing immediate cash flows like the environmental encyclopedia, those with a one- to three-year payback like insulation material and electro-gas dynamic generators, and those with a longer payback period such as the aircraft innovations. This procedure allowed Dr. Savitsky to manage funds in a more disciplined and effective manner.

Organizationally, Mikromashina underwent dramatic changes. The company's work force decreased to several hundred, part of the turnover being caused by delays in paying wages. Although the acting director had sought to retain employees and keep the company independent, other managers were more willing to consider alternatives. In late 1994, the American joint venture partner owned ten percent of Mikromashina and offered to increase its ownership position. The acting director was somewhat favorable to the offer, but was reluctant to see the company become foreign-owned. Partly due to this attitude, he was replaced by a younger manager at a stockholders' meeting early in the Nomenklatura stage.

The American firm had already purchased Mikromashina's remaining ownership in the joint venture, and its offer for additional Mikromashina stock would have infused $300,000 into the troubled Russian company. Negotiations continued through the entire Nomenklatura period, but never came to fruition. The Americans believed that the new Mikromashina owner-managers had a grossly inflated view of the company's value, and its attempts to buy the government's 20-percent share became extremely complicated. The Americans, nevertheless, did succeed in bringing their ownership of Mikromashina to nearly 50 percent by buying shares from the former acting director, the director of the joint venture, and some other employees. By the end of 1997, the joint venture ceased to exist, and the American company formed a Russian subsidiary, Nypro Moscow. This new organization negotiated business relationships with Mikromashina on an arm's length basis, in spite of Nypro's significant ownership position.

Tonar's management began to exercise increasing oversight of various projects, while still attempting to decentralize as much as seemed reasonable during uncertain times. A service team was created for each major project, and corporate control was exercised through planning and control systems which monitored project performance. The number of daughter entrepreneurial companies diminished somewhat, and the entrepreneurs were no longer given the incentive of earning ten-percent ownership of their companies. Instead, they were offered an opportunity to participate in a plan to obtain stock in the parent company. The major change in Tonar's organization was an increase in centralization of decision making.

The major changes in Ekip's organization and processes mirrored those of Tonar. In addition to developing a cash-flow classification system for its projects, the company began developing a business plan for each one. Dr. Savitsky's son and daughter, due to their training in economics and computers, were major contributors to this effort which combined both financial and technical feasibility analysis. As in Tonar, attention to planning and control increased dramatically during the Nomenklatura stage. Dr. Savitsky also refused to vote the shares he held in a key aircraft factory to support one of its high-level executives. He considered the individual to be overly ambitious and greedy, a characteristic demonstrated by many opportunists during the Nomenklatura period. Dr. Savitsky was clearly intent on retaining both majority ownership and operating control of his developing organization.

Hybrid Organizations in the Statization Stage

The economic environment during the first half of 1998 appeared positive on the surface, but masked the increasing deterioration which led to the financial crisis that erupted in August. For all three hybrid organizations, survival became the overriding objective, even as the country's economic situation improved during the first half of 1999.

In an ironic twist, Mikromashina, although hurt during the August crisis, actually benefited from the ensuing severe devaluation of the ruble. It began producing electrical appliances at an increasing rate as Russians resumed purchasing domestic products rather than the now very expensive imported goods. The company improved its quality to meet consumers' heightened expectations that resulted from their experience with imports. Employment continued to fall, but the work force leveled off at around 140 by mid-1999. In addition to a small resurgence in its traditional production strategy, the company succeeded in renting space to about 15 small businesses, including Nypro Moscow. That new company was headed by the former sales manager of the defunct joint venture, and operated five plastic injection molding machines in an advanced cleanroom facility. Nypro US executives felt that the new general director was doing a good job in steering Mikromashina through the troubled times. They, in fact, were happy to see the company's fortunes improving because they owned nearly half of the company's stock, and Nypro Moscow was a tenant in the building.

Beyond its survival focus, Ekip's mission and other major objectives did not change during 1998, even though the country's financial crisis had eroded funding for scientific research and development. The company managed to continue its activities at a reduced pace. Strategically, the firm continued working on projects that were most likely to produce cash in the short and medium terms. The company's primary business objective was the development of energy-efficient heat pump systems. Dr. Savitsky took the lead in founding a large scientific-production association devoted to promoting heat pump technology. Company scientists wrote articles and made presentations and speeches to promote the company's activities. Managers lobbied the Moscow city government for funding of its energy-saving projects. Ekip also continued work on other projects such as its electro-gas dynamic compressor. The company still received support from the Ministry of Science and Technology and the Moscow city government, but funding became more difficult after the financial crisis. Management's successful defense against a major tax liability did, however, help the company's financial position. No basic changes occurred in the ownership of the company, in the top management team, or organizational structure. More emphasis, however, was placed on merit and productivity in reward systems.

By the Statization stage, Vadim Andronov and Konstantin Ananichev, the two founders of Tonar, had died, and Dr. Andronov's son had assumed leadership of the company. Strategy changed little, but because the company's projects were so capital intensive, they progressed at a very slow pace. Much of management's time was spent seeking partners who could infuse capital into the company's projects. Tonar maintained a website which described its projects and its interest in securing partners to pursue these endeavors.

The Statization stage with its financial crisis of mid-1998 tested the staying power of most Russian organizations including these three hybrid firms. Survival for them, as for most enterprises, became the overriding concern and objective. A major concern for Ekip and Tonar was the virtual bankruptcy of the government on whom they had depended for financial support of large technical projects, while Mikromashina had long since stopped receiving government subsidies. Financing their futures had become even more problematical than in the earlier stages of the country's transition, but the improving economic situation of the first half of 1999 did provide some relief. Still, all three hybrid organizations remained under pressure to improve their financial positions if they were to follow their strategies and pursue their objectives.

Entrepreneurships in the Commercialization Stage

The Commercialization stage, with its landmark legislative changes legalizing private businesses, opened the door for entrepreneurs to develop new business opportunities. Beginning with small retail shops and other cooperative-type ventures, the entrepreneurial spirit spread throughout many sectors, especially in services since such businesses required relatively little initial investment. Some entrepreneurs started ventures within state-owned enterprises, or as spin-offs from those organizations. Other ventures were start-ups run by entrepreneurs from various backgrounds including university professors, students, scientists, government officials, and individuals from the black market economy. The newly permissive and open environment led many honest and ethical individuals to start new businesses, but unfortunately it also attracted others with lesser scruples and ideals. A major obstacle for many, regardless of intentions, was their lack of experience in a market-oriented economy. There were few rules to guide them and most were forced to learn by doing, which led to unfortunate consequences for many. Still, the entrepreneurial climate proved to be a powerful magnet of opportunity which attracted many to test their talents.

The nascent market economy called for a viable private banking sector to support the capital requirements of new entrepreneurships. Thus, promising opportunities developed early which attracted numerous entrepreneurs who hoped to participate on the ground floor of the new economy. However, the

244

Central Bank regulated the private banking industry and imposed many onerous requirements. For instance, its requirement of a deposit amounting to 20 percent of assets from all private banks severely limited loan funds available to customers. Unrealistic taxes and other restrictive government legislation also inhibited development of the banking system. Still, it was acknowledged that these institutions required some control because of their power and potential for damage to the emerging economy.

Premier Bank, founded by a professor-economist, was one of the first three commercial banks registered in the USSR. The founder often criticized the role of the Central Bank, but also acknowledged that the banking industry included some executives who violated internationally accepted business approaches. Thus, many people were suspicious of banking practices in general. Dr. Kruk viewed the banking environment as being primarily influenced by the Central Bank's regulations, governmental policies such as taxation, economic conditions including inflation, and the growth of new businesses with their great need for capital.

Premier Bank's initial capital came from the founder, as well as investments from business associates including several bankers with whom he had worked in the past. The bank's mission was to become a successful commercial bank, primarily through making loans to domestic private entrepreneurships as well as international customers. Premier Bank chose not to do business with large state enterprises so as not to be exposed to trouble in case of their failure. The strategy during the early 1990s was to commit its loan funds for a maximum of one year, and usually for much shorter periods. Given the risk associated with most loans, the company usually required a hard currency deposit from borrowers.

Organizationally, the company was directed by its founder, Dr. Kruk. He had a strong background in economics and finance, and wanted to exercise his talents in the newly developing industry. From his office situated near the Kremlin, he oversaw the growth of Premier Bank. Operations required a very small staff, and business was done primarily on a personal basis between Dr. Kruk and his customers. Eventually, he hoped to turn the bank over to his son.

As crucial as the banking system was for many start-ups, BusinessLink was one entrepreneurship that grew successfully during these years through internal financing. The company, which was created in 1991, was successful from the start due primarily to the backgrounds and networks of its educator-founders. These professors and administrators from St. Petersburg University had a wide range of associates from Western countries. Their experience and the contacts they had made provided leads and capabilities to work with Western companies which established operations in Russia during the early years of the market economy. The influx of multinationals and other Western firms was in fact the primary environmental factor affecting the growth of BusinessLink. The lure of the potentially large Russian market and the opening of opportunities for foreign companies were irresistible incentives to these organizations.

BusinessLink's managers devised a strategy to take advantage of their contacts and experience with Western business methods to offer services to these companies, beginning with consulting. The primary focus was to advise international organizations on market entry approaches, and then to recruit employees for them. These activities soon led BusinessLink to assist international firms in finding Russian partners. Procter & Gamble was its first major client, and Coca-Cola soon followed upon P&G's recommendation. Advertising also became a major opportunity for BusinessLink during this period.

Organizationally, the company was led by four founders who formed a limited partnership, while retaining their positions at the university. They were initially very active in the company's consulting activities, but their direct involvement diminished as they brought on additional employees. Key hires were also instrumental in leading the company into new services for international clients. The most important of these was an individual hired in late 1991 with experience in advertising, who developed a major effort in this area for BusinessLink. The company seemed to have unlimited opportunities as the Commercialization stage came to a close.

Aquarius was started in early 1989 as a joint venture between five Russian organizations and a West German trading company. The JV succeeded an earlier one involving relationships with the Taiwanese company Aquarius, which had the leading sales position in the Russian market. This earlier Russian-German-Taiwanese agreement was one of the first signed under the 1988 USSR joint venture law. The computer business, however, was extremely competitive, with large state-owned enterprises selling products at very low prices. Computers imported from Asia could also be purchased for relatively low prices, while Western imports were priced somewhat higher. Taxes on imported components made computers assembled in Russia very expensive, inhibiting the growth of a domestic industry.

In spite of these obstacles, the JV's strategy was to enter the computer business by assembling and selling high quality computers for the Russian market. The joint venture targeted high-level government agencies as its major market. The firm soon developed a strong reputation for quality products at reasonable prices, and offered two-year warranties to customers. Government agencies proved to be good customers for Aquarius and readily accepted its products. Initially, the computers were assembled by the company's 120 workers. Parts were purchased from the German partner's parent company as well as from the Taiwanese partner. After a short period, however, the German partner wanted to import assembled computers, a decision which the Russian partners believed went against their agreement.

This dispute led to a number of organizational changes. With the German partner's decision not to invest in more plant and equipment, the Russian partners were forced to find funds elsewhere. The dispute led to the exodus of the German partner, and relationships with the Taiwanese partner became infrequent after the latter was acquired by a larger Taiwanese firm. In late 1992, Aquarius became an independent Russian stock company. Although the firm experienced some success during these years, it lost 20 million rubles in 1992 when the government freed prices and inflation soared.

Vybor was started in 1986 as a consumer goods trading cooperative by the two Buianovskii brothers who shared ownership equally. They had explored various business opportunities and concluded that a trading company would be the most profitable. The brothers shared the top management responsibilities, and rotated the roles of president and general manager. They also set up business units as profit centers in which each brother had a 50-percent share.

The business environment during the period was very supportive of trading companies that imported consumer goods into the shortage-plagued economy. Like other service companies, these organizations required little investment, but their success depended upon capable managers and employees. Inflation was actually viewed as an advantage by some who believed that consumers would rather buy goods than hold onto rubles that might quickly devalue. On the negative side, however, shipping goods into Russia was very difficult due to uncertain tax legislation and customs regulations, and the undeveloped banking system exacerbated problems in financing transactions.

Vybor's founders planned to stay in the trading business only as long as it remained profitable, and then they would try another line of business. The firm's strategy was to remain as a wholesaler and distributor and not to develop its own retail stores. Rather, it sold to customer groups of all sizes, ranging from large enterprises to small kiosks which had proliferated on the streets of the larger cities. Vybor would also bring products directly to large state enterprises on paydays and sell goods directly to the employees. One of the company's strengths was its expediting service which transported goods from warehouses to customers. The company imported products primarily from Asian countries with low wage rates, and was thus able to sell goods at reasonable prices.

Early in the company's history, Vybor had entered into a joint venture with an Irish trading company which had substantial experience in the import-export business. Initially, the joint venture benefited greatly from the partnership, but the advantages diminished as the brothers became more experienced. Vybor operated more as an independent company, and its organizational structure included a headquarters in Moscow and 40 subsidiaries located throughout the country. In decision making, the brothers encouraged their managers to act as if they were running their own small independent companies under the Vybor umbrella. They encouraged entrepreneurship and allowed managers to make most decisions that did not require additional funding. Senior managers were eligible for profit sharing, and along with individual unit managers, earned shares in Vybor through the company's stock incentive plan. Although this system diluted the founders' ownership position, they believed these inducements were necessary to incentivize and retain their best managers.

The Commercialization stage was one of growth and relative success for all of the entrepreneurships, but all did not fare equally well during this stage. Premier Bank grew nicely, with the founder utilizing his network to gain funding as well as develop business with new private enterprises. The need for commercial banks to provide loan funds to these emerging organizations was crucial to the development of a market economy. BusinessLink prospered from the influx of large international companies which saw promising business opportunities. Aquarius also grew, but fared less well, primarily due to counterproductive government legislation and disruptive changes in relations with foreign partners. Vybor, like so many trading companies, grew profitably by bringing highly desirable imported goods to the consumer market. The Commercialization stage was a period of excitement and promise for individuals with an entrepreneurial inclination. Opportunities seemed boundless, but an understanding of operating in a more open economy was only beginning to develop.

Entrepreneurships in the Privatization Stage

Although the government's privatization program was a milestone in Russia's transition to a market economy, entrepreneurships were the organizations least affected by the process. The major exceptions were the commercial banks. Many saw a potential business opportunity in financing the newly privatized enterprises, although most recognized the risk involved.

Premier Bank entered the Privatization stage as a solid and profitable financial institution. Its success continued throughout this period with 1993 showing a 650-percent ROI, several times greater than inflation. These results were achieved in spite of numerous problems in the economy and the banking system. Dr. Kruk noted that the Central Bank was still a major obstacle to progress within the banking system because it had done little to stem inflation after the start of privatization. The Central Bank had promised to keep the money supply tied to the level of production in order to keep prices in line with supply. In actuality, it continued increasing the money supply while the output of goods and services decreased dramatically, thus fueling inflation. Government policies also continued to cause problems for businesses including the commercial banks. The newly privatized enterprises received vastly reduced levels of government support, which led banks like Premier to view them as high-risk clients. Excessive levels of taxation caused problems in cash flow for all businesses, as well as for many banks.

Although the environment improved little during the Privatization period, the new era itself did not affect Premier Bank directly. Its policy of not dealing with large state enterprises continued even after many had been privatized, although the bank did begin doing business with some of the smaller enterprises. Premier's strategy continued to focus on making loans to domestic clients for only very short periods, often as little as one month. This business was profitable, and Premier Bank even invested in the businesses of some of its better clients. The bank also continued doing business with a few foreign clients, but its most profitable activity was trading in currencies to take advantage of the wide fluctuations between the ruble and other currencies. By 1993, the bank had over 500 clients.

Organizationally, Premier Bank changed little during the period, but the founder became more and more involved in his growing business. He was guardedly optimistic about the future of his bank, as well as the country. He noted in 1993 that the shock therapy approach had caused numerous problems, but believed that it was probably unavoidable. He felt the same about privatization, noting the many problems that had erupted in the country's business infrastructure, as well as the cash crunch that affected most former state-owned enterprises. He concluded that, despite many problems with the government, President Yeltsin was the country's only hope at that time.

BusinessLink's management hardly seemed to notice any effects of the country's early privatization efforts. To a large degree, the service company was shielded from many of the negative effects of the legislation, and saw the newly privatized enterprises as potential clients. Revenues reached the $1 million level in 1993, and the company had not yet resorted to bank loans, but continued to finance growth from profits. It still dealt almost exclusively with large international clients, and added new services to its portfolio. The strategy had evolved to provide "one-stop shopping" for foreign firms. Services by this time included consulting, executive and personnel search, advertising, public relations, and real estate development. A real estate professional had been hired earlier to build this business, and an initial activity focused on renovating the company's own building. This new opportunity was the result of the shortage of quality office space in St. Petersburg to house foreign companies and new Russian entrepreneurships.

The foundation of BusinessLink's diversification strategy was to follow the needs of customers. In pricing its services, the company usually stayed below Western competitors but above the prices of domestic companies. Much of its growth was fueled by word of mouth and strong recommendations to new clients, as well as by the increasing revenues from present customers. The company developed business with international companies in Moscow and other areas outside of St. Petersburg. Competition for consulting came mainly from the Big Six American accounting firms, while numerous relatively weak Russian firms competed with all of the company's businesses. To combat competition and promote its reputation and service offerings, the company employed direct marketing techniques and seminars.

BusinessLink remained a limited partnership with a management committee coordinating the activities of individual units. In 1993, the company had 40 full-time employees and 100 part-time personnel hired on a project basis. Most full-time staff were Russians between 30 and 40 years old, and most had some experience in their fields before joining BusinessLink. A shortage of such skilled people was the company's major obstacle to growth during these years, and management tried to create an attractive environment for young professionals by providing highly competitive salaries, flexible work hours, and a family-oriented culture. Senior managers and consultants also had the opportunity to receive substantial bonuses. The partners still did not draw salaries, preferring to reinvest in their rapidly growing business.

The Privatization period provided a new beginning for Aquarius, although many problems still existed in the economic and political environments. The company's managers noted that constantly changing laws made it difficult to plan for the future. They noted also that privatization, being targeted at state-owned organizations, brought no support for entrepreneurs or other private firms. Yet, Aquarius regained profitability in 1993 due to improving computer industry conditions and a new competitive strategy. Import taxes on components decreased from 200 percent of value to 10 percent, removing an onerous burden from the company's cost structure. New Russian computer firms focused on sales and service, but no major competitor emerged that also assembled computers.

The company's strategy changed to a new emphasis on sales while maintaining quality in its products. Aquarius created an extensive dealership network throughout Russia, and initiated a highly creative approach with dealers. It began selling to them on consignment, which in turn allowed dealers to pay Aquarius after they themselves had been paid. The company's management realized the risk in this approach, but was willing to incur it in order to increase market penetration. Sales were supported by promotions at trade shows, some of which the company hosted. As the new strategy developed, customer focus shifted from government agencies to smaller private and newly privatized companies. Most sales were made in the Russian market, while around ten percent came from exports to other CIS countries.

Concurrent with successes in its improving computer business, Aquarius began a strategy of diversification, and changed its organizational structure to accommodate this new direction. The computer business became one operating unit of the new Aquarius holding company. Other businesses were added such as financial and legal services, production of window frames and heaters for homes, information systems for import-export operations, and real estate development and construction management projects. Like BusinessLink and other entrepreneurships, the company began its real estate development business by renovating the building it occupied. The holding company operated its diversified businesses as a portfolio, with funds taken from some businesses to finance the growth of others. The company also planned to have an internal bank to loan funds to its own businesses at reduced rates. The addition of so many businesses in a short period required more financing than the company could generate through its sales.

Vybor, like many trading companies, did not prosper as well during the Privatization period as entrepreneurships in banking and business services, and even some with assembly operations like Aquarius. Vybor had begun specializing in the distribution of sport shoes imported from a number of Asian countries. An increasing number of competitors, however, had entered this market and the company was forced to lower prices and increase advertising. The company supplemented sales efforts with television advertising targeted at retailers rather than consumers, but supported this with newspaper advertising to consumers. By 1993, the founders of Vybor thought that the market was becoming saturated when profits decreased by 70 percent. Yet, it was still one of the top 50 import-export firms in Russia, and had no problem getting credit from banks due to its strong reputation.

Vybor employed 500 people in its Moscow operations and five to ten in each of its 40 daughter companies. The average age of employees was under 30, and half were women. Finding experienced and reliable people was very difficult, so most employees required substantial training. The brothers felt that a major problem was the psychology of employees in Russia, and stated that it was difficult to motivate them to work hard after 70 years of socialist attitudes and work habits. Even though employees' wages were linked to performance, the founders were not confident that this was an effective incentive.

The Privatization stage was generally a positive time for the entrepreneurial companies which were largely unaffected by the landmark legislation that brought about the privatization of most of the country's state-owned enterprises. In spite of increasing competition as foreign and domestic companies entered the growing market, these entrepreneurships found ways to grow successfully. Beginning as private companies, these new ventures always had to be self-financing. They had never relied on government subsidies as had the newly privatized enterprises. They were also more attuned to the emerging market economy than were other organizations. A major obstacle to the growth of most entrepreneurships was the shortage of motivated personnel experienced in a market economy. The strategies of the entrepreneurs were almost always market driven, and often opportunistic, which caused many of them to diversify. As the complexity of their businesses increased, they developed new organizational structures and systems. The end of the

Privatization stage saw most founders of the entrepreneurships looking to the future with optimism.

Entrepreneurships in the Nomenklatura Stage

It was the banking industry, more than any other, that was dramatically affected by events of the Nomenklatura stage. The founders of many of the country's largest banks were in fact the central figures of the period as they accrued power and wealth. The most infamous of the group were called oligarchs, and they allied themselves with politicians, some becoming very close to President Yeltsin. Having gained wealth and power in the new private sector, the most ambitious secured high-level government positions to extend their influence. Bankers, government officials, and some leaders of major privatized businesses like Gazprom became locked in an incestuous power structure.

A major problem for most commercial banks during this period was the high interest rates of around 200 percent charged to them by the Central Bank. Another was the nonpayment of debts by the government and enterprises which drained the cash reserves of many banks. This was an especially serious problem since they were required by the Central Bank to have large capital reserves. In 1995, such circumstances caused three of the country's top 30 banks to be designated as bankrupt. Not all bankers, of course, joined the ranks of the nomenklatura, but it was difficult for their institutions to remain unaffected by the emerging power structure. This influential group was often responsible for ever-changing banking regulations, and engaged in lucrative financial transactions with the government.

Other banks participated in these financial activities to a much more limited extent, such as buying and selling short-term government notes and bonds, and profiting on the interest. Premier Bank was among those that engaged in purchasing and selling volatile state obligations on which they earned exceptionally high interest. Another major source of profit for Premier was its continuing involvement in currency transactions. The bank also followed its strategy of making short-term loans to selected companies, and added services such as financing receivables and real estate. Clients in these transactions were enterprises that were solid, and had valuable assets as well as good cash flow. The bank had increased its activities in all of these areas during 1994 and extended its list of customers. Active clients, however, were a relatively small percentage of the bank's nearly 1,000 customers.

Premier Bank's successful strategy continued to generate profits in 1995. Dr. Kruk resigned from the Institute of Finance in order to devote his full efforts to Premier. By 1996, the bank had 25 full-time and 30 part-time employees, and its assets reached around $10 million. The continuously profitable Premier Bank was ranked among the top 400 of the country's 2,000 banks. Having brought his institution to this level of success, Dr. Kruk passed the leadership to his 30-year-old son. The organization remained relatively small and was growing slowly, while increasing assets and the capital base. Premier Bank was, however, open to the prospect of allying itself with a Western banking partner.

BusinessLink, because of the nature of its business and customer base, was relatively unaffected by the developments of the Nomenklatura stage. The company's profits continued to be sufficient to finance growth, and it did not need to borrow from banks. In most respects, it was detached from the people and activities which characterized the Nomenklatura period, and the company continued to be extremely successful. The firm grew by responding to customer needs and emphasizing its two major competitive advantages – quality and reputation. All of its businesses prospered, and the client base increased to over 400 foreign firms and a growing number of Russian companies.

Management saw the economic environment becoming more stable, although they noted the uncertainty in the political arena. Competition was increasing for all of the businesses, but the advertising unit, renamed BL Advertising, was strong enough to compete with international advertising agencies. The company had allied itself with a leading Scottish real estate development company, and BusinessLink's newly established branch office in Finland was successful in attracting 11 of the 50 largest Finnish companies as clients.

Dr. Molchanov was the only one of the four original founders to remain active in BusinessLink after 1994. Two partners had died in an automobile accident, while a third withdrew from active management of the firm. Dr. Molchanov spent an increasing part of his time deciding where to make investments, particularly with regard to the firm's burgeoning real estate activities. His managerial focus was on establishing an organizational structure which could support the firm's growth strategy. He delegated more and more authority to the directors of BusinessLink's four business units. They were treated as autonomous businesses having their own competitive strategies, but major resource allocation decisions were made by BusinessLink's board of directors.

During the Nomenklatura stage, BusinessLink's staff increased to 200 full-time people, as well as part-timers as needed. The company's main problem continued to be attracting enough qualified professionals to support its growing client base. Management continued to use its contacts with St. Petersburg University to attract talent, and provided training including opportunities for key managers to earn MBA degrees abroad at company expense. The firm's structure and culture continued to de-emphasize hierarchy and centralized decision making, both to help people grow and to provide an atmosphere conducive to retaining them. Salaries continued to be relatively high and a team-based performance bonus system was in place for all employees. Together, the company's structure, culture, and incentive systems ensured a low incidence of turnover.

The new entrepreneurship's spiral of success resulted in a near doubling of BusinessLink's revenues during most years of the Nomenklatura stage, increasing from under $2 million in 1994 to over $14 million in 1997. Management forecasted another major increase for 1998. Even though its financial strategy of reinvesting all profits in the business continued, financial demands were increasing as the company's growth continued unabated. Still, the company borrowed only to finance real estate transactions which required substantial funding. The company had also opened a new Moscow office to serve its current clients as well as an increasing number of Russian companies which sought its services. Management was also considering starting a professional financial consulting business which would offer auditing services, primarily to Russian firms.

Like BusinessLink, Aquarius was not directly affected by the events of the Nomenklatura period, and in fact the company prospered during these years of increased stabilization in the economic and political environments. Inflation was still a serious problem, however, as was nonpayment of debts among businesses. Yet, the company was able to obtain bank loans as needed, and also became involved in trading government promissory notes, which for a time was very profitable. The computer industry was experiencing substantial growth, with firms such as Dell and Compaq from the US providing competition for standard models of Aquarius computers, while IBM and Hewlett-Packard competed with the firm's advanced model. Still, the company's computer unit grew successfully through a strategy of new product introductions. The holding company's construction business was also growing well, and plans for building a customs service center were progressing on schedule.

However, the management of the computer business unit, which was the original focus of Aquarius, became increasingly dissatisfied with the lack of support they received from the holding company. As one of eight units, and a fast-growing business, the company required cash to sustain its momentum. Management claimed, however, that the holding company was siphoning off its profits to support other business units. The computer unit's successful growth strategy involved producing standard and advanced models, as well as diversifying into assembly and distribution of electronic cash registers. This decision resulted from a government regulation requiring retail establishments to have such point-of-sale installations. The unit continued to emphasize quality and reliability through its two-year warranty, and lobbied the government to provide low-interest credit to customers who purchased home computers.

In 1995, the director of the holding company was replaced by a financial officer from the firm. Igor Galkin, who was leading the computer business unit, negotiated its purchase before the corporation went bankrupt the following year. The Aquarius computer unit became an independent stock company after borrowing enough funds to complete the transaction, and these debts were repaid before the end of 1996. The computer company's managers believed that the new strategy could now be carried out successfully without the restrictions of an unsupportive parent. Cash registers, in fact, had become more profitable than computers, and Aquarius was able to secure loans from other banks and an American fund.

Independence seemed to serve the computer company well as it grew and prospered during the remainder of the Nomenklatura period. The company focused on expanding its products and services, and improving distribution channels. It established a relationship with one of the country's strongest distributors, OCS, and became listed as an official supplier for many government ministries. As 1997 ended, Aquarius computers were serviced at more than 100 centers throughout the Federation. The cash register product and its related systems also enjoyed growing success, with more than 50,000 machines in use. The Shuya factory was in active operation, producing and assembling company products, and Aquarius was investigating the use of subcontractors as demand increased.

Mr. Galkin proved to be an effective strategist and leader for the newly independent company, and employees who had left in the past began returning to the reorganized computer company. He credited the new spirit and enthusiasm for the organization's success, and the company was even doing business with some former employees who had joined other companies. Growth, however, was not achieved without pressures and problems. It caused financial strains, as well as organizational pressures as the company attempted to balance a supportive culture with sufficient controls to ensure profitability. At the end of the Nomenklatura period, managers remained optimistic about the future of the newly independent computer firm.

As a wholesaler and distributor of imported products, Vybor was more affected by the vagaries of the economic environment during the Nomenklatura stage than were the other entrepreneurships. Periods of hyperinflation, nonpayment of debts among enterprises, and difficulties in finding reliable employees all remained issues for the company. Vybor's major problem was that customers lacked money to pay for consumer goods, causing the company to resort to bartering with customers. The environment continued to deteriorate for Vybor, with competition becoming fiercer, causing severe price erosion. Still, business remained profitable during 1994 and 1995, although profits were lower than in previous years.

During this stage, Aleksandr Buianovskii devoted more time to strategic issues, especially prospecting for and organizing new businesses, and he planned only six months ahead because of the rapidly changing environment. He increased delegation of operational decisions to the most experienced and trusted staff members. His strategy was to retain the company's joint venture, and continue to operate as a wholesaler and distributor of consumer goods such as shoes and clothing. He and his brother, however, were open to new opportunities, and in 1994 they became part owners of an investment fund, financing the purchase by bartering products in exchange for shares. The company's ability to compete and survive during this period was due to Aleksandr's new focus on strategic issues. He realized that the company had to cut costs and divest some businesses, and led those efforts. A major result of his work was a downsizing in 1994 which saw the company lay off half of its employees. In 1995, Mr. Buianovskii decided to divest a number of subsidiary companies and to focus on athletic shoes, women's footwear, and clothing. The company also purchased a nearby sewing factory to begin making its own clothing line.

The downsizing task was delegated to managers, as was the job of introducing other efficiencies. Their participation in the company's profit sharing plan provided an incentive to carry this out. The downsizing of the work force also lessened the task of monitoring and controlling employees to minimize pilferage. Managers were rewarded with shares in their own units, each of which was organized as an independent entity, and they could eventually achieve 50-percent ownership.

Although the Nomenklatura stage was not an easy time for Vybor, the Buianovskii brothers believed the company had developed four primary sources of competitive advantage: experience as an established firm, a good reputation, an effective distribution channel, and a central location in Moscow. In mid-1995, Aleksandr looked to the future with optimism. It soon became clear, however, that the company had become overextended and had incurred a dangerous level of debt. Very inexpensive goods from Asia quickly eroded its market. The joint venture was dissolved and the bank demanded payments on a $2 million loan. Valentin Buianovskii left Vybor to start a new accounting business, leaving his brother to head the firm. In early 1996, the company's myriad problems became insurmountable and Vybor went bankrupt. Aleksandr stated at the time that Vybor existed only on paper. Ever optimistic, he himself became director of a plastic pipe plant, and began organizing a new company to distribute shoes throughout Russia. He believed that the political environment was improving somewhat, and that more positive economic conditions would follow and support the growth of his new ventures. He looked back on his experience at Vybor as a time of personal growth and learning that would serve him well in his future as an entrepreneur.

As the Nomenklatura period saw some enterprises like Vybor close their doors, new entrepreneurships emerged to fill the needs of the still evolving market economy. One such new entrant was Platinum Russia, an accounting and manufacturing software company. The new entrepreneurship started operations in mid-1994 under an exclusive license from Platinum Corporation of the US to distribute its products throughout the CIS. The founder, Olga Peterson, was a native Russian who at age 30 returned to her homeland after emigrating to the US at the age of 18. While in the US, she received her university education and worked in major corporations for several years. Dr. Peterson had begun negotiations with Platinum in the fall of 1993 and reached a successful conclusion six months later. Simultaneously, she obtained her Ph.D. in management from Moscow State University.

The time was opportune for Platinum Russia's strategy of translating a number of Platinum's products and localizing them for the Russian market. Numerous multinationals required their accounting systems and software to be adapted to the Russian language and local conditions. Many private Russian companies, including newly privatized enterprises, also desired financial systems which were compatible with Western standards, in order to attract foreign investors. Both foreign and domestic companies needed systems flexible enough to accommodate the rapidly changing tax laws and other reporting requirements of the Russian government. Major international accounting firms such as the US's Big Six had entered the market in response to these growth opportunities.

To combat such formidable competition, Platinum Russia's strategy focused on providing quality products and services. Its product-market approach combined Platinum USA's sophisticated product line with Dr. Peterson's extensive knowledge of customers and market conditions. The centerpiece of the company's offerings was a general ledger package which could be offered individually, or integrated with other Platinum products to provide clients with a complete financial information system. Platinum and its competitors often had to train Russian clients in accepted accounting methods and systems. Additionally, Platinum usually became engaged in consulting on systems development prior to installing its software packages, and this service frequently continued through a project's implementation stage.

The company's strategy included establishing alliances with some of the larger international accounting firms, including two at which Dr. Peterson had worked for several years after returning to Russia. These relationships lessened somewhat the level of competition among the companies. Platinum's early customers included well-known Western companies like Mercedes-Benz and Motorola, as well as large Russian companies. By 1996, it had more than 120 clients including PepsiCo, Coca-Cola, and Caterpillar. Company revenues in 1995, the first full year of operations, were $3 million.

Dr. Peterson shared ownership of Platinum Russia with her husband who was a senior marketing manager. She was recognized as the undisputed leader, and she saw her roles as being the company's strategist and senior manager. She became involved in functional activities like marketing only when she felt she could add value, and tried to keep out of technical matters. In this area she relied on her deputy who had an extensive technological and scientific background. All Platinum employees except Dr. Peterson's husband were Russian nationals. Their age averaged 30, and many had Ph.Ds.

By 1996, the company employed 150 professionals, 60 of whom worked as consultants which was the fastest growing group in Platinum. Staff members were recruited from universities and the Big Six accounting firms, often utilizing Dr. Peterson's extensive network of contacts. The company paid highly competitive salaries, and employees were eligible for performance-based bonuses. They were also attracted by Platinum's culture which Dr. Peterson described as creative and exciting. She also recognized that people were smart and should be treated with dignity. Still, attracting and keeping qualified professionals was the company's primary obstacle to growth.

Platinum, which began at the start of the Nomenklatura period, was profitable every year and entered 1998 poised for continued prosperity. Dr. Peterson believed that the company's success might attract additional investors to fund even more rapid growth, but she wanted to retain majority ownership with her husband. She had plans to expand to many new sites within Russia as well as into Eastern Europe, and to offer some of the company's products through a distributor network. Her entrepreneurship had clearly achieved its objectives during these years.

Entrepreneurships in the Statization Stage

Although the Statization stage saw the accumulation of power in the hands of government officials and leading business oligarchs, the early years of this stage appeared to produce a relatively stable and increasingly positive economy. President Yeltsin's erratic decisions, however, led to increasing political turmoil and more government involvement in economic decisions. The entrepreneurships most affected by these decisions were the country's private commercial banks, since many banking leaders or oligarchs were becoming targets of criticism from the public and government officials. It was the oligarchs' banks which suffered major problems during the financial crisis when the government devalued the ruble, froze bank accounts, and postponed payments on its debts. Many banks which held GKOs and other forms of government debt became nearly illiquid and were unable to meet their own obligations.

Premier Bank continued its successful operations during the first half of 1998 in spite of the increasingly stringent requirements and regulations of the Central Bank. Aleksandr Kruk, who assumed leadership of Premier in 1996, was critical of the Central Bank's policies, as well as the lack of government help for business. Still, the bank had continued to increase its capital and paid full dividends to shareholders through the first half of the year. Management had decided to continue investing in government short-term bonds since they carried the government's unconditional guarantee for repayment. Such bond holdings were sufficient to cover all the bank's liabilities to its customers.

When the government defaulted on its bonds, Premier Bank, like most others, found itself in a very difficult situation, having insufficient liquidity to repay its obligations. Beyond the bank's immediate problems, Aleksandr Kruk stated that the country had been thrown into an economic morass and that it would take years for businesses and banks to recover. In spite of its difficulties, Premier Bank continued to provide services to clients.

The bank's management tried not to lay off employees but did cut salaries by 40 percent. Although Aleksandr's position as the bank's new leader was the only major managerial change in eleven years, the crisis forced a restructuring and redistribution of responsibilities. Before the crisis, management planned for continuous growth of the bank's capital and clientele. The crisis, however, forced Aleksandr to focus on survival, hoping that the government would begin to repay at least part of its frozen debt. He said in early 1999 that the country's economic situation and that of his bank were difficult, but not hopeless. Referring to the increasing role of the government in the country's economy, he expected only long-term obstacles from that source, and believed that banks and businesses could rely only on themselves for the foreseeable future.

Unlike Premier Bank and other commercial banks which were adversely affected by the government's increasing involvement in the economy, BusinessLink hardly noticed the changing environment. Most of its business units still dealt primarily with international customers, and being in this market segment effectively sheltered the firm from many disruptions caused by governmental policies. The first half of 1998 saw a continuation of the company's highly successful growth, and BusinessLink was on its way to reaching its planned profits and revenues. Dr. Molchanov, in fact, was devoting a greater portion of his time to arranging financing for the real estate development group to fund its increasing number of projects.

Although the burgeoning real estate business had become the company's most profitable unit by 1998, BL Advertising was its largest producer with 1998 revenues projected at $17 million, up from 1997's $13 million. It had become a major competitor in the St. Petersburg market, and its Moscow office was also thriving. The real estate and advertising units continued to be led by their long-term directors who had been with the company since its early days. The personnel services group, under its newly appointed director, had doubled its revenues in the 12 months ending in July 1998. The company continued to increase its areas of activity and planned a new auditing service unit to work with Russian companies.

BusinessLink's work force numbered 200 full-time professionals in early 1998, who were supplemented by a part-time work force as needed. Dr.

Molchanov had restructured the firm into a holding company during 1997 with BusinessLink as the umbrella company for its operating units. BL Advertising was growing so fast that it had virtually become an umbrella for its own operating units. The holding company's board of directors was constituted entirely of insiders in mid-1998, but Dr. Molchanov was considering inviting outsiders with particular expertise to help shape the growing company's strategy. He had delegated increasing authority to the business unit directors to give them more latitude, and to free himself to work more intensively on strategic and financial issues. Most financial needs of BusinessLink were satisfied by internal funding, and banks were happy to deal with the company in financing its real estate projects. Dr. Molchanov recognized, however, that this activity took more and more of his time because many Russian, and even some international, banks were involved. He looked upon the first half of 1998 as having been a very positive growth period for BusinessLink.

Even after the August crisis, Dr. Molchanov felt that the company was healthy and well positioned for survival, and that BusinessLink could retain a substantial amount of its business. The company, however, was affected negatively by the rapidly deteriorating economic conditions. It had been forced to cut costs which included a substantial downsizing of personnel. Clients had become much more cost conscious and BusinessLink had to recognize this in its pricing. BL Advertising was especially affected since clients had less money for advertising, and some questioned the effectiveness of advertising to consumers whose purchasing power had rapidly decreased. Obtaining funds for the real estate development unit had also become more difficult since banks had so little money to lend.

Dr. Molchanov and his directors realized that the situation would not change soon, and that their primary objective had to be ensuring the survival of BusinessLink. This involved serious attention to cost cutting, and all senior managers became more directly involved with clients to help ensure a revenue flow. Dr. Molchanov's strategy had called for all units to be self-financing, but he was willing to moderate this requirement in order for all of them to survive the crisis. He believed that BusinessLink would succeed best as one company of several business units offering varied services to clients. Regarding personnel, managers regretted the downsizing but viewed it as crucial for survival. They kept those employees who were most productive and who could perform multiple jobs. Managers realized that the situation was very difficult, but were guardedly optimistic because of the relatively solid financial and business positions of the company. All of them had grown up in the business as entrepreneurs, and even during this adversity, they retained their belief in BusinessLink and in themselves.

The Statization period proved no obstacle for Aquarius Systems Inform. The increasing government involvement in the economy was more a problem for banks and other companies which were either regulated by the government or which did substantial government business. Aquarius' customer base was quite diversified as was its product line, and the company was somewhat shielded from the vagaries of government decision making. Its computers were well accepted by commercial customers, and the new cash register line had become as important as computers. The company's technology and quality were increasingly recognized, and Aquarius became the first Russian computer firm to attain ISO 9002 certification. As further indication of its increasing internationalization, the company was testing its products for compatibility with Windows 95, Warp 4.0, and other international standards.

To enhance distribution, the company had created a strategic alliance with a major retailer and its subsidiary, Landata. That company's dealer network would, for the first time, allow Aquarius computers to be distributed to consumers and small businesses. Additional distribution capability was achieved with a broad alliance between the company and OCS, a major Russian distributor of computers, which in the past had focused on Western products as well as its own brand. The high volume generated through OCS' network was facilitated by Aquarius' attractive price and terms package. These alliances, as well as the company's growing reputation, allowed Aquarius to attract new partners and become involved in major projects. For instance, Aquarius acted as general contractor of a major project to establish a computer network for the central administration of the Social Insurance Fund of the Russian Federation, which would utilize 3,000 Aquarius computers. Partners in the project were Landata, OCS, and Newbridge Networks Corporation of Canada. Aquarius brought this project to a successful conclusion, and it was the first centralized computer technology project to be completed for a federal government ministry.

To manage its growing and complex business, Aquarius Systems Inform became the corporate parent of three operating daughter companies. Aquarius Data was created to assume responsibility for the computer business. Aquarius Register handled the cash register business, while the factory in Shuya was responsible for production. The corporate office provided support for the three units, and was responsible for overall strategy formulation and implementation oversight.

The company's success established Aquarius as a major firm in Russia's computer industry, and its solid reputation allowed it to fare quite well even during the mid-1998 financial crisis. Regardless of the economic downturn, demand for computers was still substantial, and the company was well positioned to respond. In fact, the downturn provided new opportunities for Aquarius as Russian companies sought quality computers at the best price. Because of its reputation and performance, Aquarius became a desirable supplier to fill this need. Its relationship with OCS was also solidified during this period as that supplier looked for economic solutions for its own business. As another indication of the company's vitality, Aquarius continued updating its website after the crisis. The site contained many up-to-date company announcements as well as information about the company's products, services, and organization. In spite of the crisis, the company was progressing well and had attained a leadership position in the Russian computer industry.

Entering 1998, Platinum Russia had reached an annualized revenue level of $6 million from its 300 customers. Dr. Peterson stated then that the company was highly regarded, quite profitable, and was one of the top three Western accounting software and consulting firms in the country. The first half of the year saw continued success as evidenced by growth in revenues and profits, as well as in the number of customers and employees.

The country's financial crisis at mid-year did take a toll on Platinum Russia, but because of its very solid business and financial positions, the company appeared to have weathered that storm better than most organizations. Dr. Peterson noted in the fall of 1998 that the company was still healthy and profitable, but added that the crisis had forced cost-cutting measures which included reducing the work force to 100 employees. Early in the year, both her deputy and the company's senior marketing manager left Platinum to pursue other opportunities. She also explained that many customers had become much more cost conscious given their own financial problems.

Dr. Peterson noted that competitors were becoming fewer, and that some foreign clients had cut back their operations. She added that Platinum could face more problems if many such companies left the country since most Russian companies could not afford Platinum's services. In true entrepreneurial spirit, however, she talked of adding new software products as well as new related services, and targeted a major increase in revenues over the next five years. She admitted that managing through the crisis was a challenge, but was confident she could guide her company through it.

The entrepreneurships clearly fared better during the Statization period than the state-owned or hybrid organizations, although Premier Bank suffered more disruption than did the other entrepreneurships. The nature of the entrepreneurial businesses distanced them somewhat from the government's economic policies and their repercussions. BusinessLink and Platinum Russia, for instance, dealt mainly with international companies which themselves were less directly affected by the government's increasing involvement in the economy. All organizations, however, were negatively affected by the mounting uncertainties.

There was no way for any company, even international ones, to escape the chaos that followed the August crisis. The government's very credibility had collapsed along with its ability to finance itself or pay its debts. Russian banks, as well as foreign creditors, were unable to collect debts from the government. Companies which depended upon bank loans were unable to obtain them, and even relatively healthy companies became unable to pay all their own debts including payrolls. The ruble was greatly devalued, and coupled with higher unemployment, severely weakened purchasing power. The entrepreneurships, being in stronger financial and business positions than many other organizations, were more optimistic about their survival and futures. Even these companies, however, would have difficulty making it through a protracted financial and economic crisis.

VARIABLE PROGRESS DURING THE DECADE

The progress made during the decade varied among the three types of enterprises, as well as among enterprises within each type. The flexibility and market-oriented experience of the entrepreneurships provided their managers with the ability to more effectively weather changing circumstances than was true for the other types. As the country transitioned through the decade's four economic and political stages, entrepreneurships as a group were more resilient and encountered more success. Even after the mid-1998 financial crisis, they emerged as the strongest organizations with the best probability of surviving and achieving success on their own. The other two types were unlikely to do so without government support. The state-owned enterprises, although badly battered by increasingly negative environmental forces, would likely survive as the government increased its role in the economy. The hybrid enterprises also seemed likely to survive because of their relationships with the increasingly active governmental agencies. The future of all three types, as well as the individual organizations, however, would depend upon the course that the government would set after the elections in late 1999 and 2000. Several possible scenarios are discussed in the concluding chapter.

14. Interpreting the Capitalist Experiment and a Look Ahead

INTERPRETING ENTERPRISE PROGRESS

Early in the country's economic transition, during the Commercialization stage, the ten companies, regardless of type, moved forward with optimism, seizing opportunities and beginning their adjustment to the new environment. Progress varied, however, across the three types of enterprises as the companies progressed through the four stages of the transition. And companies of the same type exhibited different rates of progress during each stage. The Privatization and Nomenklatura stages affected the state-owned enterprises and hybrid companies more negatively than the entrepreneurships. The same was true of the Statization stage, although by mid-1998 the country's financial crisis caused all companies to focus on survival as their primary objective. Even then, however, most of the entrepreneurships seemed more capable than the other types of firms of coping with the country's economic and political problems. The differences in progress can be attributed to a number of factors, primarily the way each type of firm was affected by the changing political and economic environment. Other major factors were the industries in which companies operated, the objectives they set, the strategies they adopted, and the capabilities that the management teams exhibited.

The state-owned enterprises generally fared less well than other organizations during most of the decade. They were the companies most affected by the constantly changing government policies of the four stages, and the negative economic effects of those policies. Also, these enterprises were more closely tied to objectives common in pre-perestroika Russia. Thus, they sought to maintain employment and engage in very large-scale projects similar to those they pursued earlier as important members of the defense establishment. Being still wholly or majority state-owned, they were less able to initiate new policies and practices as quickly as the other types of enterprises. Simultaneously, they saw government financial support erode as their subsidies dwindled. This negative spiral continued during most years of the decade. It became particularly acute during the last years of the

Nomenklatura stage as well as during the Statization stage when government support virtually disappeared.

In response to their deteriorating situations, both the Central R&D Institute and Toriy attempted to become more market-oriented. Both enterprises attempted to find commercial markets for their products, and to adapt their products to new potential markets. Toriy allowed its scientists to establish entrepreneurships within the enterprise, while the firm developed products for the medical instruments and commercial electronics fields. The R&D Institute formulated a strategy focused on telecommunications, and continued to develop expertise in that area. The two state-owned enterprises.struggled to survive, managed their costs diligently, and continued to lobby government agencies for financial support which they felt was their right as state-owned organizations. Even after the financial crisis, while focusing on survival, the director of the R&D Institute continued to steer his enterprise in the same strategic direction. He realized the magnitude of his task, but maintained the conviction and patriotic belief that the country would overcome its problems, and that his institute could help in that process. The untimely death of Toriy's director during the Statization period hindered the company as it sought to survive the financial crisis.

The hybrid organizations generally fared better than the state-owned enterprises during most of the decade, although Mikromashina, as a former state-owned enterprise, was more negatively affected than Tonar and Ekip by constant changes in the environment, as well as by its own internal turmoil. Tonar and Ekip were born in the early days of perestroika as new organizations and were able to adapt quite well to the changing conditions of the four stages. They grew successfully during the Commercialization and Privatization periods with financial assistance from government agencies. As new organizations engaged in attractive projects, they also succeeded in developing new sources of funds from domestic and international investors. These new hybrid organizations did not suffer severe setbacks during the Commercialization and Privatization stages. In contrast, Mikromashina was required to shed its legacy as a state-owned enterprise. The company experienced many difficulties as its supportive infrastructure disintegrated, sales suffered from international competition, and its ability to fund itself as a newly privatized company proved to be exceedingly difficult. Without government funding, the company had to develop its own revenue sources, and its diminishing sales forced a series of major layoffs of long-time employees.

The Nomenklatura stage initiated a period of difficulties for Tonar and Ekip, and exacerbated Mikromashina's problems. Although the economy appeared to be gaining strength as GDP and production increased, underlying conditions continued to deteriorate. The government continued to fund itself by issuing short-term notes, rather than collecting taxes effectively and restraining spending. Many members of the nomenklatura, including the powerful oligarchs, became wealthy at the expense of the country's economic progress. Government policies changed continuously as did senior members of the federal government. The country's wealth was plundered by those with power and position, and the government's ability to finance itself came into serious question. The executives of Tonar and Ekip noted the deterioration of the ethical foundations of business and government, and became more concerned about the future of the country and their own enterprises. Mikromashina's internal problems stemmed in part from a power struggle which centered around ownership as well as the strategic direction of the firm.

As the Statization stage began in 1998, Tonar and Ekip were still in relatively good positions, partly as a result of prioritizing their projects and paying close attention to cash flows. In these quasi-independent organizations, executives were able to set priorities and make decisions which could solidify the positions of their firms. Mikromashina had a new top management team which focused the firm on real estate, and Nypro Inc. purchased additional ownership. The financial crisis at mid-year, however, caused the hybrid firms to focus on survival and short-term cash flow. They began to recentralize decision making, a direction taken during the latter part of the Nomenklatura stage. These firms tried to maintain their longer-term missions, but exhibited the flexibility to deal with the problems caused by the country's difficulties.

The Russian government's launching of the transition to a market-oriented economy paved the way for the birth of thousands of entrepreneurships. Except for Platinum Russia, which was founded in 1993, all the other entrepreneurships in this study started during the early years of the Commercialization stage. Many enterprising Russians from various backgrounds founded organizations, but the five profiled here were created by talented professionals with strong academic, scientific, and business credentials. All sought to take part in the new freedom by starting and owning businesses, and like entrepreneurs elsewhere, tried to control their own destiny while contributing to their country's economic development.

All of these entrepreneurs started businesses that focused on particular market needs that existed as a result of the country's new openness. Premier Bank sought to engage in the functions of a commercial bank, Vybor traded in badly needed consumer goods, BusinessLink consulted with international firms on their entry strategies, and Aquarius produced computers to fill a major market need. Platinum Russia developed software for international clients when it started operations during the Privatization period. By that time, the other four firms had begun diversifying their products, services, and markets, as Platinum also did within a short time. Premier Bank engaged heavily in trading government securities, Vybor expanded its product line, BusinessLink was heavily involved in advertising, and Aquarius had entered several new businesses.

The Nomenklatura stage, like earlier periods, was a positive time for most of the entrepreneurships. They were relatively unaffected by the negative results of the country's increasing consolidation of power and ownership with the accompanying plunder of the nation's wealth. Premier Bank, however, continued to endure the vagaries of dealing with the Central Bank which imposed unreasonable restrictions and requirements upon Premier and other commercial banks. In spite of these problems, Premier Bank continued to prosper throughout the Nomenklatura stage. BusinessLink and Platinum likewise continued their successful and profitable growth by diversifying into related services, although BusinessLink had also become very involved in profitable real estate development projects. Aquarius expanded beyond its computer business into numerous other directions under a holding company structure. Because resources continued to be taken from the growing computer unit, the unit's executives engaged in what amounted to a leveraged buy-out. The newly independent Aquarius computer firm also began producing cash registers and grew successfully with an improved distribution network. Vybor's fortunes varied during this stage as the opportunistic founders looked for new directions when fierce international competition emerged, and the company declared bankruptcy in 1996.

The entrepreneurships proved to be highly flexible and opportunistic, but for the most part followed their strategic courses. Most diversification was in fields related to their original competence, or in the developing needs of their customers. The companies appeared to be well managed and able to grow profitably while adapting their organizational structures and systems in ways appropriate for their stage of development. Aquarius, as a corporation, engaged in unrelated diversifications for two years, but the computer unit upon which our study focused remained committed to its original mission. By adapting its competitive strategy to changing conditions, the company found itself on solid financial footing within a year of regaining its independence, and achieved success in all its product lines. Even Vybor, which ended in bankruptcy, provided a vehicle which fulfilled the objectives of its founders who were always willing to close a business and seek more profitable opportunities.

The other four entrepreneurships entered the Statization stage as vital and financially solid organizations fulfilling needs of growing markets. The founders had operated their businesses in a strategic fashion, surveying changing market needs, marshalling the required resources, and fulfilling their own personal values. They managed their firms as profit-oriented organizations which satisfied customers and provided rewarding opportunities for employees. They displayed the ingenuity and flexibility to capitalize upon opportunities while for the most part retaining their strategic directions. They had shown that entrepreneurships, led by talented and energetic leaders, could prosper even during the more restrictive Statization stage. The country's financial crisis, however, clearly affected even these resilient organizations, although they were better prepared to survive it than were the other types of firms.

A LOOK AHEAD WITH THREE SCENARIOS

As the decade of the 1990s was coming to a close, it was clear that Russia's Statization stage would last for the foreseeable future. President Yeltsin had continued his erratic policy of replacing prime ministers and other cabinet ministers. Prime Minister Primakov was ousted in May 1999, although he had brought a period of stability to the country during his few short months in power. All observers agreed that he had not developed a workable plan for improving the economy, but international financial institutions were willing to work with him and provide desperately needed financing. Serious doubts developed about whether such aid would be forthcoming after Primakov was replaced. The IMF, however, seemed compelled to work with whomever was in power and provided a $4.5 billion loan in mid-1999. The timing paralleled Prime Minister Stepashin's seemingly successful diplomatic meetings with the US Vice President Gore and other senior US officials. The Duma tried unsuccessfully to impeach President Yeltsin, but it was clear that the two government branches could not cooperate on any forward-looking policies. And in August 1999, Prime Minister Stepashin was abruptly replaced by the KGB veteran, Vladimir Putin. The major questions at that time were who would come to power in the Duma and presidential elections scheduled for late 1999 and 2000, and what policies would be developed after the elections. The picture became even more complicated with the August 1999 announcement that a new and powerful political coalition had been formed by Moscow Mayor Luzhkov and former Prime Minister Primakov.

We conclude our examination of Russian enterprises in the 1990s by developing three scenarios which we view as plausible for the country's future. These are a reversal of privatization, a reaffirmation of the market economy, and a mixed economy in which state-owned and private enterprises would co-exist.

Reversal of Privatization Scenario

One scenario, a reversal of privatization, would entail ever-increasing government control of the economy, and considerable dismantling of free-market mechanisms. The prospect of government control returning to the communists would make this a credible scenario. The likelihood of that occurring, however, seems unrealistic in the eyes of many, including Yevgeny Volk, a well-known Moscow political analyst who stated: "Everyone realizes that the communists have no chance of winning the election." His reasons centered around the development of a powerful new coalition led by Moscow Mayor, Yuri Luzhkov, and Volk claimed that the "Communist electorate is elderly, slowly declining, and limited to a minority of the population" (York, 1999, p. A14).

While not likely involving a return to communism, government's role in regulating the economy could still result in state ownership of much of the country's industrial base and natural resources, as well as land. A large number of enterprises deemed critical to the country's national interest would be ineligible for any form of privatization. Entrepreneurships similar to cooperatives could co-exist with state enterprises. It is not likely, however, that the types of entrepreneurships described in this book would last, because the environment would be too restrictive and opportunities too few. Little external investment or funding would be available from international sources for the country or its businesses. Government funding would be directed primarily to industries important to the country's strategic goals, which would not emphasize consumer goods or the development of a middle class. Regionalization would likely continue and fragment even further the country's political and economic landscape. This reversal of privatization scenario could well result from the elections, given the disenchantment of the Russian public in view of the negative events which accompanied the country's experiment with capitalism.

The reversal of privatization would clearly prevent the country from becoming a fully participating member of the world economy. State-owned enterprises would not be a viable model for operating in the global business arena since managers would be severely hindered by the government's objectives as the major stakeholder. Thus, they would have little flexibility to serve the needs of commercial customers, particularly in international markets. Russia would likely have to resort to high levels of protectionism in order for its own industries to find markets, and it is likely that domestic consumers would again be the last market served. In fact, the government decree of July 1996 had already designated hundreds of defense enterprises as being ineligible for privatization because of their strategic importance to the country. It is these enterprises that would likely receive the lion's share of government support. Whether called communism or another name, the negative effects on Russia's consumer market would resemble pre-perestroika times. Enterprises like the Central R&D Institute and Toriy would be revitalized, but they would no longer seek commercial markets. Their attention would revert to serving the government and its objectives. Entrepreneurships would have little opportunity to operate except in very small retail operations, smaller production enterprises, and possibly in agriculture. Though not the most probable scenario, Russia is notorious for surprising those who try to predict its future.

Free-Market Scenario

The free-market scenario is a less likely eventuality. It is one in which the elections would result in a government dedicated to continuing the country's transition to a market economy. This, in fact, was the centerpiece of the platform of presidential hopeful Grigory Yavlinsky and his Yabloko party. He would go beyond the policies of former governments and support true privatization, including privatization of land. This scenario includes reduction in the power of monopolies like Gazprom. The main argument in favor of such a future is the failure of previous Russian governments to create a vibrant and productive economy through state ownership of land and resources. This scenario would be attractive for international investment as well as funding by international agencies. International companies would again be attracted to Russia, and could again become major customers for growing Russian firms like BusinessLink and Platinum Russia. Such a scenario would not lessen the country's political and economic fragmentation, but might promote more cooperation among the regions as well as with Moscow. It is unlikely, though, that the long-suffering Russian people would opt for what could be seen as a continuation of a failed experiment. Yet, a new government could move in this direction although probably not with shock-therapy speed. The major requirement for success of such a scenario would be the development of an ethical business environment, supported by legislation which was enforced.

In spite of the apparent failures of the country's attempts at transformation to a market economy, the free-market scenario could still be appealing if the government was truly committed to its full development and provided real support for this direction. Many of the problems of shock therapy were inevitable, but the process had at least continued for a decade, and some progress had been made. For instance, entrepreneurships were able to flourish during most of the decade until the financial crisis of mid-1998, which was beyond the control of these pioneers. Firms that were established during the 1990s specifically to meet market needs were particularly successful. Often these firms were established in the service sector which required less up-front investment than production companies. Additionally, they depended primarily upon intellectual capital for success in meeting the needs of international companies as well as many Russian firms. BusinessLink and Platinum Russia are good examples of this type of company. It is unclear, however, whether production-oriented entrepreneurships could fare as well in the foreseeable future because of the large investment required. Still, Aquarius was quite successful during most of the decade because it filled market needs and operated eventually as a market-driven company.

Middle-Ground Scenario

A third scenario, which we believe to be the most likely, is the middle-ground scenario which would entail rationalization of privatized enterprises, with government involvement and support for the stronger ones. The government would be significantly involved in the development of an infrastructure to support the country's industry and develop its mineral wealth. At the same time, entrepreneurships would be allowed to fulfill the needs of the country's consumers, and to some extent its industrial base. They would also serve the needs of international firms. This scenario would result in a mixed economy where the government is significantly involved and protects what it sees as national interests, but is also relatively positive towards and supportive of business development. State enterprises would exist in the defense and natural resource sectors, as well as in energy and major infrastructure areas like transportation. Most other industrial enterprises would be of the hybrid type which enjoy some government support, but which would be majority-owned by private shareholders including professional managers of the organizations.

Tonar and Ekip are examples of hybrid organizations which exhibited flexibility and attention to market needs, while being supported by various government agencies which were often shareholders. As these organizations became more successful, government ownership would be diminished until they became truly privatized companies. This scenario would be attractive to private international investors and would likely attract funding from international agencies. Like the free-market scenario, this future would require an ethical business environment and effective enforcement of legislation. This direction clearly would take time, but it could be the best possibility for a positive future for Russia's economy.

Given the immense problems in the political and economic environments at the close of the 1990s, it will take the country years, and possibly decades, to establish a new socio-economic order. Since statization was the prevailing condition as the decade closed, there was little reason to believe that this policy would change dramatically in the near future. Still, it did not seem likely that the country would revert to the former communist model. Instead, a model would be developed which supported entrepreneurships, while the state would still be deeply involved in economic policy.

This view suggests that hybrid type enterprises could well be major players in post-election Russia. They combine in one enterprise the attributes of entrepreneurship with state involvement, support, and often partial ownership. This model offers flexible entrepreneurship concurrently with the state involvement to which Russians are accustomed, and which seems inevitable for the foreseeable future. As Tonar and Ekip have shown, hybrid firms can react to market forces while pursuing large-scale projects, and still exhibit the flexibility to change direction as circumstances require. This model might also best serve the needs of production enterprises with their large investment needs, as well as others which pursue large-scale projects involving costly technology development and applications.

In this middle-ground scenario, state enterprises could provide the business infrastructure of a properly functioning central bank, as well as transportation, raw materials, energy, and other key infrastructure elements. Some of these organizations, however, could hopefully be based upon a hybrid form which included managers with ownership positions that motivated them to run effective businesses. Government's major objective would be to support business development, rather than following the capricious and negative practices of the 1990s.

This scenario gained credibility in the fall of 1999 with the creation of a new political coalition which had positioned itself as a nationalist left-wing opposition party to both the Kremlin and the communists. The heads of the coalition, Moscow Mayor Luzhkov and former Prime Minister Primakov, attracted powerful regional governors who had supported the Kremlin, as well as the Agrarian Party which defected from the Communist camp (York, 1999). Although their platform was as yet unclear, given their objective of satisfying those with various positions on the political spectrum, it seemed feasible that the new political group could adopt policies that would be consistent with our middle-ground scenario.

Like any other program promoting economic and business development in Russia, this middle-ground scenario must be built within an environment which supports legitimate business practices. These in turn require enlightened government policies. Many failures of the 1990s could be traced to the government's ineffectiveness in developing and enforcing legislation to guide business decision making. Entrepreneurships, the organizations in which the government was least involved, proved to be the most successful firms of the capitalist experiment. They could provide the engine of a new government-supported quasi-market economy. Even more important, however, is the necessity for an ethical and honest climate among businesspersons and government officials, the lack of which was responsible for the most flagrant abuses of the decade. Only such forces as these can reverse the negative excesses of the capitalist experiment, and offer a positive scenario for Russia's future.

References

Berzonsky, V. Jr. (1998), Banking in Russia since the August crisis. *Bisnis Bulletin*, December, 1 and 5.

Bisnis Bulletin (1999), Agency spotlight: Gore-Stepashin Commission, July, 7.

Blasi, J.R., Kroumova, M. and Kruse, D. (1997), *Kremlin capitalism: Privatizing the Russian economy*. Ithaca, NY: Cornell University Press.

Boston Sunday Globe (1998), Russia plan called tactical retreat, November 1, A9.

Boston Sunday Globe (1999), Russian central bankers reported hiding assets, August 1, A4.

Boycko, M., Schleifer, A. and Vishy, R. (1995), *Privatizing Russia*. Cambridge: MIT Press.

Browning, L. (1998), A mixed-up economy: Russian analysts find that Russia is moving toward limbo; neither socialist nor capitalist. *Boston Sunday Globe*, September 20, E1 and E7.

Colton, T.J. (1999), Russia stalled; The uncertain transition from Communism. Harvard Magazine, March-April, 33-35.

Economic Newsletter (March 1993, June 1994, July 1994, August 1994, October 1998, November 1998, December 1998, January 1999, February 1999, June 1999, July 1999, August 1999), Davis Center for Russian Studies, Harvard University, Cambridge, MA.

Englund, W. (1992), Yeltsin, speaking to industrialists, vows to persevere. *Boston Sunday Globe*, November 15, 2.

Filatotchev, A., Starkey, K., and Wright, M. (1994), The ethical challenges of management buy-outs as a form of privatisation in Central and Eastern Europe. *Journal of Business Ethics*, **13**, 523-532.

Filipov, D. (1998a), Russian premier is approved, enlists old Soviet hands. *Boston Globe*, September 12, A12.

Filipov, D. (1998b), Yeltsin tells Clinton aging new leaders will pursue reforms. *Boston Sunday Globe*, September 13, A25.

Filipov, D. (1998c), Russia to unveil rescue plan without the blessing of international lenders. *Boston Sunday Globe*, October 31, F1 and 2.

References

Filtzer, D.A. (1991), The contradictions of the marketless market: Self-financing in the Soviet industrial enterprises, 1986-90. *Soviet Studies*, **43** (6), 989-1009.

Financial Times (1998), Russia's bleak future. Editorial, November 3, 15.

Goldman, M.I. (1998), Moscow moods. *Economic Newsletter*, Davis Center for Russian Studies, Harvard University, Cambridge, MA, November, 3 and 4.

Goldman, M.I. (1999), Russia's mixed-up moves reveal its dangerous divide. *The Washington Post*, June 20, B1 and B5.

Higgins, A. (1999), Russian newspaper finds itself in a tug of war over ownership. *The Wall Street Journal*, August 9, A15.

Hill, M.R. (1998), From Soviet giants to Russian survivors. *Leadership and Organization Development*, **19** (6), 325-331.

Kelley, J., and Stanglin, D. (1999), Inside Moscow's money scandal. *USA Today*, September 13, 1-2.

Kramer, D. (1998), In Nettleton, S., Russian economy – what went wrong? *CNN in Interactive, www.cnn.com*, October 24.

Kranz, P. (1994), Russia's state sell-off: Sink-or-swim time. *Business Week*, July 4, 46 and 47.

Kranz, P. (1998a), Russia: Is there a solution? *Business Week*, September 7, 25-29.

Kranz, P. (1998b), Russia: How bad this time? Only massive borrowing will keep it out of default. *Business Week*, December 21, 36.

Kranz, P. (1999), Fall of an oligarch: Can Vladimir Potanin save his empire? *Business Week*, March 1, 44 and 45.

Lawrence, P.R., Vlachoutsicos, C.A., Faminsky, I., Brakov, E., Puffer, S., Walton, E., Naumov, A., and Ozira, V. (eds.), (1990), *Behind the factory walls: Decision making in Soviet and US enterprises*. Boston: Harvard Business School Press. Published in Russian by Naumov, A.I. (ed.), (1990), *Mozhno li upravliat' predpriiatiem vmeste? (Can we manage enterprises together?)*, Moscow, USSR: Vneshtorgizdat.

Lloyd, J. (1994), Twisting and turning. *Financial Times*, November 8, 16.

Longnecker, C.O., and Popovski, S. (1994), Managerial trials of privatization: Retooling Russian managers. *Business Horizons*, November-December, 35-43.

Matlack, C. (1999), Betting on a new label: Made in Russia. *Business Week*, April 12, 122E6.

Matthews, O., and Dlugy, Y. (1999), Balancing bear: Turmoil in Moscow. *Newsweek*, May 24, 35-39.

References

Matthews, O., and Hirsh, M. (1998), Russian roulette. *Newsweek*, September 7, 26-31.

McCarthy, D.J., and Puffer, S.M. (1992), Perestroika at the plant level: Managers' job · attitudes and views of decision-making in the former USSR. *Columbia Journal of World Business*, **27** (1), 86-99.

McCarthy, D.J., and Puffer, S.M. (1995), 'Diamonds and Rust' on Russia's road to privatization: The profits and pitfalls for Western managers. *Columbia Journal of World Business*, **30** (3), 56-69.

McCarthy, D.J., and Puffer, S.M. (1997a), Mikromashina of Moscow: Problems and opportunities of privatization. *Case Research Journal*, **17** (4), 33-50. Translated in Naumov, A.I. (ed.), (1997), *Konkretnye situatsii dlia obucheniia upravleniiu. (Case studies for management education)*. Moscow: Association for Management Development, 115-136.

McCarthy, D.J. and Puffer, S.M. (1997b), Strategic investment flexibility for MNE success in Russia: Evolving beyond entry modes. *Journal of World Business*, **32** (4), 293-319.

McCarthy, D.J., Puffer, S.M., and Naumov, A.I. (1997a), Olga Kirova: A Russian entrepreneur's quality leadership. *International Journal of Organizational Analysis*, **5** (3), 267-290.

McCarthy, D.J., Puffer, S.M., and Naumov, A.I. (1997b), Partnering with Russia's new entrepreneurs: Software Tsarina Olga Kirova. *European Management Journal*, **15** (6), 648-657. Adapted version published by Naumov, A.I. (ed.), (1997), as Ekauntenk-Rossiia (Accounting-Russia), Konkretnye situatsii dlia obucheniia upravleniiu. (Case studies for management education). Moscow: Association of Management Development, 54-69.

Mikheyev, D. (1997), *Russia transformed*. Indianapolis: Hudson Institute.

Nettleson, S. (1998), Russian economy – what went wrong? *CNN in Interactive*, www.cnn.com, October 24.

Nichols, B. (1999), Yeltsin's latest firing is seen as self-preservation. *USA Today*, August 10, 1A and 12A.

Owen, T.C. (1995), Russian corporate capitalism from Peter the Great to perestroika. New York: Oxford University Press.

Puffer, S.M. (1999), Global statesman: Mikhail Gorbachev on globalization. *The Academy of Management Executive*, **13** (1), 8-14.

Puffer, S.M., and McCarthy, D.J. (1993a), Decision-making authority of American and former Soviet managers: Not so different after all? *The International Executive*, **35** (6), 497-512.

Puffer, S.M., and McCarthy, D.J. (1993b), Soviet managers view organizational change in large state enterprises. *Journal of Organizational Change Management*, **6** (3), 6-23.

275

References

Puffer, S.M., McCarthy, D.J., and Zhuplev, A.V. (1998), Doing business in Russia: Lessons from the early entrants. *Thunderbird International Business Review*, **40** (5), 461-484.

Radaev, V.V. (1998), *Formirovanie novykh rossiiskikh rynkov: Transaktsionnye izderzhki, formy kontrolia i delovaia etika*. Moscow: Center for Political Technologies, CIPE.

Radaev, V.V. (1999), Business ethics in Russia: Contract enforcement and violence in the late 1990s. Keynote address, Chemnitz IV, Ostforum Proceedings.

Reddaway, P. (1998), The roots of Russia's crisis: The Soviet legacy, IMF/G7 policies, and Yeltsin's authoritarianism: Where is the crisis now leading? *Russia Business Watch*, **3** (6), 12-15.

Russia Business Review (1998), Russia's best woman executives, April 24, 22-28.

Sachs, J. (1995), What have we learned about rule of law and economic reform in Russia? Seminar, Russian Research Center, Harvard University, May 9.

Shama, A. (1993), Management under fire: The transformation of managers in the Soviet Union and Eastern Europe. *Academy of Management Executive*, February, 22-35.

Shama, A., and Sementsov, S. (1992), The collapse of the Soviet ministries: Economic and legal transformation. *The International Executive*, **34** (2), 131-150.

Standing, G. (1997), *Unemployment and enterprise restructuring: Reviving dead souls*. Geneva: International Labor Organization.

Tappan, M.A. (1998), Grassroots business recovery in Russia, *Harriman Review*, Special issue on the Russian economy in crisis, December, 12 and 13.

The Economist (1994), Not the real thing yet. March 12, 58.

The Economist (1999a), Is anyone running Russia? February 6-12, 51.

The Economist (1999b), Russia, financial outcast. February 6-12, 17.

The Economist (1999c), Russian organised crime: Crime without punishment. August 28, 17-19.

Thornhill, J. (1998), Parliamentary chiefs back Primakov's strategy. *Financial Times*, November 3, 3.

Torch, L. (1999), U.S. Russia Fund adjusts to the banking crisis. *Bisnis Bulletin*, June, 3.

Vlachoutsicos, C.A., and Lawrence, P.R. (1996), How managerial learning can assist economic transformation in Russia. *Organization Studies*, **17** (2), 311-325.

Watson, R., and Matthews, O. (1998), Russia's real rulers. *Newsweek*, September, 31.

References

Weymouth, L. (1999), Damage has been done. *Newsweek*, August 2, 42-44.

Wheatley, A. (1998), G7 details financial reform plan. *Boston Sunday Globe*, October 31, F1 and 2.

York, G. (1999), Centre-left alliance upsets Russian power balance. *The Globe and Mail*, August 31, A14.

Zhuplev, A.V., Konkov, A., and Kiesner, W.F. (1998), Comparison of entrepreneurs' motivations and obstacles: Russia and the U.S. *European Management Journal*, **16** (4).

Index

-E-

-F-

-Q-

-R-